The Time-Life Gardener's Guide

EVERGREEN SHRUBS

A
REDEFINITION
BOOK

Other Publications:

VOYAGE THROUGH THE UNIVERSE
THE THIRD REICH
MYSTERIES OF THE UNKNOWN
TIME FRAME
FIX IT YOURSELF
FITNESS, HEALTH & NUTRITION
SUCCESSFUL PARENTING
HEALTHY HOME COOKING
UNDERSTANDING COMPUTERS
LIBRARY OF NATIONS
THE ENCHANTED WORLD
THE KODAK LIBRARY OF CREATIVE PHOTOGRAPHY
GREAT MEALS IN MINUTES
THE CIVIL WAR
PLANET EARTH
COLLECTOR'S LIBRARY OF THE CIVIL WAR
THE EPIC OF FLIGHT
THE GOOD COOK
WORLD WAR II
HOME REPAIR AND IMPROVEMENT
THE OLD WEST

For information on and a full description of any of
the Time-Life Books series listed above, please call 1-800-621-7026
or write:

Reader Information
Time-Life Customer Service
P.O. Box C-32068
Richmond, Virginia 23261-2068

This book is one of a series of guides to good gardening.

The Time-Life Gardener's Guide

EVERGREEN SHRUBS

TIME-LIFE BOOKS, ALEXANDRIA, VIRGINIA

CONTENTS

1
A PLANT FOR ALL SEASONS

2
KEEPING SHRUBS IN SHAPE

3
GROWING NEW SHRUBS

Evergreen shrubs are a dependable delight. When other garden plants go into bare-limbed dormancy, only the hardy evergreens stand firm against winter's "little death." And if they flower, as some of them do, they quicken the senses with bright colors and surprising fragrances from early spring to late summer. This volume will show you how to choose shrubs for your garden, how to improve growing conditions, and how to care for evergreens to ensure their health and vigor. You'll learn the right way to plant, mulch, fertilize, water, prune and propagate your favorite shrubs. For the more ambitious, there are instructions for creating living works of art with evergreen topiary, espalier and bonsai.

You'll also find a zone map that tells you which plants will thrive as evergreens in your area, a month-by-month maintenance checklist and a troubleshooting guide with everything you need to know to combat your shrubs' natural enemies. Finally, there is a dictionary that puts at your fingertips useful information about more than 150 genera of evergreens.

4

MAKING THE MOST OF NATURE

5

DICTIONARY OF EVERGREEN SHRUBS

1
A PLANT
FOR ALL SEASONS

The omnifarious evergreen shrub is a plant not only for all times of year, but for virtually all spaces and all purposes. Whether the need is for the privacy afforded by an impenetrable boundary hedge, or for a pleasing pattern of greenery to soften the hard verticals and horizontals of buildings, or simply to present a spectacular show of flowers and foliage, the vast plant group known as needle-leaved and broad-leaved evergreen shrubs can provide ready solutions. From the plebeian pine to the regal rhododendron, they share a legacy of persistent growth, hardiness and longevity that have made them the favorites of gardeners for centuries.

On the following pages you will learn how to choose and plant the shrubs that best serve your garden requirements and your personal tastes from the thousands of available varieties. With a little preparation, most of them can be made to thrive. The low-spreading juniper, for example, provides a rich cover for steep slopes even as its roots bind the soil to prevent erosion. And there is salvation for those who have despaired of growing azaleas and rhododendrons because of poor soil. If you place these plants in raised beds filled with the acidic material they need, they will flourish and produce the explosions of colorful blossoms for which they are renowned.

You will also find techniques for showcasing the beauty of handsome miniature and dwarf varieties by planting them atop raised earthen berms, and for maintaining them in movable containers that can be brought indoors in cold weather for year-round display.

CHOOSING THE RIGHT SHRUBS
AND GETTING THEM SAFELY HOME

P urchasing shrubs at a well-stocked nursery can be a heady adventure. With many attractive plants to choose from, the temptation is to splurge on a wide, exciting variety. This may work out, but it is safer to do a bit of homework before buying. For one thing, shrubs that seem perfect for a particular spot in the landscape when young may turn out to be the wrong shape or size later on, growing to be unexpectedly wide or tall. For help in visualizing the shapes of various shrubs, see the box on the facing page; for help in how to use them, see pages 14-17.

With this homework done, visit the nursery—on a quiet weekday if you can, to avoid weekend crowds. When making selections, take smaller, younger shrubs, which are usually cheaper and easier to transplant than older ones. Ask where the shrubs were grown; local specimens will be better adapted to an area's climate and soil than ones grown far away. And look for healthy plants with foliage that shows no signs of pests, disease or breakage, and roots that are white and springy.

A good vehicle for taking home a number of shrubs is a pickup truck. If you have (or can borrow) one, also find a tarpaulin, to protect the plants from drying winds. Pack the shrubs with care in your car or truck for the trip home, as shown in the drawings below and at right. Plant them as soon as you can; evergreen shrubs are susceptible to drying out when they are out of the ground.

Freshly dug from the ground, healthy-looking 5-foot-tall arborvitaes lie in a nursery, their roots neatly and firmly balled up in fresh sheets of burlap.

1 When taking shrubs home from a nursery, start loading the bed of a pickup truck (or the trunk of a car) from the front *(right)* and work toward the back. Lay large shrubs on their sides and set small container plants upright. Pack them snugly; put small ones in the spaces between the root balls and foliage of larger ones.

2 Secure the plants against shifting by placing heavy bags of soil or mulch against them. If your pickup truck or the trunk of your car is open to the wind, stretch a tarpaulin over the shrubs and tuck the edges under the plants and the heavy bags. Secure the tarp with rope. As soon as you get home, undo the tarp and fold it back; it can get hot underneath. □

A SELECTION OF SHRUB FORMS

The drawings below show the eight principal shapes that shrubs assume when they are mature. They range from tall, pyramidal, tree-like sorts such as Japanese yew, which may grow up to 20 feet in height, to low-spreading heather, which usually reaches only 1 foot high but may spread as wide as 4 feet. A few genera, such as juniper, have species that run the full range of shapes.

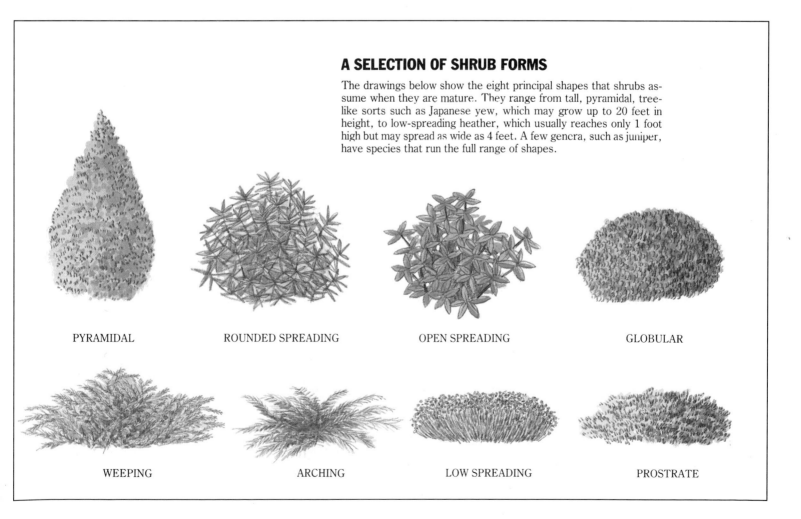

PYRAMIDAL   ROUNDED SPREADING   OPEN SPREADING   GLOBULAR

WEEPING   ARCHING   LOW SPREADING   PROSTRATE

A PROPER START
FOR CONTAINER-GROWN SHRUBS

Plant nurseries generally sell evergreen shrubs in three ways. Some larger shrubs have their roots covered in burlap. These shrubs are field-grown, then dug up and wrapped for sale. Others—those with shallow, fibrous roots—are nurtured in special beds of tree bark and other organic materials, then lifted out and put in baskets for sale. Still others—and they are generally in the majority—are grown from the start in plastic pots and are sold that way.

Balled-and-burlapped plants and basket shrubs both need to be planted with care *(pages 18-19),* but container-grown shrubs demand some special treatment *(opposite and following pages).* And for good reason: they have spent their lives in narrow confines and have been pampered with more than the usual quantities of nutrients. The transition from pot to earth is stressful.

First, they need to be planted in extra-large holes. Other shrubs make do in holes about twice as large as their root balls. Those grown in containers should be planted in holes at least twice the size of their root balls, but preferably three times as large. The additional space is filled with generous amounts of good loose soil. The extra room gives the long-confined roots plenty of space to search out nutrients and grow.

Second, the roots themselves need to be "distressed," that is, pried open and pruned here and there. A shrub that shows lots of healthy foliage is likely to have a healthy root ball, but even so, the roots may be growing in tight circles that follow the contours of the pot, and will need to be loosened and spread out before being put in the ground. This is a vital step. Unless the roots are free to grow, the plant will be stunted and may die.

Container-grown shrubs can be put in the ground any time the soil can be worked. But the best time to plant them is the early fall. By September, spring growth has become established, or "hardened off." The soil is still warm, though, and will stay that way for a couple of months, giving the transplanted roots a chance to do some extra growing in the ground before winter comes.

A rhododendron glows with clusters of pinkish white blooms in a grassy, tree-framed yard. Rhododendrons are commonly raised and sold in containers, and, when transplanted into garden soil, need plenty of room for their roots to spread out.

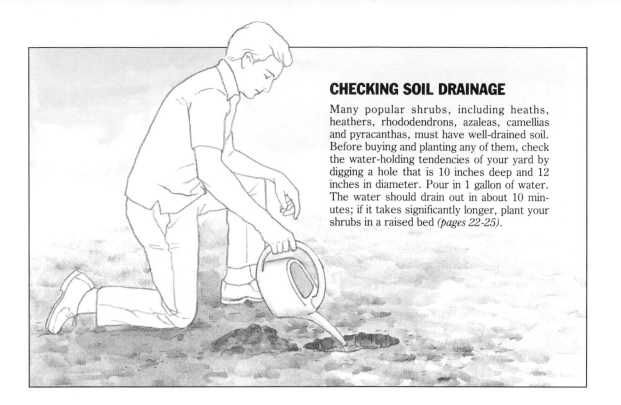

CHECKING SOIL DRAINAGE

Many popular shrubs, including heaths, heathers, rhododendrons, azaleas, camellias and pyracanthas, must have well-drained soil. Before buying and planting any of them, check the water-holding tendencies of your yard by digging a hole that is 10 inches deep and 12 inches in diameter. Pour in 1 gallon of water. The water should drain out in about 10 minutes; if it takes significantly longer, plant your shrubs in a raised bed *(pages 22-25)*.

1 When planting a container-grown shrub, use a spade to dig a hole at least twice as wide as the container. The hole should be deep enough for the shrub to sit at the same depth as it did in its pot. Do not chop up the soil in the bottom of the hole. A root ball sitting on disturbed earth will settle in time and cause the plant to sink too far.

2 Remove the shrub from its pot. If it sticks, water it to loosen the roots. Do not yank the plant by its stem or stems, or you may break them. Instead, try to maneuver the shrub by handling the root ball.

3 Work some of the compacted soil out of the root ball with your fingers; then, with a hand cultivator, loosen and straighten roots *(below)*. If there are tightly wound, coarse roots, some should be cut apart with clippers. Spread the roots outward. All this encourages the growth of new roots, which help the plant absorb moisture and nutrients.

4 Place the plant in the hole, checking to be sure it sits at the right depth, that is, with the stem or stems at the same soil level as in the pot. Fill in around the root ball with garden soil mixed with some shredded bark, which will enrich the soil and help its drainage. Firm the soil with your hands but do not press down hard: the roots will not be able to reach out through soil that is too firmly compacted.

5 Form a basin by making a circular ridge of soil around the planting hole; the basin will help keep water from running off. Water the plant well with a slow-running hose; at least 1 inch of water per week is needed during the first season. Spread mulch around the plant, for appearance and to conserve moisture, leaving 1 or 2 inches of space between the mulch and the stems. □

SITING SHRUBS
TO SUIT YOUR LANDSCAPE

Well-chosen evergreen shrubs can do more for the appearance of a house and its landscape than any other plantings. More than flower beds, even more than trees, shrubs help a house blend into its surroundings, and make the surroundings harmonious, varied and inviting.

Shrubs can do a number of vital jobs—often several at once. Hedges can delineate property lines and at the same time provide privacy, block an unattractive view and serve as a windbreak. Groupings of various shrubs are ideal for sheltering a deck or a patio and softening its contours. Banked shrubs are matchless backdrops for beds of annual and perennial flowers. Particularly handsome flowering shrubs, planted singly or in groups, add drama to an expanse of lawn. Perhaps most important, shrubs serve as foundation plantings around a house, framing windows and doors, hiding unsightly foundation walls and helping the house blend into its site.

Shrubs are marvelously versatile because they themselves are so varied—in the color and texture of their foliage, in their flowers and fruits, in shape and size. A sampling of this visual wealth is given on the following pages.

Before choosing shrubs, it is a good idea to make a checklist *(box, opposite),* noting the factors—soil type, sunlight, wind, rain—that will affect their growth. Consider also the climatic zone; winter-hardy plants may not flourish in Florida, and plants suited to the Gulf Coast may perish if planted in Michigan. Then it is vital to consider the lay of the house and the grounds, and decide where shrubs are needed, and what sorts are required *(opposite).* Hardy species are clearly best for screening harsh northerly winds. By the same token, a more delicate flowering specimen should go on the sunny, wind-protected southern side of the house. After your planning is done, consult the Dictionary of Shrubs *(pages 88-137)* to select the most appropriate shrubs for each location.

In a colorful pairing of flowers and shrubs, yellow African daisies bloom in the midst of a half-dozen pink-blossomed, low-growing Indian hawthorns. Behind them, other, taller shrubs, flanked by trees, soften the facade of the house.

HOW DOES YOUR GARDEN GROW?

Before choosing shrubs to add to your landscape, it is important to determine what sort of soil you have and how much sun, rain and wind. Many shrubs are hardy and adaptable, but some will flourish only in certain conditions. Fortunately, shrubs have such varied habits that some do well under almost any circumstances.

☐ Soil: Most evergreen shrubs like a slightly acidic growing medium that drains well. Have your soil tested before selecting shrubs to plant in it. If the soil is too clayey or too sandy, adding organic matter will improve its texture and help its drainage.

☐ Sun and shade: Determine where sunlight falls at various seasons and times of day. Some shrubs like direct all-day sun, but others are shade growers and many do well only with a combination of sun and shade.

☐ Wind: Find out where the prevailing wind comes from. There are tough shrubs that shrug off steady wintry blasts, but many more need protection from cold and from the wind's drying effects.

☐ Rain: Note your area's average rainfall. Some evergreen shrubs require large amounts of water and are almost impossible to grow in desert areas; others are highly drought-resistant.

LOOKING AT THE LAY OF THE LAND

The sketch below suggests ways shrubs may be used to beautify a house and its grounds. In planning your own plantings, consider all structures and any trees or other plantings already there, including walkways, patio and spaces that should be left open as play areas. Note where the best view is (and the worst). Think about where privacy is needed, and where you may want a hedge, a windbreak, some ornamentals and other plantings around the house. In the sketch below, an arrow indicates North, to help figure angles of sunlight and wind directions.

NORTH

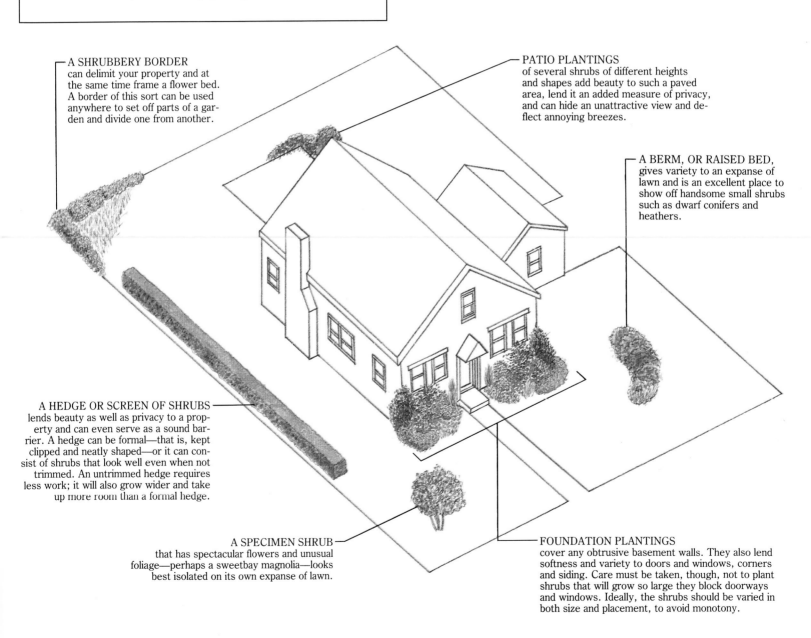

A SHRUBBERY BORDER can delimit your property and at the same time frame a flower bed. A border of this sort can be used anywhere to set off parts of a garden and divide one from another.

PATIO PLANTINGS of several shrubs of different heights and shapes add beauty to such a paved area, lend it an added measure of privacy, and can hide an unattractive view and deflect annoying breezes.

A BERM, OR RAISED BED, gives variety to an expanse of lawn and is an excellent place to show off handsome small shrubs such as dwarf conifers and heathers.

A HEDGE OR SCREEN OF SHRUBS lends beauty as well as privacy to a property and can even serve as a sound barrier. A hedge can be formal—that is, kept clipped and neatly shaped—or it can consist of shrubs that look well even when not trimmed. An untrimmed hedge requires less work; it will also grow wider and take up more room than a formal hedge.

A SPECIMEN SHRUB that has spectacular flowers and unusual foliage—perhaps a sweetbay magnolia—looks best isolated on its own expanse of lawn.

FOUNDATION PLANTINGS cover any obtrusive basement walls. They also lend softness and variety to doors and windows, corners and siding. Care must be taken, though, not to plant shrubs that will grow so large they block doorways and windows. Ideally, the shrubs should be varied in both size and placement, to avoid monotony.

RICH VARIETIES OF TEXTURE AND COLOR

Having chosen where you want shrubs to go, you can add enormous interest to your landscape by blending and contrasting foliage colors and textures, and by combining rugged-looking plants with other, more delicate species that produce spectacular flowers. Essentially, evergreen shrubs divide into two groups: the needle-leaved varieties that include the conifers, and the broad-leaved sorts that have showier foliage and blooms.

THE NEEDLE-LEAVED EVERGREENS

FINE BUT RUGGED FOLIAGE

For the tough jobs—for hedges, some foundation plantings and taller backgrounds—nothing beats the scalelike leaves of false cypress and juniper, the easily trimmed foliage of yew and the small but dense needles of spruce.

SPRUCE

FALSE CYPRESS

JUNIPER

YEW

DIVERSE AND COLORFUL FRUITS

The needle-leaved shrubs produce varied fruits, some of them brilliant in color. Most fruits are woody cones, like the arborvitae's; some are fleshy and berrylike, as in the juniper and yew.

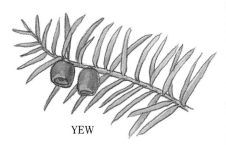

YEW

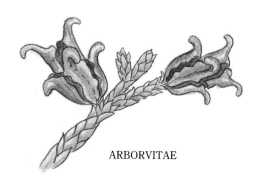

ARBORVITAE

JUNIPER

BROAD-LEAVED VARIETIES

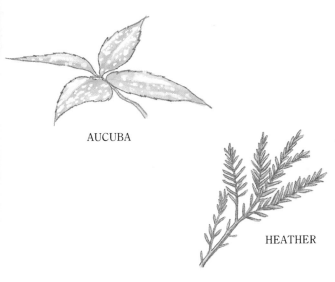

AUCUBA

FOLIAGE OF MANY SHAPES

Some of these shrubs produce small, fine leaves like the heather, but most have large, showy and often shiny foliage. The leaves are also varied in color, ranging from gray-green to yellow to blue.

HEATHER

HOLLY

PHOTINIA

BLOOMS DELICATE AND LUSH

The flowers of broad-leaved shrubs go from the spiky, bright-hued bottlebrush to the large, heavily scented gardenia. No two are alike. Mixtures of them add infinite variety to any planting.

BOTTLEBRUSH

GARDENIA

DAPHNE

ANDROMEDA

BRIGHT AND DECORATIVE FRUITS

In addition to their flowers, many broad-leaved shrubs produce colorful berries and other fruits that give a bonus of lasting color to a garden through the autumn and winter. □

OREGON GRAPE HOLLY

SWEETBAY MAGNOLIA

NANDINA

BALLED-AND-BURLAPPED SHRUBS— PICKING THEM OUT AND PLANTING THEM

Before the day of the plastic pot, nurserymen started most shrubs in beds of soil, then dug them up and offered them for sale with the roots balled in burlap. Some shrubs are still grown and sold this traditional way, and chosen with care, they remain an excellent bet. Their roots have grown naturally, unconfined by plastic containers. Further, if they have been dug up properly, with a compact ball of the earth they have grown in clinging to the roots, they adjust easily to their new environment when transplanted.

To choose fresh, healthy balled-and-burlapped shrubs, make sure that the top growth looks crisp and green, and check the burlap. It should look new and intact, indicating that the shrub has been wrapped recently. Avoid plants that have roots sticking through the burlap or a second layer of burlap hiding an earlier layer; in both cases the shrubs have been out of the ground too long. And beware of a root ball that seems soft and crumbly; that may mean that the root ball is man-made. Good root balls have a solid feel. Shop for balled-and-burlapped shrubs in early fall or in spring when, traditionally, the better nurseries put them on sale.

Planting a balled-and-burlapped shrub is not difficult either. The main steps are shown below and at right. There are just two overall precautions. First, if the root ball is heavy, it is safer to roll the shrub into position than to do any lifting. Second, the shrub should be planted soon after coming from the nursery. If there is any delay, keep the root ball moist; hose it down if it begins to look dry.

Their foliage strikingly green and full, five arborvitaes stand guard at the border of a yard, delineating the property and providing both beauty and privacy. Plants like these are frequently sold with their root balls wrapped in burlap.

1 Dig a hole twice as wide as the root ball of your newly purchased shrub. Make the hole as deep as the root ball, so that the shrub will rest at its original depth. Then maneuver the plant to the edge of the hole and gently roll it in. Do not lift it by grasping the stem; this can harm the shrub.

2 Cut the strings holding the burlap around the root ball, and remove any other fasteners. Adjust the position of the shrub, making sure that it is centered in the hole and that the stem is vertical, by pulling on the edges of the burlap *(right)*. Also make certain that the top roots are at ground level or just above. If the shrub is sitting too low or too high, lift it out and fill up or deepen the hole.

3 Remove as much burlap as you can by cutting. Natural-fiber burlap will decompose in time, but the small-mesh variety can strangle new roots, and burlap that includes synthetic fibers will do the same. Fill the hole with the earth you removed when digging, breaking up any large clods and removing big stones.

4 Build a basin of earth around the newly planted shrub to help retain water. Spread a layer of mulch about 2 inches thick in the basin but leave about 2 inches of ground uncovered at the base of the stems for air circulation. Water well. To be sure the root ball gets a good soaking, leave a hose trickling at the base of the stem for at least a half hour right after the planting is completed. □

CONTROLLING EROSION WITH LOW-GROWING SHRUBS

Looking rather like nature's version of a shag rug, massed junipers cling tightly to a sharply sloping front yard, preventing erosion, absorbing runoff during downpours and handsomely carpeting the area.

Motorists driving newly opened stretches of highway may sometimes notice large sheets of rough matting stretched over the earthen banks by the side of the road. The purpose of the matting is to secure the newly graded soil until grasses, shrubs or other plantings can be made to take root and provide natural, long-term erosion control.

Precisely the same technique can be applied in a backyard garden that includes a sloping bank—or on any other tilted bit of land that is steep enough to be in danger of erosion from rain and wind. For matting, use old-fashioned untreated burlap, which is available in cut lengths at many garden supply centers (the untreated kind will disintegrate in the soil over time). For plantings, any of several common evergreen shrubs will do; junipers are ideal because their roots spread out to anchor the soil, and their foliage makes a lovely green carpet in areas that are otherwise difficult to landscape. They are also drought-resistant, an important asset because banks are so well drained that they are often dry, especially if they stand in full sun.

The drawings at right show how to lay burlap on a slope and how to plant junipers through holes cut in the burlap sheets. For a modest-sized slope, you will not need a great number of plants; they need to be widely spaced because they will soon spread to cover the area. It is a good idea, though, to buy two different species of junipers. Some should be of the very low-growing form called prostrate, which will look well on the slope itself. The rest should be ordinary low-growers. Planted on the crest of the slope, they will cascade downward when mature.

1 Obtain enough burlap to cover the slope you intend to plant. Pin it down firmly at about 2-foot intervals with stakes or large nails. It is essential that the burlap stay in place, to prevent erosion while the shrubs root and grow.

2 Set the shrubs you have bought on the burlap, spacing them 3 to 4 feet apart in a staggered pattern. Then, using a sharp knife, make X-shaped cuts in the burlap at the spots where the plants will be located.

3 Peel back the burlap where you have made the cuts. Using a spade, dig holes as deep as the root balls and at least twice the diameter. Remove the plants from their pots and set them in the ground. Plant them as you would any container-grown shrubs (pages 10-13). Then tuck the burlap flaps into the soil around the roots. Water generously. The burlap will serve as a mulch, conserving moisture, but to disguise it you can spread a layer of fairly coarse pine bark or other organic mulch on top. □

A SOILLESS BED
FOR ACID-LOVING SHRUBS

A raised bed of pine bark mulch provides an ideal milieu for a half-dozen young, shiny-leaved rhododendrons. The pine bark, which is naturally acidic and also drains well, is contained by a simple border of logs.

The most popular stars of the shrub world, including azaleas, rhododendrons, hollies and mountain laurel, are choosy about where they will live. They demand well-drained, acidic and reasonably rich soil. If the soil is too wet, their roots will rot. If there is not enough acid, these plants may be stunted and their leaves may turn yellow.

Such demands can pose problems for gardeners who want to grow shrubs but find their plots chronically damp, or soil too alkaline—as is all too common in the Midwest and Southwest. Draining a wet area is a major undertaking best left to a contractor, and bolstering the acid level of earth that is naturally alkaline requires constant maintenance.

But there is an answer, a raised bed. In such a bed, the shrubs are planted not in but rather on top of the earth, with the bed built up around them. This effectively lifts the shrubs above the subsurface damp, and the bed can be filled with materials that are naturally acidic. Creating a raised bed, as outlined at right and on the following pages, is not a very onerous task. And once the bed has been mounded up, it can be edged with logs or stones or railroad ties that will frame the shrubs and help make the bed a handsome feature in the garden's design.

The bed need have no soil at all; it can be made of naturally acidic ground pine bark. Bark comes in 3-cubic-foot bags. To figure how much you need, determine the area of the bed and then multiply it by the depth of the plants' root balls. The best location is in an area protected from harsh winds, and where there is a mixture of sun and shade. In nature, acid-loving shrubs mostly grow on the edges of woods or in sun-dappled clearings. For further protection against too much hot sun, they should ideally be planted in groups large enough so that the plants offer each other mutual shade—with their feet, so to speak, in cool, shadowy dark and their heads reaching toward the light.

1 After deciding on a protected location for your raised bed, mark off its boundaries with some sprinkled sand; then churn up the earth with a tiller. Start at the outside of the plot, then work in diminishing circles toward the center. This tilling will break up the soil so the roots can penetrate, aerate the soil and somewhat help the drainage.

2 Once the area is thoroughly tilled, rake it carefully to remove any rocks or roots that have been turned up. But do not smooth or pack down the soil; it should remain fairly loose so that water will drain through it.

3 Remove your plants from their containers and set them out on top of the tilled earth. They should be spaced 4 to 6 feet apart in a staggered pattern. If the containers are plastic, prepare the root balls as shown on page 12. If they are in baskets (left) the root balls need no preparation.

4 Spread shredded pine bark around the shrubs. Do not stint. The bark should surround all the shrubs and come up to the tops of their root balls, that is, to the level at which the shrubs were planted before.

5 After roughly leveling the bark, you can edge the bed with logs, stones or other materials that go with your landscaping. (Do not use wood impregnated with creosote; it harms plants.) Water well and check the bed from time to time for settling. You will probably need to add bark in three to five months and each year thereafter. □

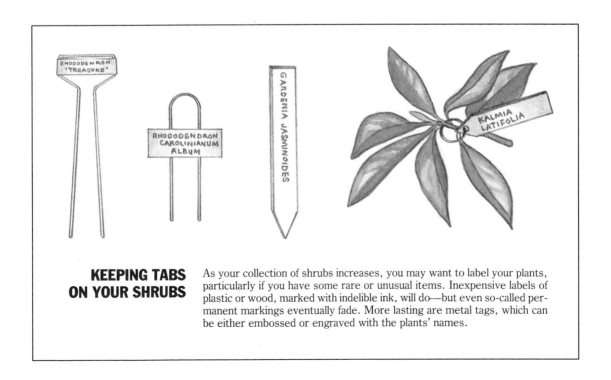

KEEPING TABS ON YOUR SHRUBS

As your collection of shrubs increases, you may want to label your plants, particularly if you have some rare or unusual items. Inexpensive labels of plastic or wood, marked with indelible ink, will do—but even so-called permanent markings eventually fade. More lasting are metal tags, which can be either embossed or engraved with the plants' names.

A BERM
TO SET OFF MINIATURE SHRUBS

Dwarf shrubs are naturally small versions of familiar species; some may grow only 18 inches high instead of 4 or 5 feet. Some of them evolved in cold, windy regions where the only way to survive was to hug the ground. Others started as genetic mutations. Either way, they are now widely cultivated—for their elegance, their ability to fit in cramped spaces and their ease of maintenance. Growing slowly, dwarfs need pruning far less often than full-sized shrubs, and they require less watering and fertilizing.

The best of all places to plant dwarf shrubs is on a berm—a shaped mound of earth, a man-made hillock that can lend variety and charm to any flat landscape. A berm, with its raised, undulating contours, perfectly shows off a collection of miniatures. If the shrubs are interplanted with some low-growing but colorful perennials and annuals, the berm can become an eye-catching part of a garden.

Making a berm, shown below and at right, is simplicity itself. You don't even have to prepare the ground. All you need is a large amount of topsoil—a truckload or two of it. To locate a reliable supplier, shop around and get advice from a local nursery. Do not buy ordinary fill; it will have few nutrients, and lots of rocks and clods. If possible, to avoid considerable wheelbarrow exercise, persuade the topsoil supplier to dump his truck where the berm will be located.

Roughly trimmed holly bushes and creeping junipers stand on a berm that, with its strategically placed rocks, resembles a small natural hillock.

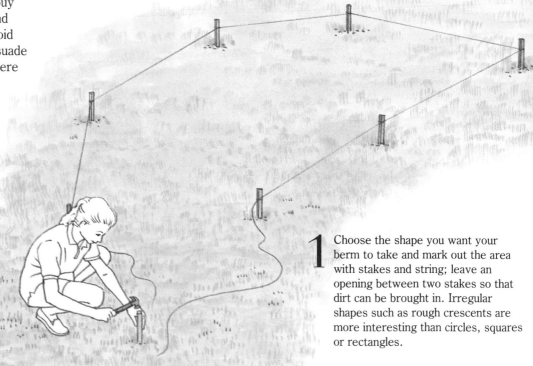

1 Choose the shape you want your berm to take and mark out the area with stakes and string; leave an opening between two stakes so that dirt can be brought in. Irregular shapes such as rough crescents are more interesting than circles, squares or rectangles.

2 Fill the marked space with topsoil. The berm should be at least 1 foot high, so there will be enough soil to cover the root balls of the shrubs and other plants you intend to put there. With a shovel, smooth and contour the soil.

3 Plant your dwarf shrubs, putting large specimens in the middle or toward the rear of the berm so that the various levels of planting will be visible. Follow the planting instructions on pages 10-13 and 18-19. If you plan to include any other permanent residents such as flowering perennials, put them in next; if you plan to include any annuals, put them in last. When the planting is finished, cover the berm with mulch and water it well. □

PINE BARK MULCH

GROWING SHRUBS IN CONTAINERS TO MOVE WITH THE SEASONS

Twin azalea specimens bring twice the color to a glass tabletop. While winter reigns outside, warm indoor temperatures coax these repotted plants into early bloom.

Specimen plants are the stand-alone stars of the garden world. Set apart from crowded beds and borders, they are meant to be seen as individuals, admired for their distinctive shapes, foliage or flowers. Evergreen shrubs grown in containers make ideal specimens because you can move them about with a minimum of effort. The "viewing season" of many flowering shrubs can be extended by bringing them indoors (to a porch or a greenhouse) in the fall, then spurring them to early bloom before setting them outside again in the spring.

Small, slow-growing shrubs, particularly dwarf varieties, are well suited to the limited confines of a container; good results can also be obtained with the early-blooming azaleas typically sold as gift plants.

The roots of plants grown in containers are more vulnerable to the cold than roots growing in the ground. If you plan to leave your container shrubs outdoors all winter, buy especially cold-hardy plants.

Since the roots have less soil to draw water from, plants in containers must be watered more frequently. This leaches out nutrients quickly, so you will have to fertilize often; for some shrubs this means every two weeks during the active growing season.

Prune regularly to control size and shape. Repot every two years. Move root-bound plants to larger pots, or cut off some roots (and some top growth to compensate) and replace the plants in their original pots. To encourage azaleas to rebloom every spring, repot them *(opposite)*. Use a mix made of 2 parts perlite, 4 parts pine bark, 1 part peat moss, 1 part vermiculite or kitty litter; kitty litter is cheaper than vermiculite and retains moisture even longer. All pots should have drainage holes in the bottom. And all should be sterilized *(box, page 31)* if they have been used before.

1 After the flowers fade from a potted azalea in spring, repot the plant in a shallow container—1½ times wider than it is tall—with a drainage hole in the bottom. The container for repotting should be either new or thoroughly sterilized. Line the bottom with a layer of broken pottery *(right),* and cover the shards with 1 to 2 inches of potting mix.

2 Remove the plant from its old pot. With a screwdriver or a stick, vigorously scrape the sides of the root ball to dislodge old soil and separate the roots. If the plant is severely root-bound, cut through the binding roots with pruning shears. Pull or cut off any dead or unhealthy roots; these are usually brownish in color, in contrast to healthy roots, which are whitish.

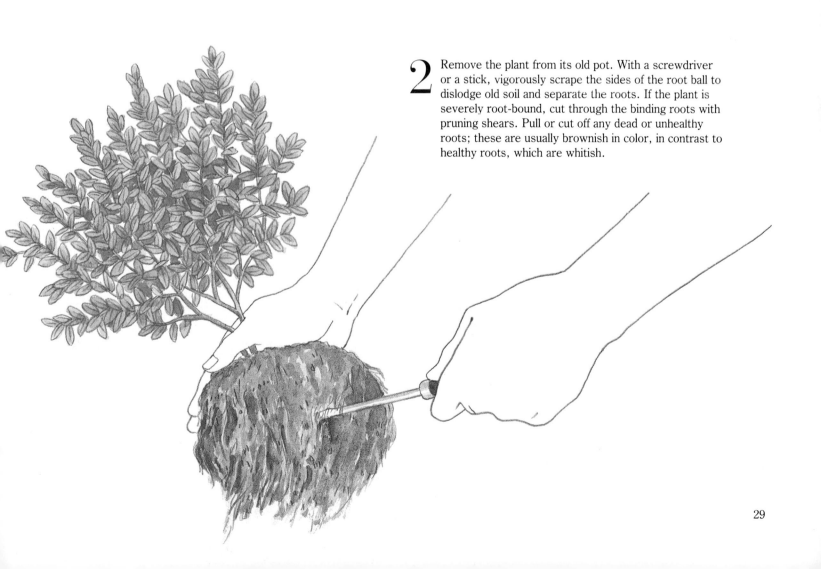

3 Place the plant in a new container. If necessary, fill in with soil until the plant sits at the same level in the new container as it did in its previous pot. Then add more soil, working it down among the roots with your fingers *(right)*. Water thoroughly.

4 Prune some foliage to compensate for damage to the root ball and to encourage fresh growth *(left)*. In spring, move the azalea outdoors to a spot that receives indirect sunlight. Feed it monthly with azalea fertilizer. Before the first frost, move the plant to a porch or a greenhouse where temperatures average 50° F; azaleas need cool nights and at least four hours of indirect sun daily to bloom early.

5 When new buds begin to swell and show color, bring the plant indoors where warmer temperatures will encourage the buds to open. While the plant is blooming, pinch off any new foliage growth; this will direct the plant's energy to flower production. After the flowers fade, prune the plant to maintain its size and shape. Move it outdoors again in spring. □

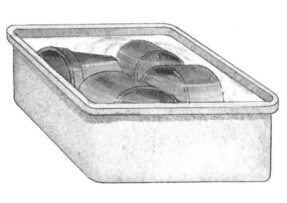

NEW LIFE FOR OLD POTS

To avoid contamination by pests and disease organisms, use only new or carefully cleaned containers. To remove the white crust that develops from salts and fertilizer and settles around the top rim, scrub old plastic and other nonporous pots in a solution of 1 part household bleach to 9 parts water; then rinse in fresh water. Clay pots, which absorb the salts, need extra treatment. Soak them eight hours in a solution of 1 part bleach to 9 parts water, scrub with a brush and rinse. Then soak the pots for another eight hours in a solution of 1 part vinegar to 16 parts water; wash with soap and water, and rinse.

2
KEEPING SHRUBS IN SHAPE

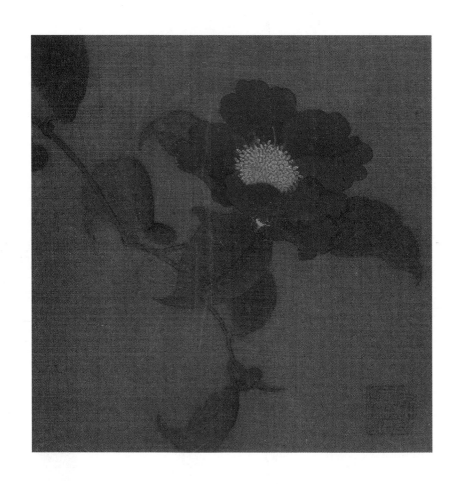

Most evergreen shrubs are so undemanding that it is easy to overlook them when tending to garden needs. In moist, well-drained and slightly acidic soil, they are apt to grow rampantly. Even in unfavorable soil they often thrive. But like all growing things, shrubs benefit from a little attention. Fertilizing will provide the roots with the nutrients to make them grow strong and robust. Watering will ensure that the nutrients are distributed from the root system to the branch tips and keep the foliage green. Pruning will keep shrubs dense, compact and shapely, at the same time encouraging the growth of new limbs. And some evergreens need protection from winter's perils. Trussing the limbs of pines, spruces and hemlocks is wise in areas where heavy accumulations of snow may weigh them down to the breaking point, and broad-leaved species such as rhododendrons and mountain laurels may need to be screened from drying winds.

Most of the foregoing are routine tasks that will repay the gardener in handsome and healthy shrubs. One of them—pruning—can be more than a routine chore; done with imagination it can be an art form of many variations. In topiary, fast-growing shrubs such as boxwood, yew and privet may be sculptured into globes, pyramids and animal forms, and flowering shrubs such as camellias may be shaped into treelike standards. Espaliering trains shrubs to grow flat against a wall, to give both the shrub and the wall architectural interest. Bonsai—an art that Japanese gardeners have practiced for centuries—involves the pruning of shrubs into delicately contorted miniatures.

Techniques for all these operations, both the routine and the artful—and the tools needed to perform them—are described in the pages that follow.

AN INTEGRATED APPROACH TO ROUTINE MAINTENANCE TASKS

Shrubs, to be at their healthiest and most attractive, need to be fertilized, watered, mulched and pruned. By combining the first three chores in an integrated maintenance program, you can do your plants the most good with the least amount of work.

Fertilizers may be organic (derived from living matter) or inorganic (chemically formulated nutrients). Organic fertilizers are slower to act than inorganics, but less likely to upset the natural balance of the soil. The required nutrients are present in most soils, but not always in the right amounts. Have your soil analyzed every two or three years. If supplements are called for, add them in the spring before growth starts, or in the fall after the plant has stopped producing new shoots.

Water plays a multitude of roles in plants: it transports nutrients, lends rigidity to leaves and stems, and is indispensable to the manufacture of new tissue. Water thoroughly so that moisture reaches the deepest roots. Water administered at a slow trickle will seep deeper into the soil than water delivered in a quick blast. Repeated light watering can actually make a plant susceptible to drought, because unless the water goes deep into the soil, the roots will not extend themselves to reach for it; hence they will be shallow-growing. But do not overwater; roots will die in constantly wet soil from lack of oxygen.

Organic mulch reduces the need for fertilizer and water. Besides returning nutrients to the soil as it decomposes, a good organic mulch conserves water by slowing evaporation, helps keep soil temperature stable and inhibits weed growth. Good organic mulches are available at garden centers, or you can make your own by mixing grass clippings and fallen leaves.

Techniques for fertilizing and watering—and tools to do the jobs—are shown below and on the following pages. For pruning information, see pages 38-43.

Given a rich, moist, acidic soil, this skimmia responds with healthy foliage and abundant blooms. Most evergreens require acidic soil, and special fertilizers are available for them.

WATERING TO ORDER

Whatever your watering chore, there is a tool available to help you do it right. To provide a gentle shower that will not wash away soil from the base of a plant, use a fine-spray nozzle *(left, top)* that attaches to your garden hose. To deliver moisture to the roots of plants with minimal evaporation loss, buy a soaker hose *(left, center)* made of permeable canvas or perforated rubber that oozes water from its entire length; stretch out the soaker hose on the surface or bury it underground for a season of irrigation. If you use a sprinkler *(left, bottom)* to water shrubs, remember to leave it on long enough to give the soil a good, deep soaking.

1 Before fertilizing with an inorganic fertilizer, remove leaves, old mulch and other debris from under and around the shrub. Following the instructions on the label, spread the fertilizer near the base of the plant *(right)*. Be careful not to let any fertilizer touch leaves, stems or your hands; wear gloves or scatter it with a trowel.

2 To water a shrub with a hose, use a nozzle attachment that breaks up the flow into a gentle spray. Water until the ground is thoroughly wet; depending on weather and the type of soil, this may take five to 10 minutes. Then give the leaves and stems a final rinse to make sure no fertilizer has landed on them; the salts in fertilizer can damage them.

3 Spread new mulch under and around the plant, leaving a clear space around the base of the stems. Build a layer 3 to 4 inches thick. The mulch should be dense enough to prevent weed growth but loose enough to let water seep through. □

SHIELDING EVERGREENS FROM WINTER'S COLD

Needle-leaved evergreens generally survive northern winters well, although steps may have to be taken to prevent snow damage *(box, opposite)*. But their broad-leaved counterparts—mountain laurels, azaleas, rhododendrons, hollies and others—can shrivel and die in cold climates for want of water. Winter winds draw moisture from the leaves, and so does winter sunshine. And dormant roots cannot replace the lost moisture.

The first defense against winter damage is to plant evergreen shrubs in spots protected from the worst winds. For shrubs already in the ground, be sure they get extra waterings as the date for the first hard frost approaches. This will send them into winter with a good supply of moisture. Then spread a thick layer of mulch around them, to help keep the water from evaporating and to provide insulation for the roots.

If more protection is needed—and it certainly may be in northerly areas, especially for new transplants—there are two further useful maneuvers, shown at right. One is to spray the leaves with an antidesiccant—a milky-looking waxy liquid that coats the leaves and retards water loss. Another is to build temporary stake-and-burlap screens on the windward sides of exposed evergreens. To find out where such blasts come from, make a miniature wind sock by tying a strip of cloth to a post. Plants can be loosely wrapped in burlap, for that matter, but screens are preferable because they let in some sunlight and allow air to circulate freely. A warning: do not wrap a plant in plastic, unless you punch holes in the plastic to allow some ventilation.

Scores of buds stand ready to supplement the dozens of flowers already in bloom on a thriving mountain laurel. Having delicate broad leaves that easily lose moisture, mountain laurel needs protection against sharp winds and winter cold.

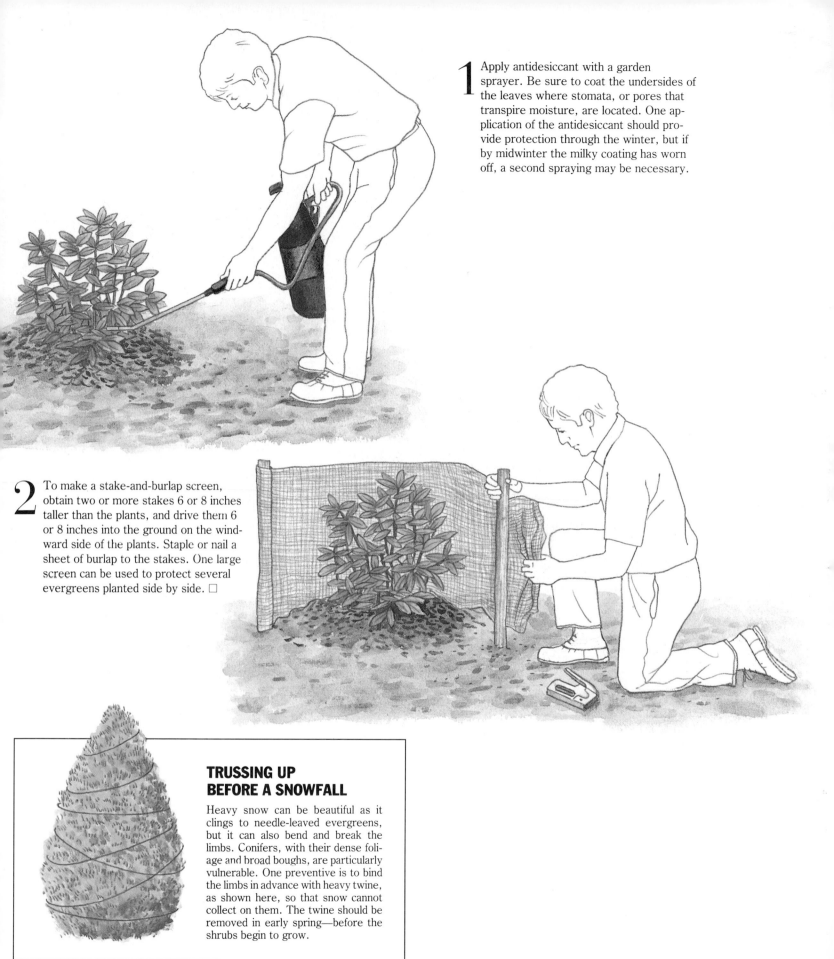

1 Apply antidesiccant with a garden sprayer. Be sure to coat the undersides of the leaves where stomata, or pores that transpire moisture, are located. One application of the antidesiccant should provide protection through the winter, but if by midwinter the milky coating has worn off, a second spraying may be necessary.

2 To make a stake-and-burlap screen, obtain two or more stakes 6 or 8 inches taller than the plants, and drive them 6 or 8 inches into the ground on the windward side of the plants. Staple or nail a sheet of burlap to the stakes. One large screen can be used to protect several evergreens planted side by side. □

TRUSSING UP BEFORE A SNOWFALL

Heavy snow can be beautiful as it clings to needle-leaved evergreens, but it can also bend and break the limbs. Conifers, with their dense foliage and broad boughs, are particularly vulnerable. One preventive is to bind the limbs in advance with heavy twine, as shown here, so that snow cannot collect on them. The twine should be removed in early spring—before the shrubs begin to grow.

PRUNING CONIFERS TO KEEP THEM IN SHAPE

Few plants require as little care as conifers do. They are rarely bothered by insects or disease, and they thrive in almost any soil that is well drained. About the only care is periodic pruning. Most can be made to grow more densely if the growing tips are cut seasonally, and some put out wayward branches that need shortening to maintain a good silhouette.

The manner of pruning and the time to do it depend on the nature of the conifer. Hemlocks, junipers, yews and other soft-needled conifers produce buds, hundreds and sometimes even thousands of them, all along their branches. Such shrubs may be pruned at any time while the growing season lasts, and at almost any point along a branch. Because of a botanical phenomenon called apical dominance, which means that most growth is concentrated at a plant's branch tips, the presence of terminal buds inhibits the growth of lateral buds. The removal of a terminal bud reroutes the shrub's hormones and thus allows the lateral buds to develop.

On pines, spruces and firs (the stiff-needled conifers) growth occurs at the branch tips, in long, cylindrical formations called candles—new shoots that are covered with soft, tiny needles. Pruning the candles will promote the growth of more candles and hence a denser, bushier plant in the long run. Pruning a full candle will prevent the conifer from further terminal growth on that limb that season; pruning half the candle will limit terminal growth by half that season. In either case, the pruning has to be done in spring before the candle has matured sufficiently for its needles to have developed.

Pruning mature branches on a stiff-needled conifer *(opposite)* should be done sparingly and selectively because mature wood has few buds to produce new growth. Try to follow the natural form of the shrub as closely as possible, and cut inside the desired silhouette, rather than at its edge, so that the stub is concealed.

A ground-hugging mugo pine—its newly formed candles ready for pruning to maintain the shrub's characteristic moundlike shape—provides a pleasant contrast in tone and texture to the surrounding ring of blue-flowering lithodora plantings.

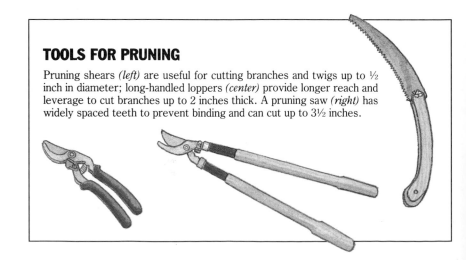

TOOLS FOR PRUNING

Pruning shears *(left)* are useful for cutting branches and twigs up to ½ inch in diameter; long-handled loppers *(center)* provide longer reach and leverage to cut branches up to 2 inches thick. A pruning saw *(right)* has widely spaced teeth to prevent binding and can cut up to 3½ inches.

1 To rid a stiff-needled conifer of wayward branches that give it an ungainly shape, cut at the juncture of two branches or at the juncture of a branch and the main stem *(inset);* this will make the surgery as inconspicuous as possible.

2 To limit branch length and promote density in a stiff-needled conifer, remove about half of each candle *(below)* before new needles mature in spring. This inhibits the branches from extending upward and outward while encouraging the production of added branches. □

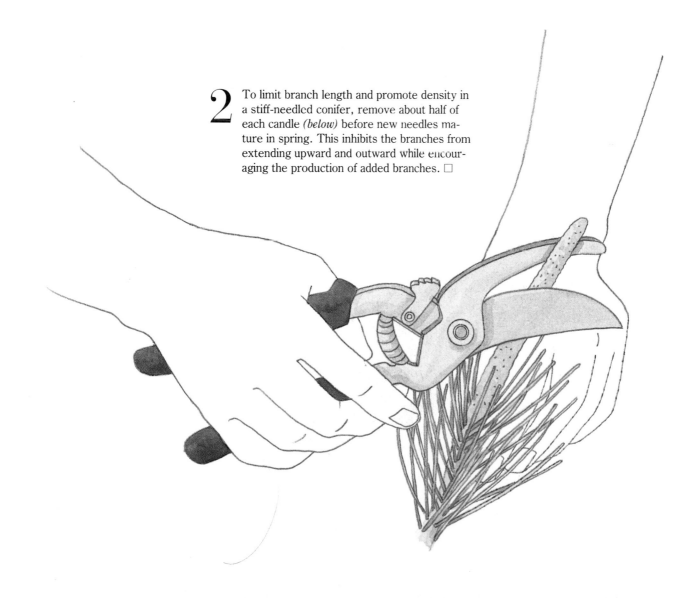

SHEARING A HEDGE FOR A FORMAL EFFECT

Many hedges planted as windbreaks, privacy screens and backdrops for flower beds look best if they are sheared rather than allowed to grow shaggy and untamed. With clean, sharp lines, they give a landscape definition and an eye-pleasing symmetry, and if they are tapered so that they are narrower at the top than at the bottom, the lower branches get the light and air they need to develop. The clipping need only be done twice a year or so, and the job, shown on the opposite page, is surprisingly easy to do well.

The task is made far easier if you have top-quality cutting tools. Hedge shears with long blades give the most control and are best for hedges of moderate size. They should have drop-forged, heat-treated steel blades and ash or hickory handles. Power shears do not cut as neatly but are more practical for extensive hedges that would simply take too long to trim by hand. Small pruning shears are needed to cut stems too thick or tough for other clippers.

Not all shrubs are good candidates for shearing. Trimming large-leaved shrubs involves cutting many leaves in half, which results in a lot of unsightly brown edges. A hedge made of such shrubs is better left unsheared. In general, small-leaved plants make the best formal hedges. Traditional favorites include Japanese and English yew, juniper, box and privet.

Trimming should be done in the spring, when new growth has appeared, and followed up with a second pruning later in the season. At neither time should new shoots be completely cut back. A hedge of evergreen shrubs must be allowed to grow slightly each year if it is to remain vigorous.

The geometric lines of two Japanese boxwoods frame a neatly shaped brush cherry. Both kinds of shrubs, with their small leaves, are ideal for shearing.

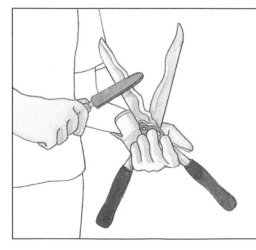

SHARP BLADES FOR CLEAN CUTS

Keen-edged shears make hedge trimming not only easier, but also far neater; dull blades can tear stems and produce uneven cuts. To sharpen them, use a medium-grit stone lubricated with oil to start, then follow with a fine-grit stone. For wavy-edged blades, which are superior since they have more cutting edge than straight ones, employ a stone that has a rounded surface.

1 Decide how wide you want the bottom of your hedge to be, and how much you want it to taper inward toward the top. Begin clipping at the bottom. To aid in making a tapered edge as you move upward, hold the shears with the blades tilted slightly inward. Trust your eye, and step back periodically to see how the shrubs are shaping up.

2 Shear a flat plane across the top surface of the hedge. After you have finished shearing, remove clippings that have not fallen to the ground by running a leaf rake over the surface of the hedge. Finally, clean your clipping tools, making sure to remove encrusted sap or resin. □

41

PRUNING BROAD-LEAVED EVERGREENS FOR FULLNESS AND VIGOR

Alternating golden privet and red barberry shrubs make a colorful border. They are kept informal but tidy by regular pruning.

The year-round beauty of broad-leaved evergreen shrubs is often enhanced by careful grooming —pruning the branches and, in some cases, removing flowers *(opposite)*. Whether the objective is to produce a spectacular display of rhododendron blooms or to regulate the size and shape of a privet, grooming results in shrubs that are more attractive and more vigorous.

There are two basic pruning techniques for broad-leaved evergreens. One is thinning, which involves the removal of entire branches from larger branches or from the main stem to encourage interior growth. The other is heading, which is the cutting back of branch ends and terminal buds to limit the height and spread of a bush and to promote interior branching and greater flowering.

Whichever pruning technique is used—and some bushes may require both—the timing is critical. Shrubs that blossom in early spring from the previous year's growth, as azaleas, camellias and magnolias do, should be pruned while in bloom, or shortly thereafter, so that the buds of next season's flowers form on the pruned branches. (The cuttings need not go to waste; they make handsome bouquets for indoors.) Shrubs that flower from new growth in late spring or summer, as privet, hibiscus and abelia do, should be pruned before the new growth appears. This will bring about denser new growth and a greater abundance of flowers. Always use quality pruning tools *(page 38)* that are clean and sharp. Dull blades make ragged cuts that invite pests and disease.

Dead and damaged branches should be pruned first and the tools should be cleaned with alcohol afterward to prevent possible infection of healthy limbs.

When drastic pruning is required to restore neglected or overgrown shrubs, it may be advisable to perform the pruning in increments over a two- or three-year period. Pruning more than a third of a shrub at a time is a risky procedure that can kill or seriously damage a plant.

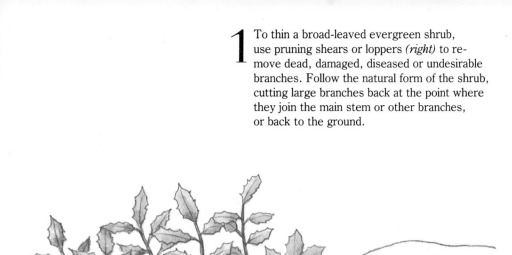

1 To thin a broad-leaved evergreen shrub, use pruning shears or loppers *(right)* to remove dead, damaged, diseased or undesirable branches. Follow the natural form of the shrub, cutting large branches back at the point where they join the main stem or other branches, or back to the ground.

2 To head a shrub, use pruning shears to snip branch tips back to buds that will eventually produce a network of lateral side shoots and result in greater displays of foliage and flowers. Buds appear at the junctures between a stem and its leaves *(inset)*. □

DISBUDDING AND DEADHEADING

For flowering shrubs to look their best, not only the branches need attention, but the flowers themselves need occasional disbudding and deadheading. In disbudding, excess buds are plucked from plants such as camellias *(left, top)* to produce larger blooms from the remaining buds. In deadheading, spent flower heads from plants such as rhododendrons *(left, bottom)* are twisted off to divert plant energy and nutrients from seed production to greater foliage and flower growth the following season. No special tools are needed; you can do both jobs with your fingers.

GIBBING—A TREATMENT TO ENHANCE CAMELLIA BLOSSOMS

Extravagant pink blossoms such as these, 3 to 5 inches across, are produced by treating the leaf buds of a mature camellia with the natural plant hormone gibberellic acid.

Camellias produce some of the largest, lushest blossoms that grow on shrubs. Their handsome flowers open late in the year to grace the fall and winter landscape with rich color. By applying a plant hormone, you can help these late bloomers produce flowers of increased size and more intense color. The treatment will also bring the blossoms to an earlier peak, which can prevent the loss of buds to frost damage.

The chemical is gibberellic acid, or gib, and it is made from a hormone that regulates growth. It is sold in powdered form, and must be dissolved in water before use. Drops of the gib solution can then be applied to an area adjoining a flower bud. The chemical enters the stem and the bud tissues, speeding the growth of the flower and producing a larger, brighter blossom.

Most camellias respond well to gibbing. But since an overdose of hormones can produce unwanted mutations, a few precautions should be taken to avoid injury to the plant. Select a shrub that is at least three years old, and treat it with gib only in alternate years. Use gib for no more than 20 percent of the flowers on a mature shrub. And once the gibbed buds have bloomed, cut them off as soon as they fade; otherwise foliage growth from the tips of treated branches may be inhibited.

1 Examine the branches of your camellia for a well-developed leaf bud next to a healthy flower bud; leaf buds are narrow and pointed, flower buds plump and rounded. Twist off the leaf bud *(left)*, leaving a cup-shaped formation of bud scales behind. If you cannot find a leaf bud next to a flower bud, look for two flower buds side by side and twist off one of the flower buds as you would a leaf bud.

2 Mix gibbing powder with distilled water as directed on the package. Using an eyedropper, place one drop of the solution in the cup of bud scales. (If there is no cup, apply the gib to the wound left by the removal of the bud.) Attach a dated label to the stem. Within two weeks, the flower bud adjacent to the treated leaf bud should show accelerated growth. After it fades, cut it off just below the nearest leaf on the stem. □

BONSAI—
THE ART OF CREATING MINIATURES

The name *bonsai* means simply "tray plant." As refined over the years by Japanese gardeners, the art of bonsai allows you to bring a taste of the wilderness—appropriately scaled down but otherwise true to life—into your home by training shrubs to grow as miniatures.

To get shrubs to grow successfully in very small containers, their tops must be repeatedly pruned and their roots carefully trimmed. A shrub that normally reaches a height of 20 feet may be no more than a foot tall as a mature bonsai.

The mastery of bonsai takes patience and experience; the fine line between just enough pruning and too much can be learned only through trial and error. But with the right tools *(below, right)* and by applying a few basic principles *(opposite),* even beginners can achieve a pleasing specimen of the art in a few years.

Many evergreen shrubs, such as azalea, camellia, juniper and cotoneaster, make good bonsai because they grow well in containers and stand up to heavy root and top pruning. Not surprisingly, dwarf varieties do best. In any case, choose a small plant with an interesting shape.

You can start bonsai in ordinary clay or plastic pots and later transplant them to special bonsai containers. These are typically flat ceramic dishes with drainage holes in the bottom. Good drainage is essential. If you use a commercial potting soil, lighten it by adding 1 part sand or perlite to 3 parts of mix. Or make your own mix by combining 2 parts perlite, 4 parts fine pine bark, 1 part peat moss and 1 part vermiculite.

Because their containers hold so little soil, bonsai need frequent watering—as often as twice a day in spring, summer and fall; every other day in winter. Since frequent watering washes nutrients from the soil, fertilize lightly once a month with a complete organic fertilizer. Avoid overpruning; once or twice during each growing season should be sufficient to achieve and maintain the desired shape. Repot every two years.

After just a few years of bonsai training, this juniper displays an artfully asymmetric, recumbent profile that might have been chiseled by an unrelenting mountain wind.

SPECIAL BONSAI TOOLS

Traditional tools used in the work of bonsai are available at many garden centers. Scissorlike shears with large curved handles are ideal for removing branches and roots. Long narrow shears with small blades allow you to get into tight spaces to snip twigs, leaves and buds. A small brush gently sweeps up clippings and smoothes soil. Ceramic containers come in a variety of shapes, sizes and colors—but should be small and low, in order to keep the roots confined.

1 To select a specimen for bonsai, look for a healthy container-grown evergreen shrub with a prominent trunk and an interesting shape. Use scissorlike bonsai shears to remove the shrub's lower branches (right) and expose its trunk.

2 Continue shaping by removing some of the branches on the rest of the trunk so that you produce an asymmetrical outline. Then remove all growth from the undersides of the remaining branches; such stripping emphasizes their shapes.

3 Remove the shrub from its container. Gently work old soil off the roots with a blunt-ended stick such as a chopstick. Be careful not to damage the small, light-colored feeder roots. Leave the impacted soil in the center of the root ball undisturbed.

4 With the scissorlike shears, trim away one-third to one-half of all the roots—except for those nearest to the trunk, which should be left as is. Remove entirely any roots that look unhealthy or that have a thick, woody appearance. As soon as you have finished trimming, place the root ball in a bowl of water.

5 Prepare the bonsai container by covering the drainage holes in the bottom with a piece of all-weather screening. This will prevent the potting mixture from washing out during frequent waterings.

6 Prepare a light potting mix and spread a thin layer of it on the bottom of the container. Set the plant on the soil and spread out its roots in all directions. Center the plant in a container that is round or square; place it slightly off-center in one that is rectangular or oval. Add more potting mix and work it down among the roots with your fingers.

PERLITE

VERMICULITE

PEAT MOSS

7 Cover the top of the potting mix with decorative pebbles. Water frequently—twice a day in hot weather. But don't overwater; the roots will rot if the bonsai constantly sits in a wet medium. □

TOPIARY—
LIVING SCULPTURE

This thick boxwood hedge, planted to follow a serpentine driveway, has been trimmed flat on the top and the sides to give it the formality of a wall. Poking through the hedge are privet bushes, trained as standards with bare stems and globular crowns.

Since the days of the Roman Empire, gardeners have taken pleasure in the challenge of topiary—sculpting plants to geometric or whimsical shapes that they would never assume naturally. Topiary is well suited to finely textured evergreens like boxwood, yew, rosemary, lavender, laurel, and small-leaved varieties of holly and privet. Simple designs, like globes and pyramids, are more in keeping with modern tastes than the elaborate animals of traditional topiary; they also take less time and effort. One popular shape known as a standard resembles a small tree, with a trunklike stem and globular top. Camellias, azaleas, gardenias and lantanas make good standards.

To create a topiary, you can plant a cutting and begin training it as soon as it is firmly rooted, or you can start with an established (one- to two-year-old) shrub and gradually prune it to the desired shape.

Both methods require patience. Prune by stages, giving the plant at least two months to recover in between. A simple geometric shape should take about two years to develop. Fertilize the shrub regularly during the training period to encourage fast growth. Once you have achieved the shape you want, you have only to remove the occasional errant shoot. Display your topiary in an ornamental pot or in a prominent location in your garden.

GARDENER'S CHOICE

With practice, you can create topiaries that form pyramids, spirals or more elaborate pompons—a series of globes of diminishing sizes piled atop one another *(above, right)*. Whichever form you choose, create the basic outline first, clearing the stem where required. Don't try for a finished look right away; it's better to trim the foliage into shape as it grows. Overenthusiastic pruning or bending of branches may hinder realization of the design or cause permanent damage to the plant.

1 Choose a container-grown plant that will lend itself to pruning. If you intend to create a standard, make sure the shrub has a straight, sturdy main stem and enough foliage on top to form a crown. With pruning shears, cut off all lower branches to expose the "trunk."

2 To trim the top of a standard, stand directly over the shrub and look down. From this perspective, use the outline of the container as a guide to prune in a circle, and then round the top surface to achieve a globular form.

3 If the stem is too thin to support the newly pruned (and somewhat top-heavy) plant, use a bamboo stake. The stake should be as tall as the trunk. Insert the stake into the soil next to the stem; tie the stake to the stem with light twine or with plastic-coated wire, being careful not to bind the stem too tightly. Prune the shrub regularly to keep the rounded top in shape and to remove any new growth from the bare "trunk." □

ESPALIER—
DESIGN IN TWO DIMENSIONS

Espalier—a form of training that first flattens a shrub against a wall or a fence, then persuades it to assume a decorative shape as it grows—is well suited to slow-growing evergreens. They can be coaxed into a broad range of designs—symmetrical, stylized representations of fans, candelabras and checkerboards, or into informal shapes devised by the gardener's imagination. The best designs follow the natural growth habit of the shrub. Vigorous and repeated pruning *(pages 38-43)* is required to set and hold the shape.

Whatever the design, espalier works best with the supple, flexible branches of young shrubs; older, drier branches may break when bent for shaping. Choose a plant between 2 and 3 feet tall. Dwarf varieties of juniper, cotoneaster, camellia, magnolia and pyracantha are easiest to train and maintain. Use nails or vine holders (wire hooks with waterproof adhesive backing) to attach the shrub to the wall or the fence.

With their flat, open arrangement, espaliers readily soak up sunlight, including the light reflected from the structure behind them. As a result, even shrubs, like pyracantha, that usually demand full sun will thrive as espaliers on northern- and eastern-facing exposures.

1 To prepare a shrub for espaliering, decide which side of the shrub will serve as the front, and prune all branches that grow outward from what will be the back *(right)*. Then plant the shrub 6 to 12 inches from a wall or a fence; the space will allow for air circulation and growth. For planting information, see pages 10-13.

Growing espalier-fashion from three stems, four rows of pyracantha branches turn a bare wall into a year-round display of living form and color.

2 Step back and think about the design you want to achieve. Try to follow the plant's natural growth habit. Stretch major branches into position and mark the places on the wall where you want to attach them. Use nails with loosely tied twine or special vine holders—wire loops that are anchored to the wall with weatherproof adhesive backing *(inset)*. Make sure the branches of the basic framework are well spaced, with leeway for future growth.

3 Remove any branches that extend out-ward from the front of the shrub; you want the plant to grow only in a flat plane. It will take several years for the espalier to mature. As new growth sprouts, continue to prune undesirable branches and to attach to the wall branches that enhance the design. ☐

3
GROWING
NEW SHRUBS

Practically no one has too many evergreen shrubs. Whether you are planning a new garden, redeveloping an old one or simply filling in bare spots, there is always room for at least one more shrub, especially if it is the twin of a prized garden specimen. Luckily, there are any number of inexpensive and reliable ways to add new shrubs to your garden by propagating them from existing plants. In the pages that follow you will find techniques for several of them.

One is to take advantage of seedlings that are produced naturally by parent plants—perhaps the result of a seed dropped by a foraging squirrel. Many such seedlings will be plants you want, but situated in the wrong places—either inches from the parent or some distance away. All you need do is transplant them.

Almost as simple is propagating by stem cuttings, a technique that is especially useful because it produces shrubs faster than growing them from seeds and guarantees plants identical to the donor shrub. That is an important factor when you want to match a particular shade of flower.

Grafting, in which portions of two plants are joined to produce a plant with the desired characteristics of both, is a time-honored method used by professionals. In cleft grafting, a scion—a portion of the plant you want to reproduce for color or form—is inserted into a cut at the top of another (usually hardier) plant's rootstock. A similar procedure, called side grafting, in which the scion is inserted into the side of the rootstock, is often used to propagate dwarf conifers.

Layering takes advantage of some plants' ability to form roots when their branches touch the ground. Many plants with low-lying branches propagate themselves spontaneously. Such plants can be encouraged to propagate on demand if you score the bottoms of their lower branches and secure them to the ground.

Finally, division—the digging up and breaking apart of stem clusters—is an excellent way to multiply such shrubs as barberry, nandina and azalea, which grow on multiple stems that often tend to spread as they mature. Division can also be used to rejuvenate an old shrub.

SPONTANEOUS SEEDLINGS, BONUSES FROM NATURE

Young shrubs often spring up spontaneously right next to established evergreen bushes, growing from seeds produced by their mature neighbors or possibly borne some distance by wind or birds. Such newcomers are more welcome than not, but they may not spring up where you want them to be—or they may be in a position to be crowded by more mature plants, which will leech away nutrients and moisture.

The sensible thing to do is to move the surprise offspring to a new location of its own. This is not a difficult operation, but it must be done swiftly; evergreen shrubs can lose moisture and suffer shock if their roots are out of the ground for long. First, a new hole should be made ready for the plant before it is removed from its original home. Then the plant should be carefully dug up *(right)* to preserve as many roots as possible. The seedling will have a long taproot, and this should be cut to encourage the growth of side roots. To compensate, some of the top growth can be trimmed after the transplanting is done.

Seedling shrubs are best moved when they have had some time to develop—at age one or two years. The best season depends upon the climate. In the North, spring is ideal; the plant can adjust to its new home through the summer months and before the onset of winter. In the South, where winters are mild but summers long and hot, autumn transplanting is preferable.

A tiny holly seedling thrusts its spiky leaves into the sunlight from a bed of fallen leaves and bark. Hollies, because they throw off many seeds, frequently produce self-sown offspring that can easily be transplanted to sites where new shrubs are wanted.

1 Before spading up your seedling, dig the hole that the shrub is to be moved into; it should be about 8 inches deep and 1 foot wide. Then start loosening the earth around the seedling itself *(right)*, keeping the spade 12 inches from the stem.

2 Continue working the spade underneath the seedling, harming as few roots as possible, until the
plant comes free. This should not take much effort;
the roots of shrubs less than two years old are not
extensive and will not have compacted earth around
them. This is what makes speedy transplanting
necessary; the bare roots dry out fast.

3 Immediately replant the shrub in its new location. The
top surfaces of the roots should be at the same level as
they were before. Using your hands, fill in around the
plant with the soil you dug up. While adding the fill,
hold the shrub by its main stem, shaking it gently from
time to time so that the earth settles about the roots.
Give the shrub some water and cover the area with 3
to 4 inches of a water-conserving layer of mulch.

4 To make up for roots lost during the transplanting
process—and for water loss as well—prune the
plant's foliage. Lower leaves can be removed entire
and some of the upper ones cut in half *(right)*. □

A CONGENIAL ENVIRONMENT
FOR ROOTING STEM CUTTINGS

*Thriving stem cuttings of Japanese euon-
ymus, displaying the shrub's fascinating
multicolored leaves, take root in a Styrofoam
cooler that has been altered to become
a miniature greenhouse.*

Homegrown plants cost far less than those bought at a nursery. The best way to grow new shrubs, if you do it yourself, is to nurture stems cut from mature plants. Cuttings produce fresh, young shrubs faster than seeds do, and the offspring will be identical to the parents in foliage and flowers, which is important to any gardener wishing to match favorite shrubs.

The key to producing healthy new shrubs from stem cuttings is having a warm, moist environment where the stems will stay alive and well while they develop roots. A greenhouse will do fine, of course, or a cold frame, but there is an easier and cheaper solution: a Styrofoam cooler of the sort often used on picnics to carry ice and chilled drinks. Properly cut and modified as described at right and on the following two pages, such an inexpensive cooler makes an ideal vehicle for propagating. It holds in moisture and warmth and allows light in. It can even be used the next year and the next if thoroughly cleaned each time with a bleach-and-water solution.

The cuttings should always be from new growth—but just how new varies among different plants. Some of the broad-leaved evergreen shrubs—notably azaleas and rhododendrons—can be propagated in the late spring from what are called softwood cuttings. A month after flowering, snip off some of the soft new shoots; they should just be showing signs of becoming firm.

From most broad-leaved shrubs, however, cuttings should be made in the late summer or early fall, when their softwood has hardened into "ripewood"—new growth that has had all summer to mature. With conifers, wait until late autumn or early winter to make cuttings. And take the cuttings from vertical shoots at the tops of these plants if upward-growing offspring are wanted. Shoots taken from the sides are apt to become low, wide-growing plants. With all shrubs, the best cuttings come from young, vigorous parent plants that are full of growing energy.

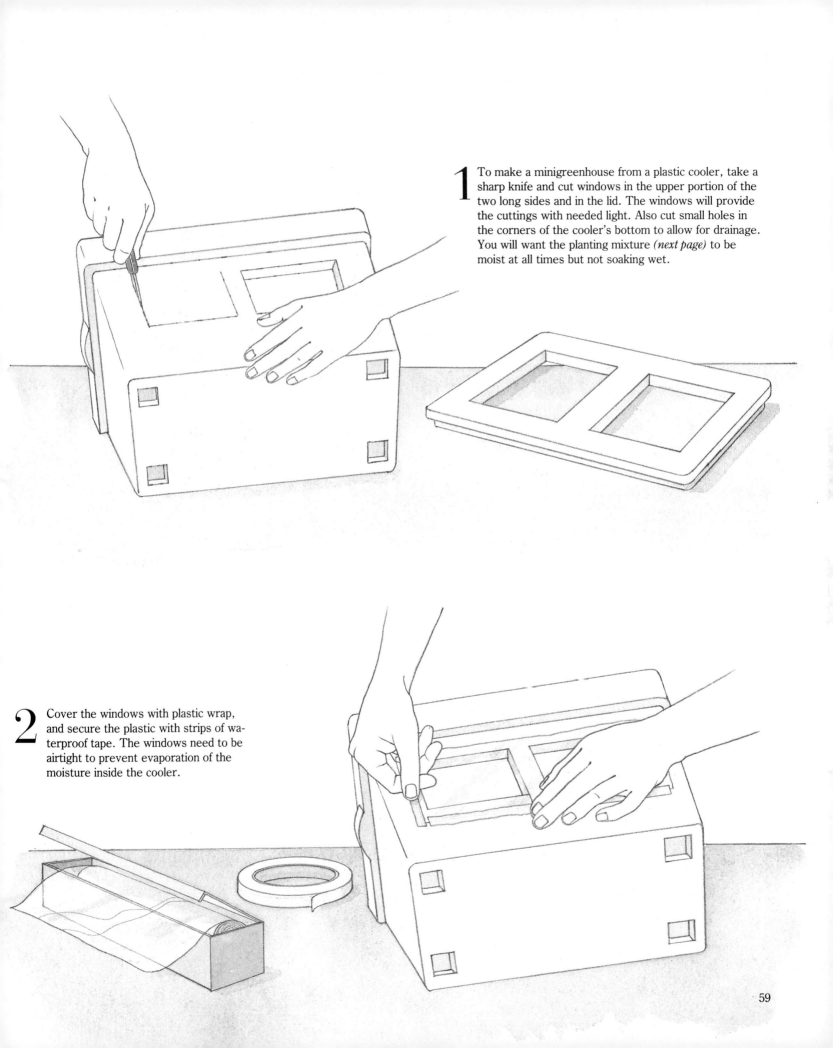

1 To make a minigreenhouse from a plastic cooler, take a sharp knife and cut windows in the upper portion of the two long sides and in the lid. The windows will provide the cuttings with needed light. Also cut small holes in the corners of the cooler's bottom to allow for drainage. You will want the planting mixture *(next page)* to be moist at all times but not soaking wet.

2 Cover the windows with plastic wrap, and secure the plastic with strips of waterproof tape. The windows need to be airtight to prevent evaporation of the moisture inside the cooler.

3 Mix a bucketful of planting medium—2 parts finely ground pine bark to 1 part perlite—and pour it into the cooler, covering the bottom to a depth of 4 inches. Water the mixture until it is thoroughly moist, then allow it to drain overnight. You can put the cooler in a sink while the water drains out the bottom, or set it outdoors on some bricks.

4 When the planter is ready, use pruning shears to make your cuttings—4-inch-long new shoots that have healthy foliage. If a cutting has a leaf bud or a flower bud, pinch it off; buds draw energy that should go into root formation. Remove the lower leaves from the cutting.

5 Place some rooting hormone powder on a sheet of paper and dip the cut end of the stem in it. The stems of some shrubs root readily enough not to need the hormone, but some require it—and it doesn't hurt any shrubs to use it.

6 Stick the cut stems 1 inch deep in the planting medium. Firm the mix around the stems but do not pack it down. Label your cuttings with plant name and date. Sprinkle with a fungicide solution (follow the manufacturer's instructions). Then close the top and place the plastic greenhouse in a warm area that has indirect light. Check from time to time; if the soil is dry, sprinkle the surface with water. Clean out any leaves that fall from the cuttings. After a month or six weeks, gently tug on one of the cuttings to see how its new root system is coming along; if it resists, roots have developed and you can begin transplanting.

7 When transplanting time comes, place the cuttings in individual pots. Make a hole in the potting soil with your finger or a round dowel so that the delicate new roots are not bruised or tangled. If the weather is mild, you can transplant directly into your garden, in a protected spot where the soil is high in organic matter. Either way, make sure the cuttings are set at the same level in the soil as they were in the planter. □

FOR MORE AND HEALTHIER SHRUBS: MULTIPLY BY DIVISION

This exuberant nandina shows the rejuvenating effect of repeated divisions—a brutal-seeming method of propagation that actually brings new life to many multistemmed shrubs as they mature.

A simple way to propagate multi-stemmed shrubs is to dig them up, break apart the clump of stems and replant the rooted segments. As brutal as it sounds, this treatment does no harm and is actually beneficial to most plants. In the case of an older shrub that has lost its shape as a result of unruly growth, propagation by division serves a dual purpose: it not only creates new plants identical to the parent, it also restores the vigor of the original plant—provided the division is left with one or more stems on top and a mass of healthy roots on the bottom.

The evergreen shrubs that can be propagated by division are generally those that are multistemmed and spreading, such as barberry, Aaronsbeard, leucothoe, mahonia, nandina, paxistima, azalea, sumac and bramble. Whatever the plant, choose one that is healthy and one that has well-developed stems growing from the crown.

The best time to divide evergreen shrubs is during their dormant period (early spring or late fall) when the plants are not actively growing. They divide most easily when they are two or three years old.

Before you start digging, plan ahead so you are prepared to replant as soon as possible; roots exposed to the air for any length of time dry out and die.

While some shock to the root system is inevitable when a plant is removed from the ground, you can keep the disturbance to a minimum by working quickly and using the right digging tool—a spading fork. After you have done the dividing, cut off about a third of the top growth to compensate for root loss. Handle the plant gently at all times.

Transfer the divisions to individual pots—or to a protected area in your garden where you can tend them until they are ready to be moved to their permanent locations. For those divided in spring, that means the fall immediately following. For those divided in fall, that means one year later.

1 To prepare for dividing a plant, dig it up, removing the soil around it carefully and lifting it gently from the ground with a spading fork. Take care not to damage the root system.

2 To divide a dug-up crown, cut it with a sharp knife or use your fingers to pull it apart into segments of roughly equal size *(left)*. Make sure each segment has plenty of roots and top growth attached.

3 Immediately replant the divisions, either in individual pots or in a protected area of your garden. When planting in the ground, leave about 1 foot between the divisions. Plant them as you would container-grown shrubs *(pages 10-13)*. Water them daily, and feed them weekly through early summer with liquid fertilizer. Stop fertilizing in midsummer. Transplant the new shrubs to permanent locations the following fall. ☐

LAYERING— NATURE'S METHOD OF PROPAGATING

Starting new shrubs from the branches of grown ones—layering —is simply a matter of prodding plants to do what they sometimes do on their own. A number of shrubs—oleanders, azaleas, mountain laurels, heaths, heathers, rhododendrons—reproduce themselves by dipping low-growing branches to the ground. The bits of branch in contact with the earth then spontaneously produce roots and give rise to fresh offspring. Layering persuades shrubs to perform this wonder on cue rather than spontaneously.

The main steps in the process are shown in the drawings below and on the opposite page. A healthy bottom branch is scored carefully with a knife and bent downward into the earth next to the parent plant. When the branch shows new growth, it has probably developed new roots. The branch can then be separated from the parent shrub.

It is best to choose the candidate for layering a full year in advance and prune its lower branches. This will promote fresh lower growth, which will bend easily and be full of the hormones that spur the formation of roots. Then, the earth under the shrub should be enriched with peat or other organic matter, loosened so that it drains well and kept moist with generous waterings.

The best season to layer shrubs is late winter or early spring—as soon as the soil can be worked. An early start gives the roots all spring and summer to grow. If things go speedily, the roots should take hold and produce a growing plant by fall. Often, however, it takes a year or longer for a new plant to become large and strong enough for transplanting.

Flowering lavishly, a bank of varied oleanders stages a dazzling spring display of pink, red and white blooms. Although they grow quite tall, oleanders produce some low-lying branches that can be bent down to the earth and rooted to propagate new plants by the technique of simple layering.

1 Select a vigorous young branch near the bottom of the shrub you have chosen for layering. Trim the leaves and side shoots from a 6- to 20-inch section of the branch but allow the leaves at the tip to remain intact.

2 Cut a shallow 1-inch-long flap in the bark, moving your knife toward the tip of the branch; growth hormones produced by the stem tip will flow to the flap and help the formation of a callus and then roots. The cut should be deep enough to penetrate the cambium layer *(page 66)* but not deep enough to weaken the branch.

3 Dig a small trench, about 3 or 4 inches deep, and bury the cut section of the branch in it. If the branch resists, weight it down with a small stone until the roots take hold, or pin it with a bent wire or a forked stick. Water the area frequently but lightly; the roots need some moisture but will rot if flooded.

4 When the roots have sent up strong new growth—it may take a year or more—cut the parent branch *(left)*. Leave the new shrub in place for another four weeks or so, to mature and gain strength. Then dig it up and move it to a protected area in your garden. □

CLEFT GRAFTING— ONE TECHNIQUE FOR PROPAGATING

Grafting is a method of propagation in which pieces of two healthy plants are united to produce one vigorous offspring. It is usually done for the purpose of combining the best characteristics of two different varieties—say hardiness or disease resistance (generally provided by the rootstock of one plant) with color, texture or flowers (provided by a shoot—called a scion—from another plant).

There are many different methods of grafting. One, called cleft grafting *(opposite and following pages),* is done by removing the top growth of the rootstock, making an incision in the upper surface of the remaining stem and inserting a stem cutting (the scion) in the incision. Another, called side grafting, attaches a scion to the side of a rootstock *(page 70).*

Cleft grafting is often done with broadleaved flowering evergreens, such as camellias, because the process generally produces mature plants that will flower earlier than plants propagated by other means. Cleft grafting can be done indoors or out, and with container-grown plants or plants growing in the ground. The rootstock may be wider in diameter than the scion; if so, two scions can be started on one rootstock and the weaker of the two can be discarded later. But the rootstock and the scion must be of the same genus. And to ensure a union between scion and rootstock, you must make sure to match up the cambium of one with the cambium of the other *(box, right).* It is also important to work quickly; the scion must not be allowed to dry out.

After the two plants have been attached, and until the bond is secure, provide a warm, humid environment by covering the attached scion and rootstock with a clear plastic bag or a large glass jar. Once new growth appears on the scion, gradually begin to accustom the grafted plant to outdoor air by poking holes in the plastic. Do not remove the bag for two or three months.

A 50-year-old camellia makes an arresting specimen. Camellias are often propagated by grafting young shoots of a colorful variety, like this one, onto the rootstock of another, hardier variety.

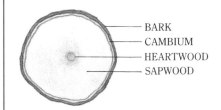

BARK
CAMBIUM
HEARTWOOD
SAPWOOD

INSIDE A WOODY STEM

The main divisions of the stem of a woody plant are seen here in cross section. Just inside the protective bark is the thin layer of cambium, where all new growth takes place. Inside that is sapwood, which transmits nutrients from the roots to the stem tips. At the center is heartwood, which gives the stem its strength.

1 Remove the top of the plant that will serve as the rootstock. Use shears or loppers (depending on the diameter of the stem) to make a clean, horizontal cut. Leave 2 to 3 inches of stem above the soil level, to receive the scion.

2 With a sharp knife, make an incision in the center of the rootstock stem, perpendicular to the surface and 1¼ inches deep. To make the cut as smooth as possible, complete the incision with a single stroke of the knife if you can.

3 Using a pair of pruning shears, snip a vigorous young shoot from the plant you have chosen to supply the scion (right). Be sure to select a shoot that has at least two or three healthy leaf buds on it.

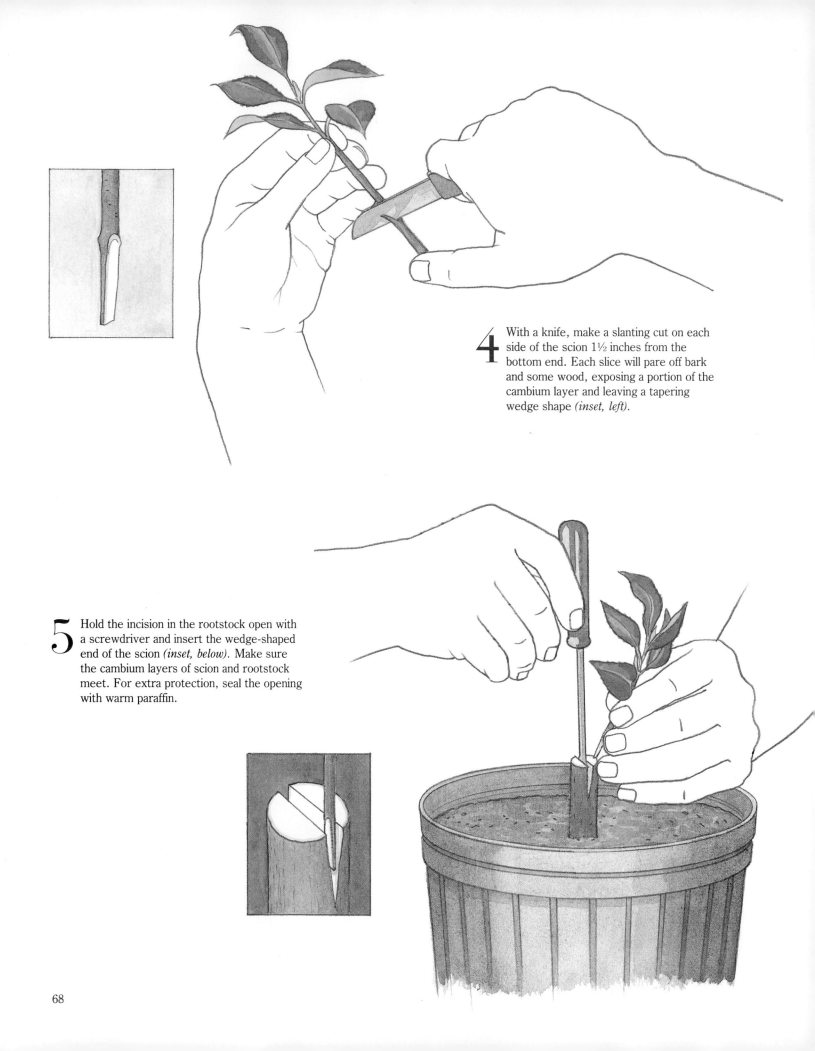

4 With a knife, make a slanting cut on each side of the scion 1½ inches from the bottom end. Each slice will pare off bark and some wood, exposing a portion of the cambium layer and leaving a tapering wedge shape *(inset, left)*.

5 Hold the incision in the rootstock open with a screwdriver and insert the wedge-shaped end of the scion *(inset, below)*. Make sure the cambium layers of scion and rootstock meet. For extra protection, seal the opening with warm paraffin.

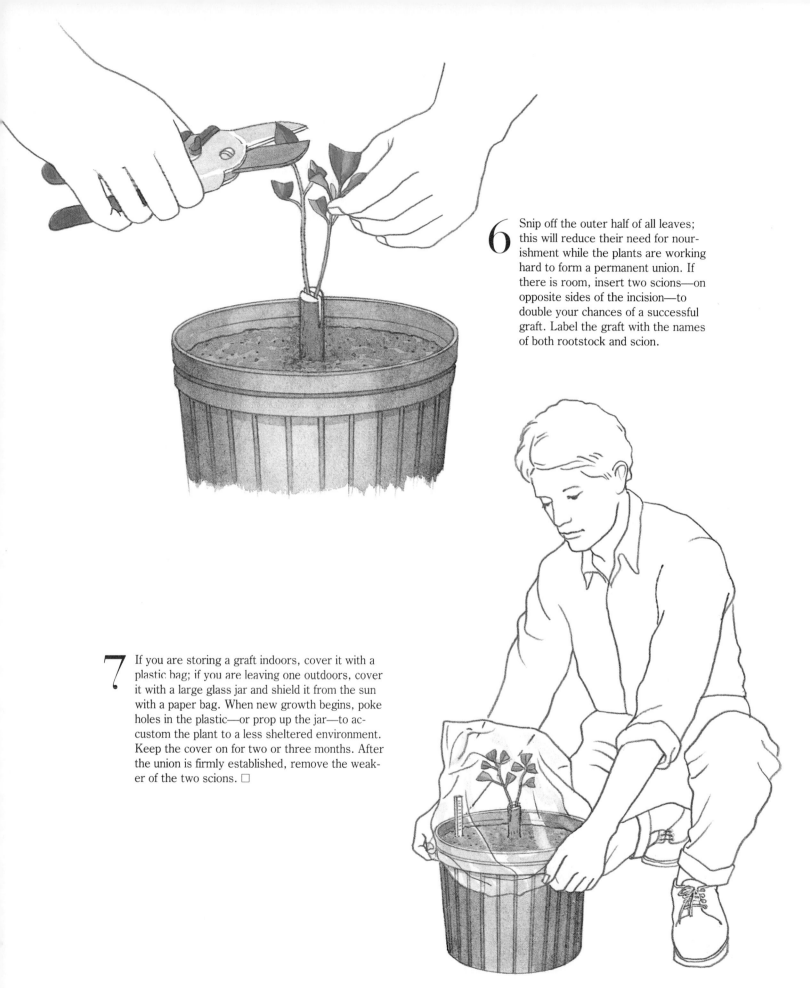

6 Snip off the outer half of all leaves; this will reduce their need for nourishment while the plants are working hard to form a permanent union. If there is room, insert two scions—on opposite sides of the incision—to double your chances of a successful graft. Label the graft with the names of both rootstock and scion.

7 If you are storing a graft indoors, cover it with a plastic bag; if you are leaving one outdoors, cover it with a large glass jar and shield it from the sun with a paper bag. When new growth begins, poke holes in the plastic—or prop up the jar—to accustom the plant to a less sheltered environment. Keep the cover on for two or three months. After the union is firmly established, remove the weaker of the two scions. □

SIDE GRAFTING—A TECHNIQUE FOR REPRODUCING DWARF CONIFERS

You may be in for a surprise if you try to raise a dwarf conifer from seed. Dwarf shrubs are cultivated mutations, so the seeds usually revert to type and grow into full-sized shrubs or trees. The only sure way to obtain a new dwarf from a favorite shrub is to propagate it asexually. For shrubs such as false cypress, Japanese cedar, juniper, Colorado spruce, arborvitae, dwarf pine and other conifers, which heal slowly when wounded, a technique that works well is side grafting.

Side grafting differs from cleft grafting (*page 66*) in that the scion is attached to the side of the rootstock stem. The top foliage on the rootstock is left uncut until the graft takes; this provides structural support and extra nutrients while the callus forms to join the rootstock and the scion.

The best time to graft conifers is late winter or early spring. Start your preparations a year in advance. The spring before you intend to graft, vigorously prune the dwarf conifer that will supply the scion. For rootstock, choose a container-grown plant that is two or three years old; in midwinter move it indoors where the warmth will stimulate new root growth.

When you are ready to graft, cut a 4- to 6-inch scion from a shoot that emerged after the previous summer's pruning. Ideally, the scion should be dormant but about to begin new growth; shoots that are already in active growth are more likely to dry out before union with the rootstock is complete.

If you want your new conifer to grow upright, take your scion from the top part of the donor plant; cuttings from lower, lateral branches typically grow sideways from the graft.

Since only smooth cuts in wood and bark will heal properly, a clean sharp knife is a must. Some conifers ooze resin when cut. To keep your blade free of resin, swab it after each cut with a cotton ball that has been dipped in alcohol. Wipe the blade dry with a clean cloth.

A mature weeping atlas cedar grows twice as wide (6 feet) as it is tall (3 feet). An unusual dwarf conifer such as this is best propagated by side grafting one of its shoots onto a hardy rootstock of a standard variety of the same species.

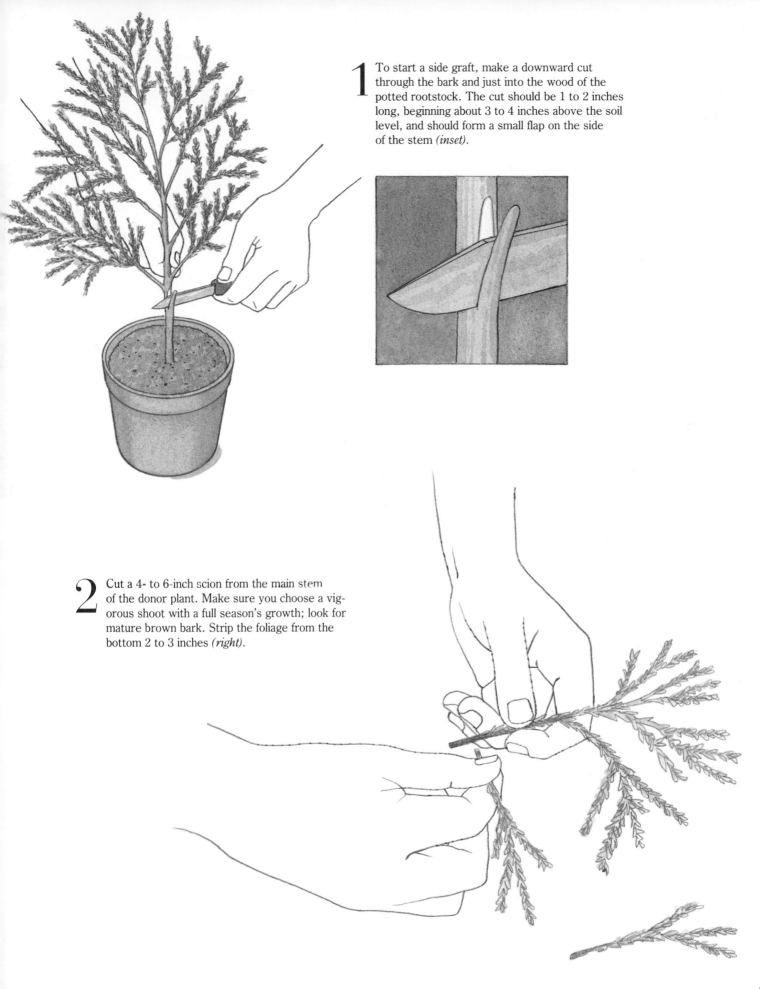

1 To start a side graft, make a downward cut through the bark and just into the wood of the potted rootstock. The cut should be 1 to 2 inches long, beginning about 3 to 4 inches above the soil level, and should form a small flap on the side of the stem *(inset)*.

2 Cut a 4- to 6-inch scion from the main stem of the donor plant. Make sure you choose a vigorous shoot with a full season's growth; look for mature brown bark. Strip the foliage from the bottom 2 to 3 inches *(right)*.

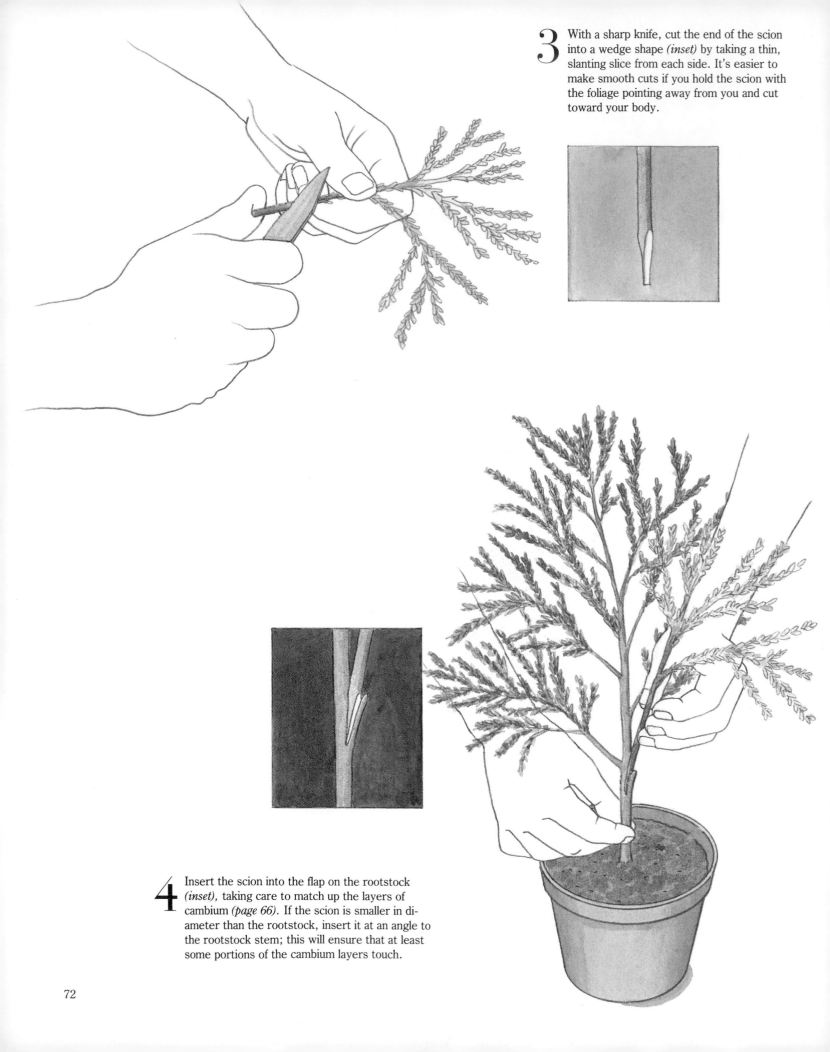

3 With a sharp knife, cut the end of the scion into a wedge shape *(inset)* by taking a thin, slanting slice from each side. It's easier to make smooth cuts if you hold the scion with the foliage pointing away from you and cut toward your body.

4 Insert the scion into the flap on the rootstock *(inset),* taking care to match up the layers of cambium *(page 66).* If the scion is smaller in diameter than the rootstock, insert it at an angle to the rootstock stem; this will ensure that at least some portions of the cambium layers touch.

5 Wrap and secure the joined sections with elastic grafting tape or a rubber band that has been cut open *(right)*. Cover the plant with a clear plastic bag to seal in moisture, and put it in a warm place that receives some indirect light. When growth from the scion begins, poke a few holes in the plastic to let in some air.

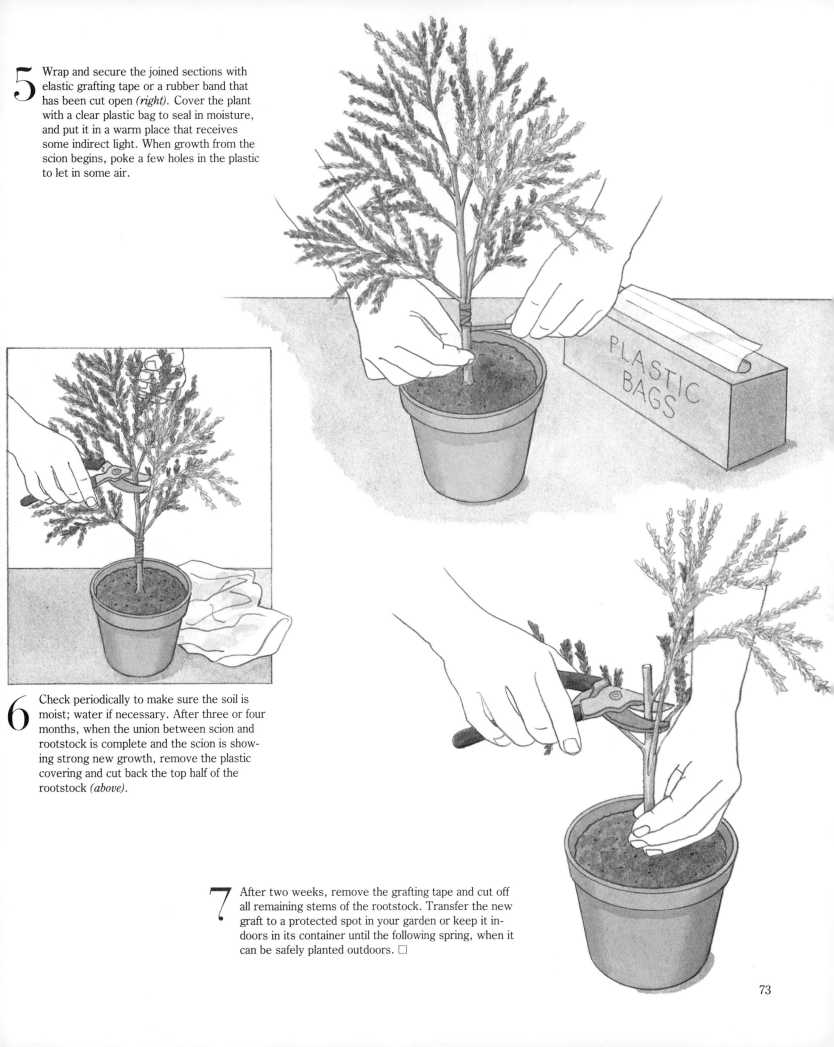

6 Check periodically to make sure the soil is moist; water if necessary. After three or four months, when the union between scion and rootstock is complete and the scion is showing strong new growth, remove the plastic covering and cut back the top half of the rootstock *(above)*.

7 After two weeks, remove the grafting tape and cut off all remaining stems of the rootstock. Transfer the new graft to a protected spot in your garden or keep it indoors in its container until the following spring, when it can be safely planted outdoors. □

4
MAKING THE MOST OF NATURE

Although evergreen shrubs have a well-deserved reputation for hardiness, many are adversely affected by extreme weather conditions; some "evergreens" even shed their foliage during severe winters. The map on page 76, which divides North America into 10 climatic zones defined by the minimum winter temperatures, will help you select and plant shrubs that are adapted to your local climate. Find your zone; then consult the Dictionary of Evergreen Shrubs *(pages 88-137)* to see which shrubs can be expected to thrive in your garden.

You can take the guesswork out of caring for evergreen shrubs by following the month-by-month maintenance checklist beginning on page 78. Since requirements vary with weather conditions, the checklist is keyed to the same zones outlined on the map. A quick glance will tell you when it's time to apply anti-desiccant spray to broad-leaved evergreens in Zone 1, when you can propagate conifers from ripewood cuttings in Zone 3 and when to divide multistemmed shrubs in Zone 10.

The section headed "What to Do When Things Go Wrong" is a comprehensive illustrated guide to coping with the ills that may strike your evergreen shrubs no matter what zone you live in. Whether the cause is an insect pest, a fungus disease or some soil deficiency, this guide will help you identify the problem and take steps to rectify it.

Finally, there is a section whose sole purpose is to help you get more pleasure from gardening. Turn to page 86 for easy-to-follow tips on how to enhance the appearance and value of your land by planting the right evergreen shrubs, how to attract more birds and fill the air with appealing scents—and how to invigorate acid-loving shrubs, like azaleas and rhododendrons, by enriching the soil with coffee grounds.

THE ZONE MAP AND PLANTING

Evergreen shrubs generally hold their shapes, textures and colors all year round, and many can be counted on to produce fruits and flowers seasonally. But for the best display of these elements, shrubs must have a congenial climate. Some shrubs cannot tolerate extreme summer heat, and some will not survive a winter freeze. Other shrubs may be evergreen or deciduous, depending on the climate. Abelia, for example, is evergreen in Florida, but may lose some or all of its leaves during the cold winters in New Mexico. And early-blooming shrubs such as winter daphne may lose their blossoms to late-spring frosts in cold regions. The Dictionary of Evergreen Shrubs (pages 88-137) describes the climatic requirements of specific shrubs and indicates the zones in which they grow best.

The zones are those designated by the U.S. Department of Agriculture, which divides North America into 10 zones based on their minimum winter temperatures. Zone 1 is the coldest, with a winter low of −50° F. Zone 10 is the warmest and is generally frost-free, with a winter minimum of 30° to 40° F. The map on the right outlines these zones and can be used to determine which shrubs will thrive in your garden.

Both the regions on the map and the temperatures should be used only as general guidelines. You can grow a shrub in a zone with a climate that is slightly warmer than ideal if you can plant it in the shade. You can grow a shrub in a zone with cooler than ideal temperatures if you can plant it in a protected location, such as the south side of a house or a wall, where it will receive the warmth of the sun.

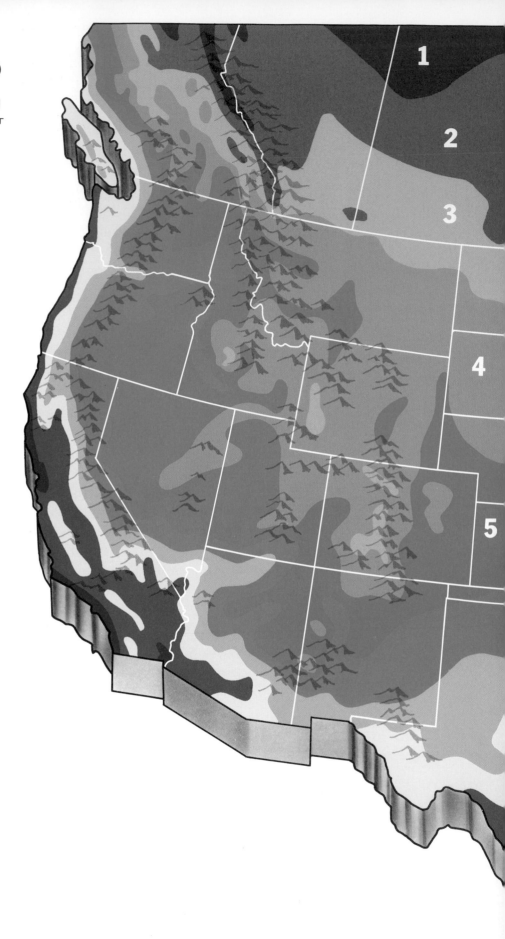

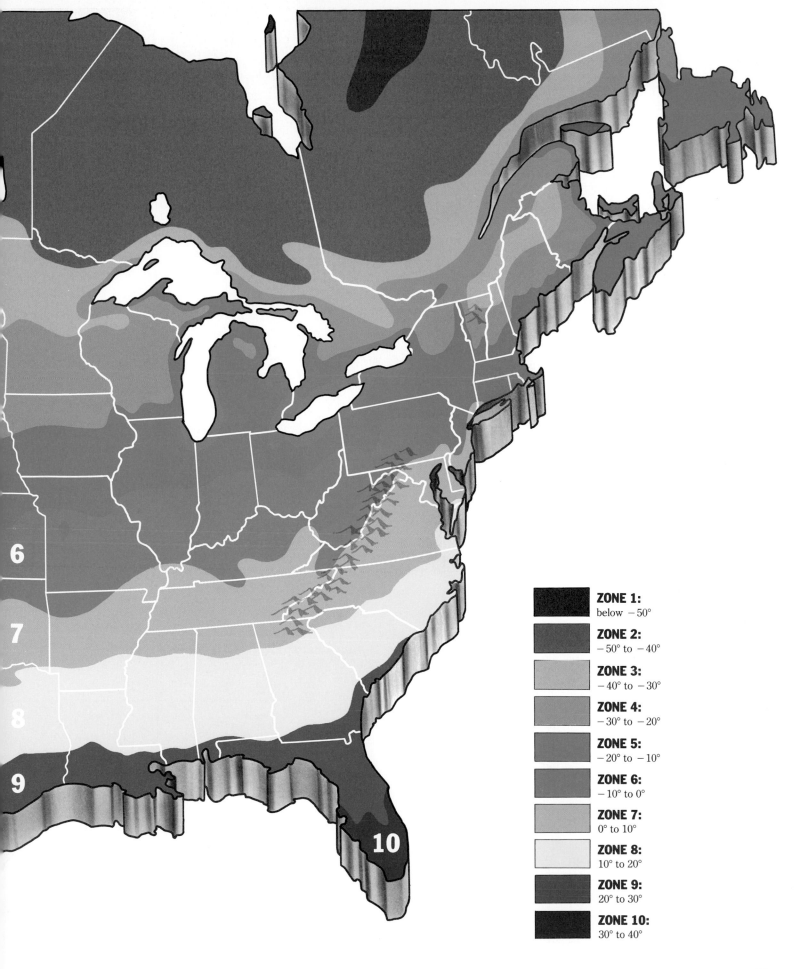

ZONE 1:
below −50°

ZONE 2:
−50° to −40°

ZONE 3:
−40° to −30°

ZONE 4:
−30° to −20°

ZONE 5:
−20° to −10°

ZONE 6:
−10° to 0°

ZONE 7:
0° to 10°

ZONE 8:
10° to 20°

ZONE 9:
20° to 30°

ZONE 10:
30° to 40°

A CHECKLIST FOR MAINTENANCE MONTH BY MONTH

	ZONE 1	ZONE 2	ZONE 3	ZONE 4	ZONE 5
JANUARY/FEBRUARY	• Remove snow and ice from shrubs after every snowfall • Replace mulch as needed • Reapply antidesiccant to broad-leaved evergreens	• Remove snow and ice from shrubs after every snowfall • Replace mulch as needed • Reapply antidesiccant to broad-leaved evergreens	• Remove snow and ice from shrubs after every snowfall • Replace mulch as needed • Reapply antidesiccant to broad-leaved evergreens	• Remove snow and ice from shrubs after every snowfall • Replace mulch as needed • Reapply antidesiccant to broad-leaved evergreens	• Remove snow and ice from shrubs after every snowfall • Replace mulch as needed • Reapply antidesiccant to broad-leaved evergreens
MARCH/APRIL	• Replace mulch as needed • Prune shrubs • Start grafts for propagation • Remove undesirable shrubs • Clean, oil, sharpen tools	• Replace mulch as needed • Prune shrubs • Start grafts for propagation • Remove undesirable shrubs • Clean, oil, sharpen tools	• Replace mulch as needed • Prune shrubs • Start grafts for propagation • Divide multistemmed shrubs • Remove undesirable shrubs • Clean, oil, sharpen tools	• Replace mulch as needed • Prune shrubs • Plant shrubs • Start grafts for propagation • Divide multistemmed shrubs • Apply horticultural oil spray • Remove undesirable shrubs • Clean, oil, sharpen tools	• Replace mulch as needed • Prune shrubs • Prune out winter damage • Start grafts for propagation • Divide multistemmed shrubs • Plant shrubs • Remove burlap screens • Apply horticultural oil spray • Remove undesirable shrubs • Clean, oil, sharpen tools
MAY/JUNE	• Prune shrubs • Prune out winter damage • Shear formal hedges • Fertilize shrubs as growth starts • Test soil pH around established shrubs • Plant shrubs • Transplant shrubs • Remove burlap screens • Apply horticultural oil spray • Weed soil around shrubs • Apply mulch for summer • Check for insects, diseases	• Prune shrubs • Prune out winter damage • Shear formal hedges • Fertilize shrubs as growth starts • Test soil pH around established shrubs • Plant shrubs • Transplant shrubs • Remove burlap screens • Apply horticultural oil spray • Weed soil around shrubs • Apply mulch for summer • Check for insects, diseases	• Prune shrubs • Prune out winter damage • Shear formal hedges • Fertilize shrubs as growth starts • Test soil pH around established shrubs • Plant shrubs • Transplant shrubs • Remove burlap screens • Apply horticultural oil spray • Weed soil around shrubs • Apply mulch for summer • Check for insects, diseases	• Prune shrubs • Prune out winter damage • Shear formal hedges • Fertilize shrubs as growth starts • Test soil pH around established shrubs • Plant shrubs • Transplant shrubs • Remove burlap screens • Weed soil around shrubs • Apply mulch for summer • Check for insects, diseases	• Prune shrubs • Shear formal hedges • Fertilize shrubs as growth starts • Test soil pH around established shrubs • Plant shrubs • Transplant shrubs • Weed soil around shrubs • Apply mulch for summer • Water as necessary • Check for insects, diseases

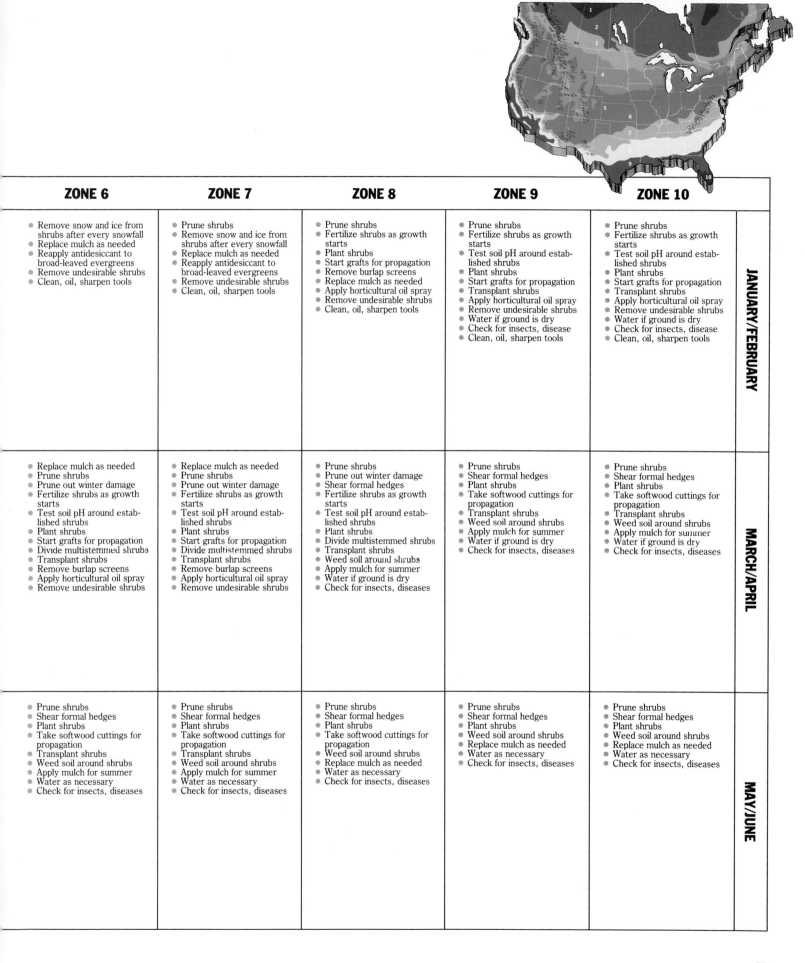

ZONE 6	ZONE 7	ZONE 8	ZONE 9	ZONE 10	
• Remove snow and ice from shrubs after every snowfall • Replace mulch as needed • Reapply antidesiccant to broad-leaved evergreens • Remove undesirable shrubs • Clean, oil, sharpen tools	• Prune shrubs • Remove snow and ice from shrubs after every snowfall • Replace mulch as needed • Reapply antidesiccant to broad-leaved evergreens • Remove undesirable shrubs • Clean, oil, sharpen tools	• Prune shrubs • Fertilize shrubs as growth starts • Plant shrubs • Start grafts for propagation • Remove burlap screens • Replace mulch as needed • Apply horticultural oil spray • Remove undesirable shrubs • Clean, oil, sharpen tools	• Prune shrubs • Fertilize shrubs as growth starts • Test soil pH around established shrubs • Plant shrubs • Start grafts for propagation • Apply horticultural oil spray • Remove undesirable shrubs • Water if ground is dry • Check for insects, disease • Clean, oil, sharpen tools	• Prune shrubs • Fertilize shrubs as growth starts • Test soil pH around established shrubs • Plant shrubs • Start grafts for propagation • Transplant shrubs • Apply horticultural oil spray • Remove undesirable shrubs • Water if ground is dry • Check for insects, disease • Clean, oil, sharpen tools	**JANUARY/FEBRUARY**
• Replace mulch as needed • Prune shrubs • Prune out winter damage • Fertilize shrubs as growth starts • Test soil pH around established shrubs • Plant shrubs • Start grafts for propagation • Divide multistemmed shrubs • Transplant shrubs • Remove burlap screens • Apply horticultural oil spray • Remove undesirable shrubs	• Replace mulch as needed • Prune shrubs • Prune out winter damage • Fertilize shrubs as growth starts • Test soil pH around established shrubs • Plant shrubs • Start grafts for propagation • Divide multistemmed shrubs • Transplant shrubs • Remove burlap screens • Apply horticultural oil spray • Remove undesirable shrubs	• Prune shrubs • Prune out winter damage • Shear formal hedges • Fertilize shrubs as growth starts • Test soil pH around established shrubs • Plant shrubs • Divide multistemmed shrubs • Transplant shrubs • Weed soil around shrubs • Apply mulch for summer • Water if ground is dry • Check for insects, diseases	• Prune shrubs • Shear formal hedges • Plant shrubs • Take softwood cuttings for propagation • Transplant shrubs • Weed soil around shrubs • Apply mulch for summer • Water if ground is dry • Check for insects, diseases	• Prune shrubs • Shear formal hedges • Plant shrubs • Take softwood cuttings for propagation • Transplant shrubs • Weed soil around shrubs • Apply mulch for summer • Water if ground is dry • Check for insects, diseases	**MARCH/APRIL**
• Prune shrubs • Shear formal hedges • Plant shrubs • Take softwood cuttings for propagation • Transplant shrubs • Weed soil around shrubs • Apply mulch for summer • Water as necessary • Check for insects, diseases	• Prune shrubs • Shear formal hedges • Plant shrubs • Take softwood cuttings for propagation • Transplant shrubs • Weed soil around shrubs • Apply mulch for summer • Water as necessary • Check for insects, diseases	• Prune shrubs • Shear formal hedges • Plant shrubs • Take softwood cuttings for propagation • Weed soil around shrubs • Replace mulch as needed • Water as necessary • Check for insects, diseases	• Prune shrubs • Shear formal hedges • Plant shrubs • Weed soil around shrubs • Replace mulch as needed • Water as necessary • Check for insects, diseases	• Prune shrubs • Shear formal hedges • Plant shrubs • Weed soil around shrubs • Replace mulch as needed • Water as necessary • Check for insects, diseases	**MAY/JUNE**

	ZONE 1	ZONE 2	ZONE 3	ZONE 4	ZONE 5
JULY/AUGUST	• Prune shrubs • Shear formal hedges • Plant shrubs • Take softwood cuttings for propagation • Transplant shrubs • Weed soil around shrubs • Replace mulch as needed • Water as necessary • Check for insects, diseases	• Prune shrubs • Shear formal hedges • Plant shrubs • Take softwood cuttings for propagation • Transplant shrubs • Weed soil around shrubs • Replace mulch as needed • Water as necessary • Check for insects, diseases	• Prune shrubs • Shear formal hedges • Plant shrubs • Take softwood cuttings for propagation • Transplant shrubs • Weed soil around shrubs • Replace mulch as needed • Water as necessary • Check for insects, diseases	• Prune shrubs • Shear formal hedges • Plant shrubs • Take softwood cuttings for propagation • Transplant shrubs • Weed soil around shrubs • Replace mulch as needed • Water as necessary • Check for insects, diseases	• Prune shrubs • Shear formal hedges • Plant shrubs • Take softwood cuttings for propagation • Weed soil around shrubs • Replace mulch as needed • Water as necessary • Check for insects, diseases
SEPTEMBER/OCTOBER	• Propagate conifers from ripewood cuttings • Divide multistemmed shrubs • Adjust soil pH and add amendments for spring planting • Spray broad-leaved evergreens with antidesiccant • Apply mulch for winter and install burlap screens • Water if ground is dry • Turn off water; drain hose	• Propagate conifers from ripewood cuttings • Divide multistemmed shrubs • Adjust soil pH and add amendments for spring planting • Spray broad-leaved evergreens with antidesiccant • Apply mulch for winter and install burlap screens • Water if ground is dry • Turn off water; drain hose	• Propagate conifers from ripewood cuttings • Divide multistemmed shrubs • Adjust soil pH and add amendments for spring planting • Spray broad-leaved evergreens with antidesiccant • Apply mulch for winter and install burlap screens • Water if ground is dry • Turn off water; drain hose	• Propagate conifers from ripewood cuttings • Divide multistemmed shrubs • Adjust soil pH and add amendments for spring planting • Spray broad-leaved evergreens with antidesiccant • Apply mulch for winter and install burlap screens • Water if ground is dry • Turn off water; drain hose	• Plant shrubs • Propagate conifers from ripewood cuttings • Divide multistemmed shrubs • Transplant shrubs • Adjust soil pH and add amendments for spring planting • Water if ground is dry
NOVEMBER/DECEMBER	• Put wire mesh around shrubs for protection against animals • Remove snow and ice from shrubs after every snowfall	• Put wire mesh around shrubs for protection against animals • Remove snow and ice from shrubs after every snowfall	• Put wire mesh around shrubs for protection against animals • Remove snow and ice from shrubs after every snowfall	• Put wire mesh around shrubs for protection against animals • Remove snow and ice from shrubs after every snowfall	• Spray broad-leaved evergreens with antidesiccant • Apply mulch for winter and install burlap screens • Put wire mesh around shrubs for protection against animals • Remove snow and ice from shrubs after every snowfall • Water if ground is dry • Turn off water, drain hose

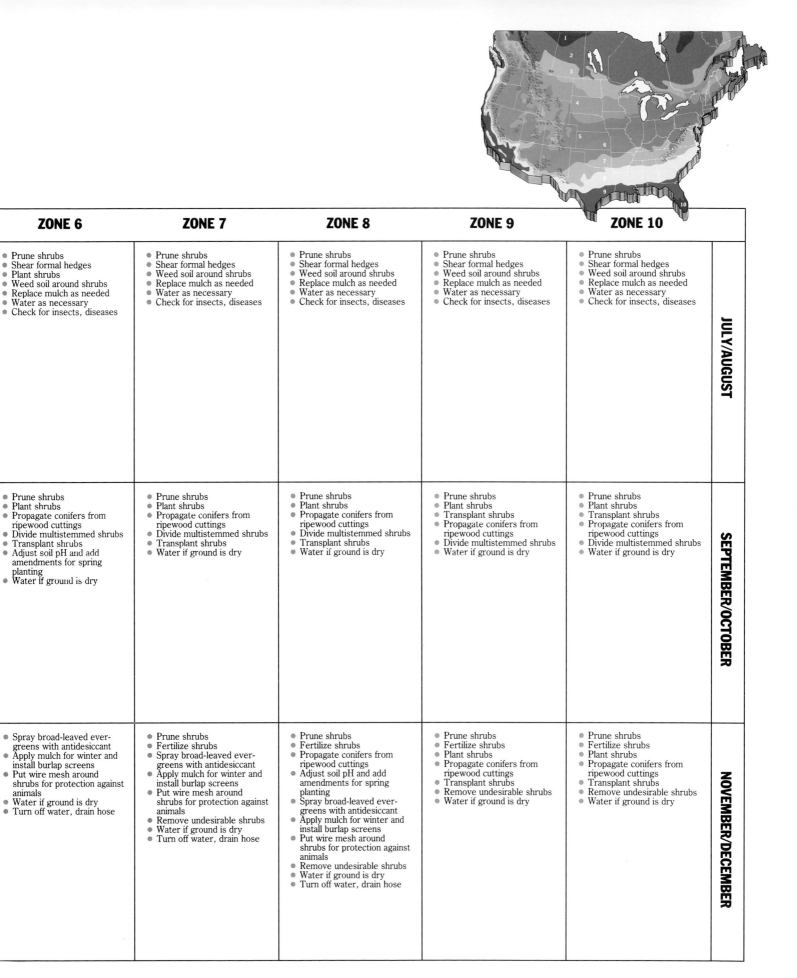

ZONE 6	ZONE 7	ZONE 8	ZONE 9	ZONE 10	
• Prune shrubs • Shear formal hedges • Plant shrubs • Weed soil around shrubs • Replace mulch as needed • Water as necessary • Check for insects, diseases	• Prune shrubs • Shear formal hedges • Weed soil around shrubs • Replace mulch as needed • Water as necessary • Check for insects, diseases	• Prune shrubs • Shear formal hedges • Weed soil around shrubs • Replace mulch as needed • Water as necessary • Check for insects, diseases	• Prune shrubs • Shear formal hedges • Weed soil around shrubs • Replace mulch as needed • Water as necessary • Check for insects, diseases	• Prune shrubs • Shear formal hedges • Weed soil around shrubs • Replace mulch as needed • Water as necessary • Check for insects, diseases	**JULY/AUGUST**
• Prune shrubs • Plant shrubs • Propagate conifers from ripewood cuttings • Divide multistemmed shrubs • Transplant shrubs • Adjust soil pH and add amendments for spring planting • Water if ground is dry	• Prune shrubs • Plant shrubs • Propagate conifers from ripewood cuttings • Divide multistemmed shrubs • Transplant shrubs • Water if ground is dry	• Prune shrubs • Plant shrubs • Propagate conifers from ripewood cuttings • Divide multistemmed shrubs • Transplant shrubs • Water if ground is dry	• Prune shrubs • Plant shrubs • Transplant shrubs • Propagate conifers from ripewood cuttings • Divide multistemmed shrubs • Water if ground is dry	• Prune shrubs • Plant shrubs • Transplant shrubs • Propagate conifers from ripewood cuttings • Divide multistemmed shrubs • Water if ground is dry	**SEPTEMBER/OCTOBER**
• Spray broad-leaved evergreens with antidesiccant • Apply mulch for winter and install burlap screens • Put wire mesh around shrubs for protection against animals • Water if ground is dry • Turn off water, drain hose	• Prune shrubs • Fertilize shrubs • Spray broad-leaved evergreens with antidesiccant • Apply mulch for winter and install burlap screens • Put wire mesh around shrubs for protection against animals • Remove undesirable shrubs • Water if ground is dry • Turn off water, drain hose	• Prune shrubs • Fertilize shrubs • Propagate conifers from ripewood cuttings • Adjust soil pH and add amendments for spring planting • Spray broad-leaved evergreens with antidesiccant • Apply mulch for winter and install burlap screens • Put wire mesh around shrubs for protection against animals • Remove undesirable shrubs • Water if ground is dry • Turn off water, drain hose	• Prune shrubs • Fertilize shrubs • Plant shrubs • Propagate conifers from ripewood cuttings • Transplant shrubs • Remove undesirable shrubs • Water if ground is dry	• Prune shrubs • Fertilize shrubs • Plant shrubs • Propagate conifers from ripewood cuttings • Transplant shrubs • Remove undesirable shrubs • Water if ground is dry	**NOVEMBER/DECEMBER**

81

WHAT TO DO
WHEN THINGS GO WRONG

PROBLEM	CAUSE	SOLUTION
A brownish gray moldy growth appears on flowers and foliage. Flowers collapse, foliage loses its color and new growth dies back. Most shrubs are susceptible.	Botrytis blight, also known as gray mold, a fungus disease. The problem is especially severe during cool, humid weather.	Spray with a fungicide once a week until symptoms disappear. Prune out and discard damaged flowers and foliage.
New leaves are yellow, but leaf veins remain green. Older foliage may turn yellow around the leaf margins. Shrubs planted near the foundation of the house may be severely affected. Acid-loving broad-leaved evergreens such as andromeda, azalea, camellia, gardenia, holly, mountain laurel and rhododendron are susceptible.	Iron deficiency, which occurs when soil is too alkaline. The elements in alkaline soil bond with iron to form an insoluble salt and thus prevent the iron from being absorbed by plants.	Add acid to the soil; acid keeps the iron from bonding and enables it to be available to plants. Test the soil pH and adjust the level to between 4.5 and 5.5. Spray the foliage and the soil around the shrub with a solution of chelated iron, or work coffee grounds, which are highly acidic, into the soil.
Leaves are covered with round spots or uneven blotches. On azalea, holly, leucothoe, mountain laurel, rhododendron and wild lilac, the spots may be yellow, red, brown or gray. On photinia, the spots are purple, and as they enlarge, they turn brown with purple margins. On all shrubs, the markings will grow together until the entire leaf is covered, turns yellow and dies.	Leaf spot, a fungus disease. The fungus is spread by water and wind, particularly during hot, humid weather.	There are no chemical cures for infected leaves; they should be pruned off and destroyed. To prevent the disease, spray shrubs with a fungicide when new growth develops in spring, and continue spraying once every two weeks as long as the weather is hot and humid.
Foliage and branches of conifers turn brown. Needles may drop. Entire sections of the shrub may die back.	Twig and needle blight, a fungus disease that is common in damp, humid conditions. The fungus spreads in water.	Prune out infected areas and sterilize pruning tools after each cut. In spring, spray shrubs with a fungicide and repeat the application until the symptoms disappear.
Conifer needles turn orange or are mottled with orange. Broad-leaved evergreen foliage develops small water-filled blisters that burst, leaving brown areas on the leaf surface. Leaves may be flecked with yellow, and the leaf margins and areas between veins turn brown. Symptoms usually appear first on new growth.	Air pollution and exhaust fumes.	There are no cures for damage from pollution. Plant pollution-tolerant shrubs such as arborvitae, balsam fir, juniper, mugo pine or privet.

PROBLEM	CAUSE	SOLUTION
Upper surfaces of leaves are covered with small yellow spots. Undersides of leaves are covered with an orange powder. Affected leaves may drop from the shrub. Azalea, mahonia and rhododendron are susceptible.	Rust, a fungus disease that spreads rapidly among damp leaves.	There are no chemical cures or preventives for the rust that attacks azalea and rhododendron. Remove infected leaves to prevent spread of the disease. Mahonia can be sprayed with a fungicide in spring when growth begins.
Leaves wilt, turn yellow, then brown and die without dropping from the plant. Roots are dark and decayed. Many evergreen shrubs are susceptible.	Root rot, caused by a fungus that thrives in wet soil.	There are no chemical controls. Infected shrubs and the surrounding soil should be removed. Before planting shrubs, make sure that your soil has good drainage.
Azalea and rhododendron flower petals develop small, rounded brown spots; camellia flower petals (right) develop brown streaks and blotches. The brown markings spread rapidly until the entire flower turns brown and collapses.	The fungus diseases azalea petal blight and camellia petal blight. Symptoms can be distinguished from normal fading because flowers turn brown almost overnight.	There are no chemical cures. Remove diseased flowers and rake up any debris on the ground under the shrub. To prevent the disease, spray with a fungicide as soon as the flower buds start to show color, and repeat applications every five days until flowering ends.
Conifer needles turn brown, starting at the tips and progressing to the bases. Broad-leaved evergreen leaf tips and margins turn brown or black. The symptoms usually appear first on older needles and leaves, and eventually may also appear on new growth.	Damage caused by salt applied to icy roads and walkways during winter.	To melt ice, use sand or sawdust instead of salt. Spray shrubs near roadsides with an antidesiccant. Plant salt-tolerant shrubs such as euonymus, oleander, pittosporum and pyracantha.
Cotoneaster and pyracantha foliage suddenly wilts, turns brown or black, and appears to have been scorched. Bark at the base of affected areas may turn dark, dry out and crack.	Fire blight, a bacterial disease that spreads in warm, wet conditions.	There are no chemical cures. Prune out damaged branches and disinfect pruning tools after each cut. To prevent the disease, spray shrubs with a recommended antibiotic every five to seven days in spring while new growth develops.
Leaves of broad-leaved evergreens have a dull, silvery appearance. The leaves may wilt and fall from the shrub. Foliage may be covered with black specks.	Thrips, tiny insects that feed on the sap of leaf tissue.	During the summer, spray shrubs every two weeks with an insecticide until all signs of infestation are gone.
Needles on branch tips appear to have been chewed. Eventually, the damaged needles are webbed together with silk. The branch tips die back and the entire shrub may die. Fir, hemlock, pine and spruce are the most susceptible shrubs.	Spruce budworms, 1-inch caterpillars that have brown bodies with yellow stripes along the sides.	Spray with an insecticide in midspring when new growth starts to open.

83

PROBLEM		CAUSE	SOLUTION
New foliage of andromeda, aralia, azalea, boxwood, gardenia, holly or rhododendron may have a distorted shape. Eventually leaves may become speckled with yellow or gray (A). Needles of arborvitae, fir, hemlock, juniper, pine or spruce lose their sheen and are streaked with yellow (B). Eventually, the needles turn brown and may drop from the plant. Thin, silken webs appear on the branches of all susceptible shrubs.		Mites, microscopic spiderlike pests that may be red, green, black, yellow, pink or white. Mites thrive in a hot, dry environment.	Keep shrubs well watered to discourage the pests. Spray with an approved miticide in spring or summer when symptoms appear. Repeat applications may be necessary. After an infestation, spray shrubs with horticultural oil early the following spring to smother eggs.
Leaves have yellow spots and leaf margins may curl. Affected areas may be covered with a clear, sticky substance. When an infested shrub is shaken, a cloud of tiny flying insects appears. Azalea, camellia, gardenia, privet and rhododendron are susceptible.		Whiteflies, $\frac{1}{12}$-inch white insects that feed on the undersides of leaves.	When symptoms appear, spray with an insecticide and be sure to cover the undersides of leaves. Repeat the application at one-week intervals until all signs of infestation are gone.
Yew and hemlock do not develop new growth in spring. Needles turn yellow, then brown and holes appear in the margins (A). Branches wilt, and the shrub may die. Azalea and rhododendron leaves turn yellow, wilt and curl up. Holes appear in the leaf margins (B).		Black vine weevils, also called taxus weevils. In early spring, the grubs feed on roots. In early summer, the weevils, which have $\frac{3}{8}$-inch black or brown bodies covered with yellow hair, feed on foliage at night.	Remove weeds and fallen leaves around shrubs in the fall; weevils lay their eggs in weedy areas during the winter. When symptoms appear, spray the foliage and the ground around the shrub with an insecticide, starting in early summer. Repeat applications three times, three weeks apart.
Shrubs cease to grow and the tips of branches may die. Foliage wilts and loses its color. Branches, twigs or leaves are covered with small rounded or oval masses. Most evergreen shrubs are susceptible.		Scale insects, which have hard or soft shells ranging in size from $\frac{1}{10}$ to $\frac{3}{8}$ inch. The shells may be white, yellow, green, red, brown or black.	Prune out severely infested branches. Spray shrubs with horticultural oil in early spring to smother the eggs. If insects appear in summer, spray with an insecticide.
Azalea, rhododendron or mountain laurel leaves turn yellow, then brown. Main branches have small holes from which sawdust emerges. Patches of bark may peel off. Entire branches may wilt or break off.		Rhododendron borers, $\frac{1}{2}$-inch yellow-white caterpillars that bore into and under the bark.	There are no controls for borers once they get under the bark. Cut off infested branches. In spring, spray or paint the bark at two-week intervals with an insecticide developed especially for borers; this will kill the larvae when they hatch.
Upper surfaces of leaves are speckled with white or yellow. Undersides of the leaves are covered with dark specks. Shrubs may fail to grow. The most susceptible shrubs are andromeda, azalea, cotoneaster and rhododendron.		Lace bugs, small flat bugs that are $\frac{1}{16}$ to $\frac{1}{8}$ inch long and have clear, lacy wings and hoodlike coverings on their heads.	Spray with an insecticide in late spring. Repeat the application two or three times, 10 days apart, until all signs of infestation are gone.

PROBLEM	CAUSE	SOLUTION
Leaf tips of conifers such as arborvitae, cypress and juniper turn yellow, then brown *(A)*. Boxwood leaves are spotted with yellow. The spots enlarge to blisterlike patches and turn brown. The spots first appear on the undersides of leaves, and then as they enlarge, they penetrate the upper leaf surfaces *(B)*. Holly leaves are marked with yellowish or brown serpentine trails *(C)*.	Leaf miners, the larvae of beetles, flies or moths. The larvae are $\frac{1}{8}$ to $\frac{1}{4}$ inch long and may be yellow or green. They hatch from eggs laid inside the leaves and feed on leaf tissue.	Prune out severely infested branch tips and leaves. Spray conifers with an insecticide in early summer. Spray boxwoods in late spring. Spray hollies in midspring when new leaves develop.
Foliage turns yellow and wilts. Entire branches may die back. Roots are covered with small, irregular swellings. The most susceptible shrubs are boxwood, gardenia and pine.	Nematodes, microscopic worms that feed on shrub roots. The only way to confirm their presence is by a soil test.	Remove damaged shrubs and the surrounding soil. In severe cases, professional soil treatment may be necessary.
Leaves turn yellow. Cottonlike white masses appear on branches and stems. Affected areas may be covered with a clear, sticky substance that attracts ants. Azalea, camellia, gardenia and yew are the most susceptible shrubs.	Mealybugs, $\frac{1}{8}$- to $\frac{1}{4}$-inch oval insects covered with white, waxy hairs.	Spray with horticultural oil in midspring. If insects appear in early summer, spray with an insecticide. Repeat applications may be necessary.
New growth on pines is deformed and bends downward instead of growing straight. Branch ends turn yellow, then brown and may die back. A mass of resin forms at the base of needles.	European pine shoot moths, which lay their eggs on branch tips. The eggs hatch $\frac{3}{4}$-inch-long brown caterpillars that bore into the base of the needles.	Prune off the deformed growth as soon as it appears. Spray shrubs with an insecticide in midspring and again in early summer.
Green, bulblike galls from $\frac{1}{2}$ to 2 inches long appear at the base of needles on the tips of conifer branches in spring. The galls turn brown as they age and eventually split open. Colonies of small insects are visible along the branches. In severe cases, entire branches may die and break off. Spruce is the most susceptible shrub, but other conifers may also be affected.	Spruce gall aphids, $\frac{1}{8}$-inch insects that have dark bodies often covered with a white, waxy substance. When the aphids feed on the foliage, they deposit a toxin that causes the galls.	In midspring, apply horticultural oil to the ends of twigs and branches to smother egg masses. In late spring, spray the same areas with an insecticide. If galls appear, spray with an insecticide in early fall as soon as the galls break open. The galls should not be pruned off, since removal of branch tips may destroy the shape of the shrub.
Cocoonlike, 1- to 2-inch bags that look like brown, dry foliage hang from branches. The most susceptible shrubs are arborvitae, hemlock, juniper and pine.	Bagworm, a caterpillar that grows to 1 inch long and has a brown or black body with a white or yellow head. It uses leaves and twigs to construct its shelter.	In winter or spring, the bags can be picked off shrubs before caterpillars appear. In late spring, if caterpillars appear, spray with an insecticide or with *Bacillus thuringiensis*, called Bt, a bacterium fatal to caterpillars but harmless to other animals.

TIPS AND TECHNIQUES

ADDING FRAGRANCE

Some shrubs produce fragrant blossoms in spring and summer; others have foliage that is fragrant all year round. Both can be used to sweeten the air in your garden. Aromatic shrubs are particularly enjoyable when they are located near frequently used areas—patios, porches and decks—alongside front walkways and garden benches, and beneath windows that are sometimes left open.

Evergreen shrubs with fragrant blossoms include daphne, gardenia, honeysuckle, magnolia, Mexican orange, Natal plum, osmanthus, sweet box, skimmia and viburnum. Shrubs that have aromatic foliage include the conifers arborvitae, cedar, cypress and fir, which smell especially sweet after a rain. Breath of heaven, rosemary and myrtle are particularly fragrant when their foliage is bruised, and they should be located where they will be brushed against when people walk by.

SHRUBS IN THE SHADE

Tall, graceful trees provide summer shade for the gardener, but they often provide too much shade for evergreen shrubs. With certain shrubs, you can create an attractive woodland garden and enjoy colorful foliage and flowers even in a shady yard.

Evergreens that have attractive foliage and grow in deep shade include aucuba, euonymus, aralia and leucothoe. Shrubs that flower in the shade include leucothoe, mahonia, mountain laurel, rhododendron *(right),* skimmia and wheel tree.

To get the best results in a shady area, remove the lowest tree branches and thin out higher branches so more sunlight comes through. Water the shrubs frequently, since they are competing with tree roots that draw a lot of moisture from the soil. Use an organic mulch such as shredded bark to help keep the roots moist and to add to the woodland appearance.

FILLING IN AN EMPTY LANDSCAPE

When you move into a new house that has not been landscaped, or if you redesign an existing yard, you may want to use fast-growing shrubs to fill in empty spaces quickly.

Most evergreen shrubs grow 3 to 4 inches a year, but a few may sprout up more than a foot per year. The fastest-growing shrubs include acacia, broom, elaeagnus, escallonia, Japanese aralia, Mexican orange, pyracantha, rockrose, sumac, sweet hakea and wild lilac. Many conifers, including arborvitae, hemlock and juniper, excluding dwarf species, also grow rapidly. Once established, these rapid growers may require heavy annual pruning to keep their size within bounds.

A design should include a mix of rapid growers and slow-growing shrubs. Many fast-growing shrubs are not long-lived, and others may become scraggly after years of severe pruning. These will eventually need to be removed, and the slow growers can be allowed to fill in the empty spaces.

LURING BIRDS

You can draw birds to your yard year round if you plant shrubs that offer them shelter and food.

Sprawling shrubs that provide dense cover are ideal locations for bird nests. Conifers provide food when their cones break open in late winter and early spring, and yield seeds. The colorful berries of such shrubs as barberry, bearberry, cotoneaster, elaeagnus, holly, loquat, Natal plum, photinia, privet and pyracantha provide fall and winter fruit for birds. Spring- and summer-flowering shrubs such as bottlebrush, lantana and pineapple guava produce nectar that is especially attractive to hummingbirds.

You can supplement the natural attractions your shrubs provide with a birdbath or with a dispenser for drinking water. You may want to add a feeder to your yard. Feeders should be located in the sun and out of the reach of squirrels and cats. Prime locations are near windows and patios, where you can enjoy bird watching.

A COFFEE BREAK FOR SHRUBS

If you live in a newly constructed house, your soil may be littered with scraps of mortar left behind by the builder. If so, the consequences can be severe for shrubs such as azalea and rhododendron, which need acid soil to thrive. Mortar is made from lime and magnesium, substances that are alkaline.

An easy way to increase the amount of acid in the soil is to spread used coffee grounds over the soil, especially around the house foundation, where mortar is most likely to be concentrated. The coffee grounds provide an additional benefit—they also improve the soil texture and make it more porous.

SHRUBS AS BARRIERS

When you want to protect an area of your yard with an attractive barrier, you can plant any of a number of shrubs in various arrangements. Several shrubs together as a hedge provide a solid screen. A single well-placed shrub at the edge of a lawn can discourage people and animals from taking a shortcut across a corner of your yard.

Especially effective as barriers are shrubs with thorns or sharp foliage, since animals are less likely to trample or dig beneath spiny plants. And these shrubs may have security value as well. Located beneath a window, the sharp foliage of shrubs such as holly and mahonia and the thorny branches of barberry *(above)*, elaeagnus, Natal plum and pyracantha can deter prowlers.

SHRUBS FOR THE SEASHORE

Gardening at the seashore is a special challenge. The soil is usually sandy and dry, and there are often drying winds and salt spray to deal with. The gardener can meet this challenge with the right choice of shrubs and a little preparation prior to planting.

Shrubs tolerant of seashore conditions include acacia, bayberry *(below)*, bearberry, cotoneaster *(right)*, elaeagnus, juniper, myrtle, plum yew, pittosporum, podocarpus and wild lilac. To make the soil moisture-retentive and help the shrubs become established, add organic matter to the soil before planting. To help maintain the shrubs once they are planted, give them an occasional heavy watering to leach out the salt in the soil, and hose down the foliage to wash off the salt spray.

5
DICTIONARY OF EVERGREEN SHRUBS

Evergreen shrubs are especially welcome in the garden, since they retain their form and color year round and keep the garden well furnished even after cold weather has stripped deciduous plants of their leaves and faded their colors. Two distinct kinds of plants fall into that category—the conifers, such as pines and firs, which have narrow, often needlelike leaves, and the broad-leaved evergreens, such as American holly and boxwood.

As a group, broad-leaved evergreens have a smaller climatic range than their needle-leaved counterparts. Most of them are best suited to the relatively mild climates of the East, the South and the Pacific Coast, though a few especially hardy ones, like inkberry *(Ilex glabra),* remain verdant ornaments throughout hard Northern winters. The category of broad-leaved evergreens is not a hard-and-fast one. Depending on the hardiness zone, the severity of a particular winter and the microclimate of a particular garden, a broad-leaved plant may be fully evergreen or semievergreen: it may not drop its leaves until late fall or early winter and may even have some stubborn leaves still clinging to its branches at winter's end. Prague viburnum, for instance, is fully evergreen in the South. North of Richmond, Virginia, however, it may retain its leaves in the sunny shelter of a courtyard, while in an exposed spot 100 feet away another specimen might be half bare by January.

The 151 genera of shrubs included in this dictionary are justly prized for their foliage, which comes in many shades of green and other, less expected colors such as gold, as in the golden Hinoki cypress. Some plants—yews and Japanese holly, for instance —are enormously versatile, serving as formal or informal hedges, screens, foundation plantings and mixed shrub borders. Evergreen shrubs with unusually beautiful forms make ideal focal points in a garden; others offer attractive seasonal displays of flowers or fruit.

Though the line between trees and shrubs is by no means distinct, this dictionary describes plants that usually have multiple stems and that rarely exceed 20 feet in height. Taller plants, which may be very closely related to species included here, are considered trees and are the subject of other volumes.

ABELIA × GRANDIFLORA

ABIES CONCOLOR 'COMPACTA'

ABUTILON HYBRIDUM

ACACIA FARNESIANA

Aaronsbeard see *Hypericum*

—

Abelia (a-BEE-lee-a)

Graceful, rounded shrub that bears 1-inch clusters of fragrant, bell-shaped white to pink flowers from early summer through autumn. Foliage is glossy. Evergreen Zones 8-10; deciduous or semievergreen Zones 6 and 7.

Selected species and varieties. *A.* × *grandiflora*, glossy abelia, is 2 to 6 feet tall and wide, with arching stems. Leaves are oval-shaped, 1 inch long, bronze when young, dark green in summer and reddish bronze in winter. 'Francis Mason' grows 3 to 6 feet tall and wide and has flowers of white flushed with pink. 'Prostrata' has flowers of the same color, but is a spreading plant 2 feet tall. *A.* × 'Edward Goucher' has pinkish lavender blooms and grows 4 to 5 feet tall.

Growing conditions. Plant abelia in full sun or partial shade in moist, acid, well-drained fertile soil. Leaves are more evergreen if the plant is protected from wind. Prune the plant in early spring. To rejuvenate an overgrown shrub, prune out stems at ground level.

Landscape uses. Plant abelia in a foundation planting, shrub border, mass planting or hedge. 'Prostrata' makes a good ground cover.

—

Abies (AY-beez)
Fir

Conifer ranging in size from large trees to dwarf shrubs. All forms have soft, needlelike, 1- to 2-inch foliage of green or blue with silver or gray on the undersides of the leaves. Zones 3-7.

Selected species and varieties. *A. balsamea* 'Nana', dwarf balsam fir, grows 12 inches high and round and has aromatic needles densely circling horizontal spreading branches. *A. concolor*, Colorado fir, white fir, has blue-green needles. Four cultivars grow to 3 feet in height: 'Conica' is conical in shape; 'Compacta' is densely branched; 'Globosa' has a rounded shape; and 'Pendula' has drooping branches.

Growing conditions. Plant firs in full sun in moist, well-drained, slightly acid, sandy soil. They need little pruning. Colorado fir tolerates heat and drought.

Landscape uses. Use dwarf firs in the front of a shrub border or in a rock garden.

—

Abutilon (a-BEW-ti-lon)
Flowering maple

Rapid-growing, vining shrub with drooping, 3-inch bell-shaped flowers of white, pink, orange, yellow and red. Foliage, which may be solid green or variegated, is five-pointed and similar to the foliage of the maple tree. Zones 9 and 10.

Selected species and varieties. *A. hybridum* can grow 8 to 10 feet tall and wide, but usually reaches only 4 to 5 feet. It blooms primarily in spring. White- and yellow-flowered varieties bloom almost all year.

Growing conditions. Plant flowering maple in full sun or light shade in rich, moist, well-drained soil. Pinch out growing tips to keep the plant bushy.

Landscape uses. Flowering maple is attractive enough to be used as a specimen. It also makes a good hedge, or can be trained as a standard or an espalier. In areas where it is not hardy, flowering maple can be grown in a container on a patio in summer and moved indoors in winter.

—

Acacia (a-KAY-sha)
Acacia, wattle

Rapid-growing tree or large shrub with feathery, divided foliage. Flowers are cream to yellow, and bloom in clusters in winter and spring. Acacia is a short-lived plant (20 years). Zones 9 and 10.

Selected species and varieties. *A. baileyana*, Bailey acacia, grows 20 feet tall, and has blue-gray leaves and yellow, fragrant flowers. 'Purpurea', purple leaf acacia, is similar but has purple foliage. *A. farnesiana*, sweet acacia, grows 15 feet tall, with deep yellow, fragrant flowers. *A. melanoxylon*, blackwood acacia, grows to 20 feet with cream- or straw-colored flowers.

Growing conditions. Grow acacia in full sun in dry, sandy, well-drained soil. Limit water to keep the plant low-growing. Remove the main shoot when the plant is young to encourage bushiness.

Landscape uses. Acacias are most effective when massed or in screens and hedges. They tolerate seashore conditions.

Acmena (ak-MEE-na)

Tall, wide-spreading shrub that has 3-inch shiny green to pinkish green leaves. Small white flowers bloom in clusters at the tips of the branches in summer. Zone 10.

Selected species and varieties. *A. smithii*, lilly-pilly, is best known for the display of white, lavender or purple ½-inch edible berries that appear in clusters all winter. It grows 10 to 25 feet tall.

Growing conditions. Grow lilly-pilly in full sun and average, well-drained garden soil. Prune to shape the plant and control its height.

Landscape uses. Because of its height, lilly-pilly is best used as a screen or a hedge.

African boxwood see *Myrsine*
African shrub daisy see *Felicia*
Alexandrian laurel see *Danae*

Alyogyne (AL-yo-gin)
Blue hibiscus

Rounded, compact shrub with trumpet-shaped blooms that have prominent stamens. The flowers are lilac, often spotted at the base of the petals and bloom on and off all year. Zones 9 and 10.

Selected species and varieties. *A. huegellii* 'Santa Cruz' grows to 6 feet tall. It has dark green, coarse, deeply lobed 3-inch leaves and glossy, dark lilac-blue flowers 4 to 5 inches across.

Growing conditions. Grow blue hibiscus in full sun in dry, well-drained soil. Pinch or prune growing tips to maintain a compact plant.

Landscape uses. Use blue hibiscus in a shrub border. It can also be trained as an espalier.

Andromeda (an-DROM-e-da)
Bog rosemary

Small, slow-growing, spreading shrub with oblong, gray-green leaves and tiny bell-shaped flowers that occur in small, drooping clusters and bloom in spring. Zones 2-6.

Selected species and varieties. *A. polifolia* grows 12 inches high, with 1½-inch leaves and 1¼-inch clusters of white flowers that are touched with pink.

Growing conditions. Grow bog rosemary in sun or light shade in very moist, cool, acid soil that is very rich in organic matter.

Landscape uses. Because it prefers wet soil, bog rosemary is best used near water or in a low, moist area. It can also be grown in a rock garden if given moist soil.

See also *Pieris*

Anise tree see *Illicium*
Aralia ivy see *Fatshedera*
Arborvitae see *Platycladus; Thuja*

Arbutus (ar-BEW-tus)

Slow-growing shrub or small tree with shiny, dark green, pointed, 3-inch leaves. New growth has a reddish cast. Tiny white flowers appear in 2-inch clusters and are followed by orange-red berries. Old bark peels away, revealing a bright red inner bark. Zones 8-10.

Selected species and varieties. *A. unedo*, strawberry tree, blooms in fall and winter and bears edible but tasteless berries resembling strawberries that often appear with the flowers. It can grow to a height of 30 feet. 'Compacta' and 'Elfin King' are dwarf cultivars that reach only 8 to 15 feet tall.

Growing conditions. Grow strawberry tree in full sun or light shade in sandy, well-drained acid soil. Prune after the plant flowers.

Landscape uses. Singly, the strawberry tree makes a good specimen. Because of its height, it can be used in a massed planting at the back of a shrub border or as a screen. It tolerates seashore conditions.

Arctostaphylos
(ark-to-STAF-i-loss)
Bearberry

Low-growing, spreading shrub that has glossy, smooth, dark green, 1-inch oblong leaves. Clusters of small, bell-shaped pink or white flowers bloom in spring. Bark is red to brown and branches grow in a crooked manner. Berries are red, ¼ inch wide and last all winter. Zones 2-8.

Selected species and varieties. *A. uva-ursi*, kinnikinick, is a prostrate shrub growing 12 inches tall and spreading to 15 feet. Stems root as

ACMENA SMITHII

ALYOGYNE HUEGELLII

ANDROMEDA POLIFOLIA

ARBUTUS UNEDO 'ELFIN KING'

ARCTOSTAPHYLOS UVA-URSI

AUCUBA JAPONICA 'VARIEGATA'

AZARA MICROPHYLLA

BAUHINIA BLAKEANA

they grow along the ground. New foliage has a reddish cast; fall foliage turns bronze. 'Big Bear' is slightly larger than the species and has larger leaves. Zones 2-7. 'Emerald Carpet' is 6 inches high and has bright green foliage. 'Massachusetts' is denser and lower-growing than the species and has smaller leaves. Zones 2-7.

Growing conditions. Grow bearberry in full sun or light shade, in dry, sandy soil with excellent drainage. It tolerates wind and salt spray. Prune the plant only to control its size.

Landscape uses. Because of its low-growing habit, bearberry should be planted as a ground cover, on a slope or spilling over a rock wall. It is a good plant for a seashore garden.

Aucuba (a-KEW-ba)

Rounded shrub with thick, glossy, 7-inch green leaves that are often marked with gold or yellow. Tiny purple flowers bloom in panicles in spring and are followed in fall (on female plants) by bright red berries that last all winter. Zones 7-10.

Selected species and varieties. *A. japonica,* Japanese aucuba, grows 6 to 8 feet tall. 'Mr. Goldstrike' has dark green leaves splashed with gold. 'Picturata' has leaves with bright yellow centers and dark green edges. 'Serratifolia' has dark green, serrated leaves. 'Sulphur' has foliage with green centers and yellow edges. 'Variegata', gold dust tree, has green leaves speckled with yellow. *A. japonica borealis* grows 2½ to 3 feet tall and has solid green foliage.

Growing conditions. Grow aucuba in light to deep shade. It prefers moist, rich, acid soil but once established will tolerate drought. It also tolerates air pollution. Prune to keep plants compact. Both male and female plants are needed to produce berries.

Landscape uses. The variegated foliage of aucuba makes it a good addition to a foundation planting. It also grows well in hedges, shrub borders, massed plantings and containers.

Australian fuchsia see *Correa*
Azalea see *Rhododendron*

Azara (a-ZA-ra)

Large, spreading shrub that has clusters of small fragrant flowers in early spring. Zones 9 and 10.

Selected species and varieties. *A. microphylla,* boxleaf azara, has ¾-inch, glossy, dark green leaves, yellow-green flowers and orange berries. It grows in a fanlike manner, reaching 12 to 18 feet in height and 8 to 12 feet in spread.

Growing conditions. Grow azara in shade in rich, moist, well-drained, heavily fertilized soil. Pinch growing tips to keep plants compact.

Landscape uses. Azara's height and shape make it a useful screen. It is also easily trained as an espalier.

Balsam fir see *Abies*
Banana shrub see *Michelia*
Barberry see *Berberis*

Bauhinia (baw-HIN-ee-a)

Tall, broad shrub with spectacular, orchidlike flowers. Foliage is round, bright green and uniquely cleft, shaped like a butterfly. Zone 10.

Selected species and varieties. *B. blakeana,* Hong Kong orchid tree, has 6-inch flowers of red to rose purple blooming in racemes during fall and winter. The plant grows 20 feet high and wide and has large leaves that are 6 to 8 inches across.

Growing conditions. Plant Hong Kong orchid tree in full sun or light shade in slightly acid, dry, sandy soil. After it flowers, prune it to shape it.

Landscape uses. Because of its showy flowers, Hong Kong orchid tree is a good specimen. Its height makes it useful in a screen.

Bayberry see *Myrica*
Bay laurel see *Laurus*
Bearberry see *Arctostaphylos*

Berberis (BER-ber-is)
Barberry

Deciduous or evergreen, rounded, thorny shrub that has clusters of glossy leaves at the end of short spurs. Flowers are yellow and bloom in spring. Zones 3-8.

Selected species and varieties. *B. candidula,* pale-leaf barberry, grows 2 to 4 feet tall and 5 feet wide. It has solitary ½-inch flowers and 1- to 2-inch bright green leaves that are white on the undersides. Fruit is grayish blue and downy. Zones 6-8. *B. julianae,* wintergreen barberry, grows 6 to 8 feet tall and has spiny, narrow, 4-inch-long leathery leaves that are dark green in summer and turn red in fall and winter. The undersides of the leaves are light green. Flowers appear in 2-inch clusters. Fruit is downy and blue-black. Zones 6-8. *B. sargentiana,* Sargent barberry, is 7 feet tall and has spiny leaves up to 4 inches long. Foliage is glossy, dark green on the upper surface and pale yellow-green on the underside. Small flowers bloom in clusters. Zones 7 and 8. *B. verruculosa,* warty barberry, grows 3 to 4 feet tall and has small warts on its stems. Leaves are spiny, leathery, 1 inch long, dark green on the upper surfaces and white on the undersides, and turn bronze in fall. Flowers are solitary; berries are downy and purple to black. Zones 6-8.

Growing conditions. Grow barberry in sun or partial shade in average, moist, well-drained garden soil. Prune lightly to shape the plant. Mature shrubs do not transplant well.

Landscape uses. Because of its thorns, barberry makes an excellent barrier plant. It can also be planted as a hedge or in a foundation planting or a shrub border. Low-growing varieties may be used as ground cover and in rock gardens.

—

Bird's eye bush see *Ochna*
Blue hibiscus see *Alyogyne*
Bog rosemary see *Andromeda*
Bottlebrush see *Callistemon*
Boxwood see *Buxus*
Bramble see *Rubus*
Breath of heaven see *Coleonema*
Broom see *Cytisus; Genista*

—

Brunfelsia (brun-FEL-see-a)

Rounded, upright plant with wavy-petaled flowers appearing in clusters at the ends of the branches. Zone 10.

Selected species and varieties. *B. pauciflora* may be erect or spreading; usually grows to 2 feet but may reach 9 feet. Flowers are 2 inches wide and dark purple with a white eye. 'Eximia', yesterday-today-and-tomorrow, is so named because its tubular, fragrant, five-part, 2-inch

flowers change color from purple on the first day, to lavender on the second day and white on the third. Bloom is heaviest in spring and appears off and on throughout the year. The plant grows 2 to 3 feet tall. Its leaves are oblong and 6 inches in length.

Growing conditions. Grow yesterday-today-and-tomorrow in full sun or light shade in rich, moist, acid, well-drained soil. Water and feed it heavily and keep it well mulched. Prune in spring to shape the plant. When grown in a container, it likes to be root-bound.

Landscape uses. The unique flowers of yesterday-today-and-tomorrow make it a good specimen. It can also be included in a flower bed or grown in a container.

—

Brush cherry see *Syzygium*
Buckthorn see *Rhamnus*
Bush germander see *Teucrium*
Bush poppy see *Dendromecon*
Butcher's broom see *Ruscus*

—

Buxus (BUK-sus)
Boxwood

Dense, compact shrub with small, round, leathery leaves and inconspicuous flowers that bloom in spring. The stems arch slightly, giving the shrub a soft appearance. Zones 4-9.

Selected species and varieties. *B. microphylla,* littleleaf box, has leaves 1 inch long and grows 3 feet high. Zones 6-9. The variety *japonica,* Japanese boxwood, grows to 6 feet tall and has light green, 1-inch leaves. Zones 5-9. The variety *koreana,* Korean boxwood, grows 2 to 2½ feet tall and has ½-inch leaves. It is hardy in Zones 4-8, but its leaves turn brown in winter in the colder zones. 'Kingsville' and 'Morris Midget' are both 18 to 24 inches tall. 'Morris Dwarf' grows 2 to 2½ feet tall. 'Wintergreen' stays green in winter. *B. sempervirens,* common or English boxwood, can grow to 20 feet. Leaves are larger than those of littleleaf box, up to 1¼ inches long. Flowers are sweetly scented. 'Arborescens', American box, is conical in form. 'Suffruticosa', edging box, is dwarf, growing to 3 feet tall and having ¾-inch leaves. Zones 5-8.

Growing conditions. Grow boxwood in sun or partial shade in well-drained, rich, moist soil. The roots

BERBERIS JULIANAE

BRUNFELSIA PAUCIFLORA 'EXIMIA'

BUXUS SEMPERVIRENS 'ARBORESCENS'

CALLIANDRA HAEMATOCEPHALA

CALLISTEMON CITRINUS

CALLUNA VULGARIS 'H. E. BEAL'

CALOCEDRUS DECURRENS 'INTRICATA'

are shallow and should be heavily mulched. Plants withstand pruning and shearing. Protect from winds.

Landscape uses. Boxwood is a formal plant that is best used in a hedge, an edging or a foundation planting. It can be trained into a topiary. Taller varieties make good screens.

Calico bush see *Kalmia*

California incense cedar
see *Calocedrus*

Calliandra (kal-ee-AN-dra)
Powderpuff

Upright shrub with very showy, round flower heads that appear above feathery, compound leaves on long, arching branches. Zone 10.

Selected species and varieties. *C. haematocephala,* red powderpuff, grows 15 feet tall and 8 feet wide. Red, silky, fluffy 2-inch flowers bloom in fall and winter, and are followed by long, flat, sometimes curled seedpods. Leaves are 4 inches long. They are bronze when young and change to dark green as they mature.

Growing conditions. Powderpuff will do well in full sun or light shade in moist, well-drained soil. Water heavily. Prune after the plant has flowered.

Landscape uses. The flowers of powderpuff make it a good specimen. Its size makes it a good screening plant. It can also be trained as an espalier.

Callistemon (kal-i-STEE-mon)
Bottlebrush

Shrub that may be upright or weeping; both forms have hundreds of silky, 1-inch stamens that protrude from tiny flowers on long, tubular spikes. Blooms appear primarily in summer but may form on and off throughout the year. Leaves are leathery, long and narrow, bronze when young and later dark green. Zones 9 and 10.

Selected species and varieties. *C. citrinus,* crimson bottlebrush, grows upright and has 4-inch spikes of red flowers and 3-inch leaves. The plant generally grows 10 to 15 feet tall, but sometimes reaches 25 feet. The leaves have a citrus aroma when crushed. *C. viminalis,* weeping bottlebrush, grows 20 feet tall and has a distinctively weeping habit. Flower spikes are red and 3 inches long. Leaves are 6 inches long.

Growing conditions. Plant bottlebrush in full sun in well-drained acid or alkaline soil. It does best when well watered, but will tolerate drought. It also tolerates wind and salt spray. For maximum flowering, prune the plant heavily every three years.

Landscape uses. The striking flowers of bottlebrush make it a good specimen plant. Because of its height, it is a useful screen or hedge. It can be trained as an espalier and is a good plant for a seashore garden.

Calluna (ka-LOO-na)
Heather

Low-growing shrub covered with fine leaves and 10-inch spikes of tiny, nodding, bell-shaped flowers of white, pink or lavender. Zones 4-7.

Selected species and varieties. *Calluna vulgaris,* Scotch heather, grows to 24 inches tall and can spread from 2 to 4 feet wide. Blooms appear in late summer or fall at the ends of ascending branches that are covered with dark green, scalelike leaves. 'County Wicklow' grows 18 inches tall and has double pink flowers. 'Dainty Bess' forms a low 4-inch mat and has lavender flowers. 'H. E. Beal' has silvery shell pink flowers and grows 24 to 30 inches high. 'Mrs. Pat' is bushy and 8 inches tall with light purple flowers. 'Spring Torch' grows 12 inches tall. Its foliage is bright yellow when new and fiery red in winter. Blooms are lavender-pink.

Growing conditions. Heather needs full sun and poor, moist, acid, well-drained soil. Roots are shallow and should be kept mulched. Prune in early spring to keep plants compact.

Landscape uses. Heather makes a good ground cover on sandy banks, and can be used in seaside gardens, dwarf gardens and rock gardens.

Calocedrus (kal-o-SEE-drus)

A broad genus of coniferous trees and shrubs having shiny, dark green, aromatic, scalelike needles that grow in flat, vertical planes. Bark is red-brown. Zones 6-10.

Selected species and varieties. *C. decurrens* 'Compacta', dwarf California incense cedar, reaches 3 feet tall and has dense branches. Foliage grows in tight, twisted sprays and has a bronze cast in winter. 'Intricata' grows 2 feet tall and 1½ feet wide; it is upright and compact, with dense branches that turn brown at the tips.

Growing conditions. Grow dwarf California incense cedar in full sun or light shade in moist, well-drained soil. Watering deeply but infrequently when the plant is young will increase its drought resistance when it matures. Little pruning is needed.

Landscape uses. Dwarf California incense cedar is useful as a foundation plant and in a hedge.

—

Camellia (ka-MEEL-ya)

Rounded shrub that has waxy flowers of white, pink, red or combinations of all three; the flowers may be single, having one ring of petals, or double, having numerous overlapping petals. The leaves are glossy, leathery and dark green. Zones 7-10.

Selected species and varieties. *C. japonica,* Japanese camellia, reaches 5 to 12 feet in height. Leaves are thick, oval and 3 to 4 inches long. Flowers are 3 to 5 inches across and bloom in winter and spring. There are literally thousands of named cultivars. 'Carter's Sunburst' has double, ball-shaped blooms of medium pink streaked with dark pink; 'Chandleri Elegans' has semidouble flowers of rose pink mottled with white and prominent stamens; 'Daikagura' has double flowers of rose red splotched with white; 'Debutante' has light pink, double, ball-shaped blooms; 'Glen 40' has a deep red, semidouble flower; 'Kramer's Supreme' has deep red, double, ball-shaped flowers; 'Kumasaka' flowers are bright rose pink and double; 'Magnoliaeflora' flowers are light pink and semidouble; 'Mathotiana Supreme' has large semidouble flowers of flaming crimson; 'Mrs. Charles Cobb' has large semidouble dark red blooms. *C. sasanqua,* Sasanqua camellia, is a looser shrub, with slender, 2-inch leaves. It grows 6 to 15 feet tall. Flowers are 2 to 3 inches across and bloom in fall and early winter. 'Bonanza' has semidouble flowers of rich scarlet; 'Jean May' has double, shell pink blooms; 'Mine-No-Yuki' has double white flowers; 'Shishi Gashira' flowers are semidouble and bright rose; 'Yuletide' has single flowers of orange-red and distinctive yellow stamens. Zones 8-10.

Growing conditions. Plant camellia in partial shade in very rich, moist, acid, well-drained soil. Mulch around the roots and do not cultivate around them; they are shallow and easily damaged. Fertilize very little. Prune the plant after it has flowered. Protect from winter sun. Buds may be damaged by late-spring frosts.

Landscape uses. Camellias are outstanding enough to be used alone as specimens and as accents. They can also be used in foundation plantings, hedges and containers, and trained as espaliers.

—

Canary-bird bush see *Crotalaria*

—

Cantua (KAN-chu-a)

Loose, open shrub that has magnificent tubular flowers that bloom in clusters at the ends of arching branches. Zone 10.

Selected species and varieties. *C. buxifolia,* magic flower, sacred flower of the Incas, grows 6 to 10 feet tall. Flowers are 4 inches across, rose or cerise striped with yellow, and bloom on and off all year. Leaves are hairy and 1 inch long.

Growing conditions. Grow magic flower in partial shade in light, well-drained soil. It may need to be staked when young. Prune the plant after it flowers.

Landscape uses. Cantua may be used as a container plant or in a hedge.

—

Cape honeysuckle
see *Tecomaria*

—

Carissa (ka-RIS-a)

Bushy, heavily thorned shrub with leathery leaves and fragrant, star-shaped, tubular flowers that bloom in clusters at the ends of the branches throughout the year. Zones 9 and 10.

Selected species and varieties. *C. grandiflora,* natal plum, has 2-inch white blooms at the ends of branches laden with 1- to 3-inch, dark green, shiny leaves. Plants reach 8 to 15 feet in height. Fruits are egg-shaped, 2 inches long, red and edible; they taste like cranberries. The fruits are produced all year long.

Growing conditions. Plant natal plum in full sun or light shade in average garden soil. Fertilize two to three times each year. Natal plum does best in moist climates and tolerates wind and salt spray. Prune or shear at any time of year.

CAMELLIA JAPONICA 'GLEN 40'

CANTUA BUXIFOLIA

CARISSA GRANDIFLORA

CARPENTERIA CALIFORNICA

CASSIA ARTEMISIODES

CEANOTHUS FOLIOSUS 'ITALIAN SKIES'

CEDRUS ATLANTICA 'PENDULA'

Landscape uses. Because of its thorns, natal plum makes a good barrier plant. It is also useful as a screen, hedge or foundation plant. It is a good plant for a seashore garden.

Carpenteria
(kar-pen-TEER-ee-a)

Slow-growing, multistemmed, formal shrub that has thick, leathery leaves and fragrant flowers with five to seven petals and large centers. Zones 7 and 8.

Selected species and varieties. *C. californica,* tree anemone, grows 3 to 6 feet tall. Leaves are narrow, 4 inches long, green on the upper surfaces and gray on the undersides. White, 3-inch flowers bloom in spring and summer.

Growing conditions. Plant tree anemone in full sun or light shade in light, sandy, well-drained soil. Water very sparingly, especially in winter, and shelter from drying winds.

Landscape uses. Use tree anemone in massed plantings, hedges and shrub borders.

Cassia (KASH-ee-a)

Deciduous or evergreen tree or shrub with showy clusters of small, yellow, four-petaled flowers and fine, compound leaves that look like conifer needles. Flat, 3- to 4-inch pods follow the flowers. Zones 9 and 10.

Selected species and varieties. *C. artemisiodes,* wormwood cassia, feathery cassia, is a 4-foot shrub with silky gray foliage. It blooms in winter and spring. *C. eremophila,* desert cassia, resembles *C. artemisiodes* but tends to be bushier. *C. leptophylla,* gold medallion tree, can reach 20 feet and has a more open, weeping form. It blooms in spring and summer.

Growing conditions. Grow cassia in full sun in well-drained, infertile soil. Cassia is very drought-resistant and should not be overwatered. Prune the plant after it flowers.

Landscape uses. Cassia is effective in massed plantings and in borders.

Ceanothus (see-a-NO-thus)
Wild lilac

Upright shrub or ground cover grown for its showy, dense, cone-shaped clusters of flowers, which may be blue, white or lavender. Zones 7-10.

Selected species and varieties. *C. × delilianus* has oval, dark green,

3-inch leaves and 4- to 6-inch clusters of blue flowers that bloom in summer and fall. It grows 3 feet tall. 'Gloire de Versailles' grows to 8 feet with fragrant lavender-blue flowers. *C. foliosus* grows to 1 foot or more in height and is densely branched. Leaves are oblong, ¾ inch in length and pale on the undersides. Clusters of blue flowers bloom in spring. 'Italian Skies' has lavender-blue flowers and light green leaves. *C. × pallidus* 'Marie Simon' is 3 to 5 feet tall, with oblong leaves and light blue flowers that bloom in spring.

Growing conditions. Plant wild lilac in full sun in sandy, light soil. Water deeply but infrequently. Prune the plant before it flowers.

Landscape uses. Use wild lilac in a mass planting or as a ground cover. It also makes a good seashore plant.

Cedar see *Cedrus*

Cedrus (SEE-drus)
Cedar

Coniferous tree or shrub with aromatic wood and 1- to 2-inch pointed needles of green or blue that appear in clusters. Large cones stand upright along the branches. Zones 5-10.

Selected species and varieties. *C. atlantica* 'Pendula', weeping atlas cedar, grows 3 feet tall with a 6-foot spread. Needles are dull green. Zones 6-10. *C. deodara* 'Compacta', dwarf deodar cedar, is a dense, low-growing, rounded shrub. 'Cream Puff' is conical, 6 to 8 feet tall and has creamy white needles mixed among the green. 'Descanco Dwarf' is conical and grows 6 to 8 feet tall with drooping foliage. 'Prostrata' grows flat on the ground. Zones 7-10. *C. libani* 'Compacta', dwarf cedar of Lebanon, is a dense 4-foot shrub with dark green needles. 'Nana' is a globe-shaped, bushy shrub that has bright green needles. It reaches 2½ feet in height. 'Pendula' has dark green needles and spreading, drooping branches. Zones 5-9.

Growing conditions. Grow cedar in full sun in rich, well-drained soil. The needles may brown in winter if the plant is exposed to cold winds.

Landscape uses. The small size of dwarf cedars makes them useful at the front of borders and foundation plantings, and in rock gardens.

Cephalotaxus (sef-a-lo-TAK-sus)
Plum yew

Broad, multistemmed conifer with soft, dark green needles that have a white stripe on the underside and purplish to dark green, 1-inch almond-shaped berries. Zones 6-10.

Selected species and varieties. *C. fortunei,* Chinese plum yew, has 2- to 3-inch shiny green needles that taper slightly to a point. It is a spreading shrub 10 feet high and wide. Zones 7-10. *C. harringtonia,* Japanese plum yew, is bushy and rounded, 6 feet high and wide, with 2-inch dull needles. 'Fastigiata' has a columnar shape, with needles spiraling around the branches. It grows 5 to 10 feet tall. 'Nana' is 2 to 4 feet tall and spreads by root suckers.

Growing conditions. Grow plum yew in full sun or partial shade in well-drained, acid to neutral, moist soil. It prefers cool, humid summers and needs protection from hot, drying winds. Prune or shear at any time.

Landscape uses. The density of plum yew makes it a good plant for a hedge or a screen. It can also be used as a foundation plant. It tolerates seashore conditions.

Ceratostigma
(ser-at-o-STIG-ma)

Mounded shrub or perennial valued for its clusters of rich, deep blue, single flowers that bloom from early summer to late fall. Zones 6-9.

Selected species and varieties. *C. plumbaginoides,* dwarf plumbago, spreads by underground stems to form a ground cover 6 to 12 inches tall. The foliage is 3 inches long and tufted, glossy green in summer and reddish bronze in winter.

Growing conditions. Grow dwarf plumbago in sun or light shade in average garden soil. It can become quite invasive unless it is heavily pruned.

Landscape uses. The low-growing habit of dwarf plumbago makes it useful as a ground cover. It can also be used in a flower border.

Cestrum (SES-trum)

Tall shrub with long leaves and clusters of conspicuous, tubular flowers that are followed by white berries. Zone 10.

Selected species and varieties. *C. aurantiacum,* orange cestrum, grows to 8 feet tall. It has 4-inch oval, deep green leaves and brilliant orange flowers in spring and summer. *C. nocturnum,* night jessamine, is 12 feet tall. Foliage is thin, shiny and 4 to 8 inches long. Greenish yellow to cream-colored flowers open only at night and emit a powerful fragrance on and off throughout the year.

Growing conditions. Grow cestrum in partial shade in rich, moist soil. Fertilize and water generously. Protect from drying winds. Prune the plant heavily to keep it shapely.

Landscape uses. Use cestrum as a hedge or a screen, or train it as an espalier.

Chamaecyparis
(kam-a-SIP-a-ris)
False cypress

Coniferous tree or shrub with foliage of green, yellow or blue that may be soft and scaly or feathery and stringlike. Leaves have white markings on the undersides and usually appear in flat sprays. Cones are small, and some varieties do not have them. Zones 3-9.

Selected species and varieties. *C. lawsoniana,* Lawson false cypress, has flat sprays of dark green scalelike foliage. 'Globosa' is globe-shaped and grows to 2 feet tall. 'Nana' has a rounded shape, grows to 2½ feet tall, and is distinguished from the similar 'Minima Glauca' in that 'Nana' has a main trunk and 'Minima Glauca' is multibranched from the ground. 'Minima Glauca' has sea green foliage. 'Tortuosa' has a conical shape. Zones 5-9. *C. nootkatensis,* Nootka or Alaska false cypress, has dull gray-green or blue-green aromatic foliage. 'Compacta' is 3 to 5 feet tall with a narrow, pyramidal shape, like a small tree. 'Pendula' grows 6 to 9 feet tall with an open, weeping habit and a broad pyramidal shape. Zones 4-8.

C. obtusa, Hinoki cypress, Hinoki false cypress, has dark green, scalelike foliage that is often curled on flat, spreading branches. 'Compacta' has a broad conical form and grows to 6 feet. 'Crippsii', golden Hinoki cypress, has branches that droop slightly; the foliage is golden yellow at the branch tips and green near the trunk. The plant grows 6 to 8 feet tall. 'Filicoides', fernspray cypress, is 5 feet tall, with fernlike foliage of moss green and upward-arching branches that give the shrub a pyramidal form. 'Gracilis' grows 6 feet tall with droop-

CEPHALOTAXUS HARRINGTONIA 'FASTIGIATA'

CERATOSTIGMA PLUMBAGINOIDES

CESTRUM NOCTURNUM

CHAMAECYPARIS OBTUSA 'NANA'

97

CHOISYA TERNATA

CHORIZEMA CORDATUM

CISTUS × PURPUREUS

ing branches in a narrow, conical form. 'Graciosa' is 5 to 6 feet high and pyramidal in shape. 'Kosteri' has layered, horizontal branches, twisted twigs and a pyramidal form 2½ feet tall. 'Magnifica' is a fast grower with bright green foliage. 'Nana' has a mounded habit with a flat top and fan-shaped needles; it grows 4 feet tall and 5 feet wide. 'Nana Aurea' is 12 to 18 inches tall and pyramidal in shape. Its foliage is golden yellow when new and dark green at maturity. 'Nana Gracilis' is a 6- to 10-foot pyramid with needles so dark they are almost black. 'Nana Lutea' is a 2-foot pyramid with foliage that is golden yellow when new and fades to white. 'Pygmaea' grows 9 to 18 inches tall and spreads to 24 to 30 inches wide, with fan-shaped, horizontal branches and bronzy foliage. 'Reis Dwarf' is 3 feet high, upright and rounded. 'Spiralis' is a stiff, 4-foot plant with twisted foliage. 'Torulosa' has contorted branches and scalelike foliage and grows to 3 feet. 'Torulosa Nana' is similar but slightly smaller. Zones 4-8.

C. pisifera, Sawara cypress, has soft, scalelike foliage of varying colors in flat sprays. 'Aurea' is a 6-foot pyramid with golden yellow foliage at the tips of the branches. 'Boulevard' has plumed, blue-gray foliage with a silvery cast. It grows 6 feet tall. 'Filifera', threadleaf cypress, has long, thready leaves on weeping branches that form a broad pyramid. 'Globosa' is low-growing and rounded. 'Minima' is mounded and 2 to 3 feet tall. 'Squarrosa' grows to 20 feet, with soft, mossy, blue-gray foliage. 'Squarrosa Veitchii' has a similar but lighter appearance. 'Squarrosa Minima' is 3 feet tall, compact and mounded. 'Tsukumo' is 3 to 4 feet tall and has fine foliage. Zones 4-8. *C. thyoides,* white cedar, has blue to gray-green scalelike foliage. 'Andelyensis' grows to 10 feet in a form that may be pyramidal to columnar and short, fanlike foliage that turns bronze in winter. 'Andelyensis Conica' and 'Andelyensis Meth Dwarf' have similar foliage and grow in a conical shape 3 to 4 feet tall. Zones 3-8.

Growing conditions. Grow false cypress in full sun in mild climates and in partial shade where the climate is hot. Soil should be fertile, rich, moist, well drained and acid to neutral. Most false cypresses prefer cool and moist climates; Hinoki false cypress and Sawara cypress are most tolerant of drier climates and poorer soils. All need protection from hot and drying winds. Lower branches and inner foliage often die out. Prune before growth starts in spring.

Landscape uses. False cypresses can be incorporated in foundation plantings and in rock gardens. They grow well in containers. Taller varieties are useful as hedges. Hinoki false cypress is often used in bonsai.

—

Chamaedrys germander
see *Teucrium*
Cherry laurel see *Prunus*
Chilean guava see *Ugni*
Chinese snowball see *Viburnum*

—

Choisya (SHOY-see-a)

Dense, broad, 6- to 10-foot shrub having aromatic 3-inch leaves that resemble fingers. Fragrant, 1-inch single flowers appear in clusters. Zones 8-10.

Selected species and varieties. *C. ternata,* Mexican orange, has white blooms at the ends of the branches in spring. Foliage is yellow-green, and each leaf is divided into three 3-inch fingers.

Growing conditions. Grow Mexican orange in full sun or light shade in acid soil with excellent drainage. Water deeply but infrequently. Frequent pruning is necessary to keep the plant shapely and compact.

Landscape uses. The density of Mexican orange makes it a good plant for an informal screen or a hedge. It also does well in massed plantings.

—

Chorizema (ko-RIZ-e-ma)

Weak-stemmed shrub or vine that has showy, ¾-inch orange or red flowers that bloom in clusters at the ends of the branches during winter and spring. Zones 9 and 10.

Selected species and varieties. *C. cordatum,* flame pea, has 2½-inch, dark green leaves that are heart-shaped at the base, and 6-inch clusters of scarlet and purple flowers. The plant may grow as a 2-foot shrub or as a 10-foot vine, depending on how the weak branches are pruned or trained.

Growing conditions. Flame pea grows well in full sun, but flower colors are richer if it is grown in partial shade. Soil should be well drained and infertile.

Landscape uses. If flame pea is pinched and pruned regularly, it can be kept as a 2-foot shrub. When shrubby, flame pea is good as a ground cover, as an edging or as a source of color in a flower garden. Left unpruned, it will sprawl to 10 feet and can be trained on a trellis, or used to spill over a wall, on a bank, in a container or in a hanging basket.

—

Christmas berry see *Heteromeles*

—

Cistus (SIS-tus)
Rockrose

Bushy, rounded to sprawling shrub with soft, hairy leaves and flowers that resemble single roses. Zones 8-10.

Selected species and varieties. *C. × hybridus* grows 4 feet tall and wide, and in spring and summer has 1- to 1½-inch flowers of white with yellow centers. Leaves are oval, 2 inches long and fragrant during warm weather. *C. × purpureus* grows 4 feet tall and wide. It has narrow, 2-inch-long leaves and 3-inch flowers that are mainly rose red, with yellow centers and spots of maroon.

Growing conditions. Grow rockrose in full sun in well-drained, slightly alkaline soil. It tolerates poor soil and drought. It is very difficult to transplant when mature.

Landscape uses. Use rockrose in a rock garden, in a seashore garden, in a massed planting or as a ground cover. Most species resist burning and are therefore useful plants for dry areas that are prone to forest fires.

—

Cleyera (KLAY-e-ra)

Graceful shrub with arching branches that grow equally wide and high. Zones 8-10.

Selected species and varieties. *C. japonica*, sakaki, grows from 6 to 15 feet tall and wide. Leaves are oblong, 2 to 6 inches in length, dark reddish brown when young and glossy green with a red midrib when mature. Fragrant single, ½-inch flowers appear in clusters in fall. Black, ¾-inch berries follow and last all winter.

Growing conditions. Grow cleyera in partial shade in rich, moist, well-drained soil. Prune the plant after it flowers.

Landscape uses. Grow cleyera as a specimen, as a foundation plant or in a hedge.

Cocculus (kok-YEW-lus)

Multistemmed shrub with an arching habit. Palm-shaped leaves have three prominent veins from base to tip. Flowers are inconspicuous. Zones 9 and 10.

Selected species and varieties. *C. laurifolius*, laurel leaf cocculus, grows 10 to 15 feet tall with foliage that is shiny, leathery, 6 inches in length and slightly drooping. The flowers are small and yellow; berries are black.

Growing conditions. Cocculus grows equally well in full sun or dense shade. It prefers moist soil but will tolerate a wide range of soil conditions. Prune to keep the plant low-growing and compact.

Landscape uses. Plant cocculus in a hedge or as a screen where its foliage will be shown off. It can also be trained as an espalier.

—

Coffee berry see *Rhamnus*

—

Coleonema (ko-lee-o-NEE-ma)
Breath of heaven

Delicate, multibranched shrub with thin stems and linear leaves that are fragrant when rubbed. Small flowers bloom heavily in winter and spring and occasionally throughout the rest of the year. Zone 10.

Selected species and varieties. *C. album*, white breath of heaven, grows to 6 feet with ½-inch leaves and ½-inch white flowers. *C. pulchrum*, pink breath of heaven, is 4 to 6 feet tall and has 1½-inch leaves and ¾-inch reddish pink flowers.

Growing conditions. Plant breath of heaven in full sun or light shade in average soil with excellent drainage. Prune after the heaviest flowering to keep the plant compact.

Landscape uses. Breath of heaven is most effective as part of a massed planting or in a hedge.

—

Convolvulus (kon-VOL-vew-lus)

Bushy to trailing annual, perennial or shrub having funnel-shaped flowers. Zones 8-10.

Selected species and varieties. *C. cneorum*, silverbush, grows 4 to 6 feet high and wide. Leaves are smooth, silvery in color and lance-shaped. Pale pink or white flowers, ½ inch across, appear singly or in

CLEYERA JAPONICA

COCCULUS LAURIFOLIUS

COLEONEMA PULCHRUM

CONVOLVULUS CNEORUM

COPROSMA REPENS 'AUREA'

CORREA PULCHELLA

COTONEASTER DAMMERI 'ROYAL BEAUTY'

clusters of up to six blooms throughout spring and summer.

Growing conditions. Grow silverbush in full sun or light shade. Soil should be light, dry and with excellent drainage. Water infrequently. Prune heavily to keep compact.

Landscape uses. Silverbush is most effective when massed on a bank or used in a hedge.

—

Coprosma (ko-PROS-ma)

Upright or spreading shrub that has flowers of greenish white in short dense heads. Female plants bear fleshy fruits, but both male and female plants are needed to produce them. Zones 9 and 10.

Selected species and varieties. *C. repens,* mirror plant, grows 10 feet tall and 6 feet wide. Leaves are very thick, shiny, oval to oblong, 2 to 3 inches long and notched at the tips. Foliage is glossy and dark green on the upper surfaces, paler and duller on the undersides. On female plants, flowers are followed by clusters of orange-yellow ⅓-inch berries. 'Aurea' has green leaves with a splash of gold at the center.

Growing conditions. Mirror plant needs full sun in cool climates, partial shade in hot climates. Soil should be dry and well drained. Prune twice a year to keep the plant compact.

Landscape uses. Use mirror plant as part of a hedge, a screen or a foundation planting. It tolerates seashore conditions. It can be trained as an espalier.

—

Coral pea see *Hardenbergia*

—

Correa (KOR-ee-a)
Australian fuchsia

Dense, spreading shrub with bell-shaped, drooping flowers that resemble hoopskirts. The blooms hang from the branches throughout winter. Leaves are round and 1 inch across, green on the upper surfaces and felty gray on the undersides. Zones 9 and 10.

Selected species and varieties. *C.* × *harrissi* is 2½ feet tall and has 1½-inch clear red flowers. *C.* × *magnifica* grows 4 to 5 feet tall and has 1½-inch green flowers. *C. pulchella* is 2½ feet tall, spreads to 8 feet in width and has 1-inch light pink flowers.

Growing conditions. Plant Australian fuchsia in full sun in cool climates and in partial shade where it is hot. Soil should be dry, sandy and well drained.

Landscape uses. The spreading habit of Australian fuchsia makes it a good ground cover. It also grows well in a container.

—

Cotoneaster (ko-toh-nee-AS-ter)

Evergreen or deciduous shrub with stiff, spreading branches and small, shiny, thick green leaves. Small white or pink flowers bloom in spring. They are followed in fall and winter by ¼-inch berries that may be red or black. Zones 3-9.

Selected species and varieties. *C. congestus,* Pyrenees cotoneaster, grows 1½ to 2½ feet tall in a rounded shape, with dull blue-green leaves, pink or white flowers and red fruit. Zones 6-8. *C. dammeri,* bearberry cotoneaster, grows 12 to 18 inches tall with trailing branches that spread to 6 feet. Leaves are 1 inch long, shiny dark green in spring and summer, and reddish purple in winter. Flowers are white; berries are red. 'Royal Beauty' is similar but has more abundant fruit. Zones 6-9. *C. lacteus,* Parney cotoneaster, has arching branches and grows 8 feet tall and wide. White flowers appear in 2-inch clusters; fruit is red and extremely profuse. Leaves are deep green and may be as much as 3 inches long. Zones 7-9. *C. microphyllus,* littleleaf cotoneaster, grows 6 to 24 inches tall and spreads to 10 feet wide. Flowers are white; fruit is red; leaves are ½ inch long and dark green. *C. microphyllus thymifolius* is more compact and has leaves that are ⅛ to ¾ inch long. Zones 6-9. *C. salicifolius,* willowleaf cotoneaster, has narrow, 1½- to 3-inch leaves that turn purple in winter, 2-inch clusters of white flowers and red fruit. The plant grows 15 feet high and wide with arching branches. 'Repens' is a prostrate grower 12 inches tall; 'Emerald Carpet' is compact, 6 to 12 inches tall and has smaller flowers. Zones 6-9.

Growing conditions. Grow cotoneaster in full sun or partial shade in well-drained, neutral to slightly alkaline soil. Mature plants will tolerate drought and wind. Cotoneaster does not transplant well when mature. Prune only to control the plant's shape.

Landscape uses. Plant cotoneaster in a rock garden or where it can spill over the top of a rock wall. It also makes a good hedge or foundation plant, and a good ground cover on a slope. It tolerates seashore conditions and can be trained into an espalier.

Crotalaria (kro-ta-LAY-ree-a)

Rapid-growing, upright, broad shrub that has showy flowers that appear in drooping spikes, with petals curved in such a way that the flower resembles a bird. Zones 9 and 10.

Selected species and varieties. *C. agatiflora,* canary-bird bush, can grow to 12 feet high and wide. Three-part, gray-green leaves are 3 inches long and 1 inch wide. Bright yellow-green flowers with brown lower petals bloom in 14-inch terminal clusters in summer and fall, and are followed by 3-inch seedpods. *C. capensis* grows to 5 feet, with 1-inch leaves and bright yellow flowers that occur in racemes.

Growing conditions. Grow canary-bird bush in full sun or partial shade. Prune two or three times a year to encourage compact growth.

Landscape uses. Canary-bird bush makes a good screen or hedge.

Cryptomeria
(krip-toh-MEER-ee-a)
Japanese cedar

Coniferous tree or shrub that has ¼- to ½-inch bright green to blue-green needles that hug the branches closely. Foliage often turns bronze in winter. Branch tips generally droop, giving the appearance of many fingers. The bark is reddish brown and peels off. Cones are 1 inch across and globe-shaped. Zones 5-9.

Selected species and varieties. *C. japonica* 'Albo Variegata' is a 10- to 15-foot pyramid with green and white foliage. 'Bandai Sugi' grows to 3 feet in a globular form with irregular branching and dark green foliage. 'Compacta' has a compact, conical form with blue-green leaves. 'Compressa' is 2 feet tall and flat-topped. 'Cristata' grows 10 feet tall and has foliage that is rich green and feathery when new. 'Elegans Compacta' has a pyramidal shape with drooping branches and is 10 feet tall. 'Globosa' is a neat, rounded shrub 15 inches tall and 30 inches wide. 'Jindai Sugi' is 4 feet tall and pyramidal with an open

habit. 'Knaptonensis' has white foliage on a 12-inch plant. 'Lobbii Nana' grows to 6 feet and is rounded. 'Pygmaea' grows 2 feet tall and slightly wider and has twisted branches. 'Tansu' is 3 to 4 feet high and rounded. 'Vilmoriniana' is rounded and 3 feet tall.

Growing conditions. Plant Japanese cedar in full sun or light shade in rich, moist, well-drained soil. Water deeply and frequently. Protect from drying winds. Little if any pruning is needed.

Landscape uses. The tall species of Japanese cedar may be used as specimens. The low-growing ones fit well in foundation plantings, in rock gardens and in containers.

Cupressus (kew-PRESS-us)
Cypress

Coniferous tree or shrub that has soft, tiny, scalelike, aromatic foliage of blue-green to dark green. Cones are round, brown and 1 inch in diameter. Zones 6-10.

Selected species and varieties. *C. arizonica,* Arizona cypress, has green to blue-green foliage and red bark. 'Compacta' grows 18 to 24 inches tall in a globe shape. 'Glauca' is similar but has bluer foliage. Zones 8-10. *C. macrocarpa,* Monterey cypress, has bright green foliage. 'Golden Pillar' is a large, pyramidal shrub that is golden yellow when grown in sun and lime green if grown in shade. Zones 8-10.

Growing conditions. Plant cypress in full sun or light shade in rich, well-drained soil. It tolerates heat and drought, wind and saltwater spray. It may be pruned to shape at any time.

Landscape uses. Singly, cypress makes a good accent shrub; several together make a good hedge. Most species grow well in seashore gardens, and the cultivar 'Compacta' grows well in a rock garden because of its small size.

Cypress see *Cupressus*

Cytisus (SIT-i-sus)
Broom

Spreading, multistemmed, deciduous or evergreen shrub ranging in height from 1 to 15 feet. Stems are graceful and slender, and remain green throughout the winter. Leaves

CROTALARIA CAPENSIS

CRYPTOMERIA JAPONICA

CUPRESSUS ARIZONICA

CYTISUS RACEMOSUS

DALEA GREGGII

DANAE RACEMOSA

DAPHNE × BURKWOODII

DAPHNE CNEORUM 'EXIMEA'

vary from being minute and inconspicuous to 1 inch long. Flowers are yellow, and bloom in racemes in spring. Zones 5-10.

Selected species and varieties. *C. racemosus* grows 3 to 8 feet tall and spreads 5 to 6 feet wide. Leaves are bright green with a silvery cast; each leaf has 1-inch leaflets. The flower clusters are 4 to 6 inches long and fragrant. Zones 9 and 10.

Growing conditions. Plant broom in full sun in dry, poor, infertile, acid to neutral, well-drained soil. It is drought-resistant but performs better if regularly watered. Prune the plant after it flowers to keep it compact. Broom is difficult to transplant.

Landscape uses. Use broom as a specimen or in a shrub border. It is especially effective as a ground cover on banks and slopes, and its root system will help control soil erosion.

Dalea (DAY-lee-a)
Indigo bush

Upright or spreading, evergreen or deciduous, multistemmed shrub that has slender branches and divided leaves. Pealike flowers bloom in racemes in spring. Zones 5-10.

Selected species and varieties. *D. greggii,* trailing indigo bush, grows to a height of 3 to 4 feet and spreads 5 to 6 feet across. Leaves are small and gray-green. Purple flowers bloom in spring.

Growing conditions. Plant indigo bush in full sun in dry, alkaline, infertile, well-drained soil. Prune in spring after the plant flowers.

Landscape uses. Spreading indigo bush is best used as a ground cover or planted on a slope.

Danae (DAN-a-ee)

Small, erect shrub with scalelike foliage. What appear to be leaves are actually modified branches. White flowers bloom in short spikes at the branch ends in summer and are followed by red berries. Zones 8-10.

Selected species and varieties. *D. racemosa,* Alexandrian laurel, grows to a height of 3 feet. The modified branches are 4 inches long and 1 inch wide.

Growing conditions. Grow Alexandrian laurel in partial to full shade in average, well-drained soil.

Landscape uses. The unusual shape of the modified branches makes

Alexandrian laurel a good accent plant. It may also be used as ground cover on a slope.

Daphne (DAF-nee)

Dense, low-growing shrub that bears small, fragrant bell-shaped flowers that bloom in clusters at the ends of branches covered with narrow leaves. Bark, leaves and berries are poisonous. Zones 4-9.

Selected species and varieties. *D. × burkwoodii,* Burkwood daphne, grows 3 to 4 feet tall in a rounded shape and has 1½- to 2-inch grayish leaves. Flowers, white turning to pink, bloom in 2-inch clusters in late spring. 'Carol Mackie' has white leaf margins and pale pink flowers. 'Somerset' has deep pink flowers and grows slightly taller. Zones 6-9. *D. cneorum,* rose daphne, forms a creeping mat 12 inches tall and 2 feet across. Foliage is dark green on the upper surface and gray-green on the underside. Flowers of pink bloom in 1½-inch clusters in late spring. 'Eximea' has deep pink flowers. Zones 5-8. *D. odora,* fragrant or winter daphne, is the most fragrant of the group, with rosy purple flowers appearing in late winter or early spring in 1-inch clusters. The plant grows 3 to 4 feet high with 2- to 3-inch dark green leaves. 'Alba' has white flowers; 'Rubra' has deep red flowers; 'Variegata' has leaves edged with yellow and pale pink flowers. Zones 7-9.

Growing conditions. Plant daphne in full sun or light shade in a loose, sandy soil that may be slightly acid to alkaline. Protection from afternoon sun in summer is beneficial. Excellent drainage is critical to growing success; where drainage is not excellent, grow in raised beds. Do not overwater. Mulch the shallow roots. Prune after flowering to keep compact. Daphne does not transplant well and is difficult to grow, often being short-lived. Apply winter protection where temperatures drop below freezing in winter and protect from drying winds and winter sun.

Landscape uses. Daphne's neat habit makes it useful in borders, beds and rock gardens. Low-growing forms make good ground covers.

Dendromecon
(den-dro-MEE-kon)

Multibranched shrub that has long, stiff leathery leaves. Flowers are golden yellow and have four petals. Zones 9 and 10.

Selected species and varieties. *D. rigida,* bush poppy, has 1- to 3-inch flowers blooming in spring on rounded plants up to 10 feet tall. Leaves are 4 inches long and ½ inch wide. Bark is yellow-gray and shreds.

Growing conditions. Grow bush poppy in sun in a sandy, well-drained soil. It prefers a hot, dry location. To keep the plant neat, prune it heavily after it flowers.

Landscape uses. Plant bush poppy on banks or slopes, or train it against walls.

—

Deodar see *Cedrus*

Devilwood see *Osmanthus*

—

Dodonaea (doh-don-EE-a)

Multistemmed shrub with sticky foliage and small, insignificant flowers that bloom at the ends of the branches. Zone 10.

Selected species and varieties. *D. viscosa,* hop bush, grows 15 feet high and wide with narrow, willow-like, 5-inch leaves. 'Purpurea' has purplish red foliage that darkens in winter.

Growing conditions. Plant hop bush in full sun in any garden soil. It is smog- and drought-resistant, and needs pruning to keep it compact.

Landscape uses. Hop bush's height and size make it a good plant for hedging or screening; its weather and pollution tolerance makes it useful at the seashore. It can be trained as an espalier.

—

Douglas fir see *Pseudotsuga*

—

Duranta (dew-RAN-ta)

Large, multistemmed shrub with tubular flowers that bloom in racemes during the summer and are followed by long clusters of ½-inch yellow berries. Zones 9 and 10.

Selected species and varieties. *D. repens,* golden-dewdrop, grows 15 to 20 feet tall with drooping branches. Leaves are glossy, round to oval in shape and 2 to 4 inches long. Flowers are lilac, ½ inch across; the racemes are 6 inches long. Thorns are often found on the plants.

Growing conditions. Plant golden-dewdrop in full sun in moist garden soil. Although it tolerates heat, it should be kept well watered. Prune it regularly to keep it neat.

Landscape uses. Use golden-dewdrop as a tall screen or hedge. Thorned varieties are especially useful as barrier plants.

—

Echium (EK-ee-um)

Broad, mounded shrub with hairy leaves and showy spikes of small flowers. Zones 4-10.

Selected species and varieties. *E. fastuosum,* pride of Madeira, grows 3 to 6 feet tall with long, narrow gray-green leaves and ½-inch purple to dark blue flowers that bloom on long, stiff spikes above the foliage in spring. Zone 10.

Growing conditions. Plant pride of Madeira in full sun in any well-drained garden soil. It tolerates poor, dry soil, and also salt spray and wind. Cut off flowers as they fade, and prune the plant to keep it bushy.

Landscape uses. The showy flowers of pride of Madeira add color and accent to the back of a flower garden. It can also be used in a garden at the seashore.

—

Elaeagnus (el-ee-AG-nus)

Broad genus of deciduous and evergreen trees and large, spreading shrubs grown primarily for their showy foliage, which is silvery on the undersides. Inconspicuous tubular flowers may bloom in spring or fall. Zones 2-10.

Selected species and varieties. *E. × ebbingei* grows 9 feet tall; its leaves are 4½ inches long and shiny green on the upper surfaces. Zones 9 and 10. *E. pungens,* thorny elaeagnus, is 15 feet tall. Its leaves are 2 to 4 inches long, olive green on the upper surfaces and have wavy margins. The flowers are fragrant, and the plant is often thorny. 'Fruitlandii' is more compact, with larger, more silvery leaves and bears edible red fruit in spring. 'Variegata' is fast-growing, and has leaves edged in white or yellow. Zones 7-10.

Growing conditions. Grow elaeagnus in sun or partial shade. It prefers sandy soil, but will grow in any garden soil, including poor and dry soil. Do not overwater. Do not fertilize. Elaeagnus tolerates

DENDROMECON RIGIDA

DODONAEA VISCOSA 'PURPUREA'

DURANTA REPENS

ECHIUM FASTUOSUM

ELAEAGNUS PUNGENS 'FRUITLANDII'

ERICA CARNEA 'SPRINGWOOD PINK'

ERIOBOTRYA JAPONICA

ERIOGONUM ARBORESCENS

wind. Prune or shear to shape and control growth.

Landscape uses. Elaeagnus may be used singly as an accent plant, or massed in hedges, screens and borders. It tolerates seashore conditions well. Thorned varieties make effective barriers.

English laurel see *Prunus*
English yew see *Taxus*

Erica (ER-i-ka)
Heath

Bushy low-growing or upright shrub that has small, needlelike foliage. Clusters of bell-shaped flowers of white, pink, rose, red or purple bloom in nodding spikes. Zones 3-9.

Selected species and varieties. *E. carnea,* spring heath, grows 6 to 18 inches tall and spreads 1 to 6 feet wide. Flowers bloom in winter and spring and last from three to five months. 'Anne Sparkes' grows 6 inches high and has deep rose pink flowers. 'Aurea' is 9 inches tall and has lilac-pink flowers. Branch tips are golden yellow. 'Pink Spangles' grows 8 inches high and has deep pink flowers. 'Springwood Pink' grows 10 inches high with pure pink flowers. 'Springwood White' grows 8 inches tall with white flowers. Zones 6-9. *E. cinerea,* twisted heath, grows 8 to 24 inches tall and spreads 2 to 4 feet across. White, rose or purple flowers bloom in summer. Foliage turns bronze in winter. 'Atropurpurea' grows 9 inches high and has deep violet flowers. 'P.S. Patrick' is 12 inches tall and has purple flowers. Zones 6-9.

Growing conditions. Plant heath in full sun or, in hot-summer areas, in partial shade. Soil should be rich, well drained and acid. Water when the soil starts to dry out. The roots are shallow and need mulching. Heavy fertilizing will discourage flowering. Heath does best where humidity is high and where there are no drying winds. Prune or shear after the plant has flowered to keep it compact and encourage new growth.

Landscape uses. Spring heath and twisted heath are good plants for ground covers, for rock gardens and for low borders because they are both low-growing. They are very effective massed on banks and slopes.

Eriobotrya (er-ee-o-BOT-ree-a)

Multistemmed shrub with open branching habit and large, toothed foliage of dark green with brown hairs on the undersides. Leaves are 10 inches long and have prominent veins; new foliage is reddish bronze. Off-white fragrant flowers covered with brown hairs bloom in fall and winter but are often hidden by the foliage. Zones 7-10.

Selected species and varieties. *E. japonica,* loquat, grows 15 to 25 feet tall. Flowers appear in clusters 6 to 8 inches long. Edible, pear-shaped, yellow aromatic fruit forms in spring. Zones 8-10.

Growing conditions. Plant loquat in full sun or partial shade in moist, well-drained soil. Keep well watered from the time flowering starts until fruit is picked. Prune and fertilize in spring after harvest.

Landscape uses. The toothed and colorful foliage of loquat makes it a good specimen or accent plant. It can also be massed as a hedge or screen. It may be trained as an espalier, but only on a north wall as it does not fare well in reflected heat.

Eriogonum (er-ee-OG-o-num)

Spreading shrub with tiny flowers that bloom in flat clusters at the ends of long stems. Zones 3-10.

Selected species and varieties. *E. arborescens,* Santa Cruz Island buckwheat, grows 3½ feet tall and spreads to 5 feet wide. Leaves are 1¼ inch long, oblong and gray-green on the upper surfaces; the undersides are covered with fine, white hairs. Flowers of pale pink to rose bloom in spring and summer. Zone 10.

Growing conditions. Plant Santa Cruz Island buckwheat in full sun in loose, sandy, well-drained soil. It tolerates wind and drought. It also self-seeds quite readily and may need yearly thinning out.

Landscape uses. The spreading habit of Santa Cruz Island buckwheat makes it a good plant for banks, mass plantings and rock gardens.

Escallonia (es-ka-LO-nee-a)

Spreading, multistemmed shrub with dark glossy leaves and showy single flowers that bloom singly or in clusters at the ends of the branches during summer and fall. It may bloom on and off all year in the warmest climates. Zones 8-10.

Selected species and varieties.
E. × exoniensis is 15 feet tall and has narrow 1½-inch leaves that are pale on the undersides. Flowers are white tinged with pink, and occur in clusters. *E. × langleyensis* grows to 8 feet with slender, arching branches and ½- to 1-inch leaves. Flowers are large, may be red or pink, and may bloom singly or in short clusters.

Growing conditions. Plant escallonia in full sun or light shade in any well-drained acid to neutral soil. Once mature, it will tolerate drought, wind and saltwater spray. Prune or shear the plant after it flowers.

Landscape uses. Its height and spreading form make escallonia a good hedge, screen or tall border plant. It may be used at the seashore.

Euonymus (yew-ON-i-mus)

Genus of compact shrubs and vines that may be deciduous or evergreen and are prized for their easy care and smooth, waxy, oval leaves. Inconspicuous spring-blooming flowers are followed by small but decorative berries in summer and autumn. Zones 3-10.

Selected species and varieties.
E. fortunei, wintercreeper, grows as a shrub and as a vine. 'Colorata', purple leaf wintercreeper, is a vining ground cover growing 12 inches tall with small leaves that turn purplish green in winter. 'Emerald Gaiety' has round leaves with white margins and grows into a 4-foot shrub. 'Emerald 'n' Gold' is similar but its leaves have gold margins. 'Gracilis' (sometimes called 'Variegata', 'Argenteo-variegata' or 'Argenteo-marginata') is a vining plant with yellow, white or pink markings on the leaves. 'Kewensis' has ¼-inch leaves and is low-growing. 'Longwood' is also low-growing, with ½-inch foliage. Zones 5-9. *E. japonica,* Japanese euonymus, is an upright shrub growing 10 to 15 feet tall with narrow, 1- to 3-inch leaves. 'Aureo-marginata' has foliage edged in golden yellow; 'Aureo-variegata' (also called 'Gold Spot') is the reverse, with centers of deep yellow and margins of green. 'Grandifolia' has somewhat larger leaves of deep green and is also stiffer and more upright than the species. 'Microphylla' is a dense, compact grower with leaves of ½ to 1 inch. 'Silver King' has green leaves with

silvery white edges. Zones 7-10. *E. kiautschovica,* spreading euonymus, is 6 to 10 feet tall with oblong leaves 2½ to 4 inches long. 'Manhattan' is lower-growing at 4 to 6 feet, with dark green, shiny, 2½-inch foliage. Zones 5-8.

Growing conditions. Euonymus may be planted in full sun to full shade in any well-drained soil, but does best in acid to neutral soil. Prune or shear at any time.

Landscape uses. The attractive form and foliage of euonymus make it a good foundation plant, accent or hedge. It can be trained as an espalier. The lower-growing types are good ground covers.

Eurya (YEW-ree-a)

Spreading shrub grown for its ornamental, teardrop-shaped, dark green, leathery foliage. Insignificant greenish white flowers bloom in spring. Zones 8-10.

Selected species and varieties.
E. japonica grows 6 to 8 feet tall, with leaves 2½ inches long and 1 inch wide. Flowers have an unpleasant odor. 'Winter Wine' has a burgundy cast to its leaves in fall.

Growing conditions. Plant eurya in partial shade in rich, moist, acid, well-drained soil. Prune at any time.

Landscape uses. Use eurya as a hedge plant where its ornamental foliage will show.

Euryops (YEW-ree-ops)

Small, dense, leafy shrub with daisy-like yellow flowers that bloom at the ends of stems held above the foliage. Leaves are fine, deeply cut and fern-like. Zones 8-10.

Selected species and varieties.
E. pectinatus, gray-leaved euryops, is 3 feet tall and has 3-inch, gray-green foliage. Branches and leaves are covered with white hairs. Flowers are 1½ to 2 inches across and bloom at the ends of 6-inch stems. Flowers appear all year but are most abundant in spring.

Growing conditions. Plant euryops in full sun in any well-drained, dry soil. It tolerates wind and saltwater spray. Remove flowers as they fade, and prune the plant in late spring.

Landscape uses. The fine foliage and long-blooming flowers make

ESCALLONIA × LANGLEYENSIS

EUONYMUS FORTUNEI 'EMERALD 'N' GOLD'

EURYA JAPONICA

EURYOPS PECTINATUS

× FATSHEDERA LIZEI

FATSIA JAPONICA

FEIJOA SELLOWIANA

FELICIA FRUTICOSA

euryops a good choice for the middle to back of a flower border. It is a good plant for the seashore.

False cypress see *Chamaecyparis*

× Fatshedera (fats-HED-er-a)
Aralia ivy, tree ivy

Semi-climbing shrub that is a cross between *Fatsia* (Japanese aralia) and *Hedera* (ivy) and has characteristics of both plants. Stems are weak and covered with large, glossy, leathery, dark green leaves with three to five lobes similar to the foliage of ivy. Zones 8-10.

Selected species and varieties. *F. lizei* grows 6 feet tall. Foliage is 5 to 10 inches across. Small, light green to cream-colored flowers bloom in fall in large, showy, branched clusters 8 to 10 inches long. Young branches are covered with rust-colored hairs. 'Variegata' is more vining than the species, with cream-colored leaf margins.

Growing conditions. Plant aralia ivy in full sun in cool areas and in partial to full shade where summers are hot. Soil should be rich, slightly acid and well drained. Water heavily and protect from drying winds.

Landscape uses. Train aralia ivy on a trellis or against a wall as an attractive screen or background plant.

Fatsia (FAT-see-a)
Japanese aralia

Large, bold, tropical-looking shrub with broad, shiny, stiff, deeply cut foliage that has five to nine lobes. Zones 9 and 10.

Selected species and varieties. *F. japonica* grows 6 to 10 feet high and wide, with 15-inch leaves at the ends of 12-inch leafstalks. Small, off-white flowers bloom in fall in large, showy, branched clusters 18 inches long. Small black berries appear in spring. 'Variegata' has leaf margins of golden yellow to white.

Growing conditions. Grow Japanese aralia in full sun in cool areas and in partial to full shade where summers are hot. Soil should be rich, sandy, slightly acid and well drained. Feed and water heavily during the growing season. Protect from winter wind and sun. Prune in early spring. Removal of flower buds in fall produces larger leaves.

Landscape uses. Its bold, tropical look makes Japanese aralia a good accent plant. In cold areas, it can be grown in a container and moved indoors during winter.

Feijoa (fay-JO-a)

Broad, fast-growing, multistemmed shrub with oblong leaves and small, single flowers with long, showy stamens that bloom in spring and summer. Egg-shaped, edible, yellow or green fruit with white flesh follows in fall. Zones 9 and 10.

Selected species and varieties. *F. sellowiana,* pineapple guava, grows 10 to 20 feet tall and has glossy green 2- to 3-inch leaves with white undersides. Flowers are white with a purple cast on the inside and have long red stamens. Fruit flavor resembles that of the pineapple. It may be necessary to have two plants to ensure cross-pollination and therefore produce fruit.

Growing conditions. Grow pineapple guava in full sun or light shade in sandy, rich, well-drained soil. Fertilize in early spring and again in early summer. Prune the plant before it flowers.

Landscape uses. The tall, bushy habit of pineapple guava makes it a good background for other plants and useful in hedges and screens.

Felicia (fe-LIS-ee-a)

Group of annuals, biennials, perennials and small shrubs, all of which have daisylike flowers of blue, pink, lavender or white with yellow centers. Zones 9 and 10.

Selected species and varieties. *F. fruticosa,* African shrub daisy, grows 2½ feet tall with narrow ½-inch leaves. One-inch flowers, usually purple but sometimes white or pink, are borne at the ends of 3-inch-long stems and bloom on and off all year.

Growing conditions. Plant African shrub daisy in full sun in sandy, dry, well-drained soil. Cut off flowers as they fade, and prune heavily in late summer to promote new growth and keep the plant compact.

Landscape uses. Use African shrub daisy in a container as an accent on a patio. It is also useful in a low border planting or mixed with annuals and perennials in a flower garden.

Fir see *Abies*

Fire thorn see *Pyracantha*

Flame pea see *Chorizema*

Flowering maple see *Abutilon*

Fortune's osmanthus
see *Osmanthus*

Fragrant box see *Sarcococca*

Fragrant tea olive
see *Osmanthus*

Gardenia (gar-DEEN-ya)

Compact shrub with glossy, leathery leaves and very fragrant, white, waxy, single, semidouble or double flowers. Zones 8-10.

Selected species and varieties. *G. jasminoides* grows 2 to 5 feet tall and has 2½- to 3-inch flowers in spring and summer. Leaves are 2 to 4 inches long. 'Mystery' is 6 to 8 feet tall with 4- to 5-inch flowers. 'Radicans' grows 12 inches high and 3 feet across, with 1-inch flowers. 'Radicans Variegata' is similar, but has leaves edged in white. Zones 9 and 10. 'Veitchii' is 3 to 4 feet tall with 1- to 1½-inch flowers.

Growing conditions. Grow gardenia in full sun in cool areas and in partial shade where summers are hot. Soil should be moist, acid, rich and well drained. The roots are shallow; mulch well and be careful when weeding near them. Fertilize heavily during the growing season. Protect from winds. Gardenia blooms best where days are hot and humid and nights are below 65° F.

Landscape uses. Gardenia makes a handsome accent or specimen plant. It also adds beauty to foundation plantings and to hedges. It can be trained as an espalier. In areas colder than Zone 8, it can be grown in a container and moved indoors for the winter. 'Radicans' makes a good ground cover.

Garrya (GAR-ee-a)
Silk-tassel

Upright shrub with leaves that are dark green and leathery on the upper surfaces, woolly and gray on the undersides. Flowers bloom in winter and spring. Zones 7-10.

Selected species and varieties. *G. elliptica* has 2- to 4-inch elliptical leaves and grows 4 to 8 feet tall. Flowers on male plants are 3 to 8 inches long, slender and yellow to green; those on female plants are 2 to 3 inches long and pale green. Both male and female plants are necessary for the female plants to bear clusters of purple, silky, grapelike berries in summer. Zones 8-10.

Growing conditions. Grow silk-tassel in full sun or partial shade in sandy, well-drained soil. Water when soil starts to dry out. Prune the plant in late summer.

Landscape uses. The form and foliage of silk-tassel make it useful as a screen, an informal hedge or a shrub border.

Gaultheria (gawl-THEER-ee-a)

Low-growing or prostrate shrub with small, drooping, bell-shaped white flowers in spring and berries in fall. Zones 3-10.

Selected species and varieties. *G. procumbens*, wintergreen, grows 3 inches high and spreads to 12 inches across. Foliage is 2 inches long, glossy green in spring and summer, and red in cold winters. The plant bears edible red berries that have a wintergreen flavor. Zones 4-8.

Growing conditions. Grow wintergreen in partial shade in rich, moist, acid, well-drained soil. Prune the plant to shape and control its size.

Landscape uses. The low-growing, creeping habit of wintergreen makes it a good ground cover, especially in a woodland setting. It is also attractive draped over rocks and spilling over walls.

Genista (je-NIS-ta)
Broom

Small, spreading shrub with many slender, almost leafless, green stems. Foliage, where present, is very small. Yellow flowers bloom in racemes at the ends of the branches in spring. Zones 2-10.

Selected species and varieties. *G. pilosa*, silky-leaved woodwaxen, grows 12 to 18 inches tall and spreads to 7 feet wide. Gray-green branches root along the ground and are covered with tiny, silvery leaves. The plant may be deciduous in cold climates. It gives the appearance of being evergreen because its dense branches retain their gray-green color all winter. Zones 6-10.

Growing conditions. Grow silky-leaved woodwaxen in full sun in dry,

GARDENIA JASMINOIDES

GARRYA ELLIPTICA

GAULTHERIA PROCUMBENS

GENISTA PILOSA

GREVILLEA × 'NOELLII'

GREWIA OCCIDENTALIS

GRISELINIA LITTORALIS 'VARIEGATA'

HAKEA SUAVEOLENS

infertile, well-drained acid or alkaline soil. Prune the plant after it has flowered to encourage a second bloom. Silky-leaved woodwaxen does not transplant well.

Landscape uses. Its spreading habit makes silky-leaved woodwaxen good as a ground cover and in mass plantings on slopes and banks.

Germander see *Teucrium*
Glory bush see *Tibouchina*
Golden-dewdrop see *Duranta*
Gold medallion tree see *Cassia*

Grevillea (gre-VIL-ee-a)

Tree or shrub with feathery foliage and clusters of long, showy, narrow, curved flowers at the ends of the branches in spring. Zones 8-10.

Selected species and varieties. *G. lanigera,* woolly grevillea, is a mounded shrub that grows 3 to 6 feet tall and spreads 6 to 10 feet across. Its dense foliage is silky, gray-green and ½ inch long. Blooms are red and cream-colored. *G.* × 'Noellii' grows up to 4 feet tall and 4 to 5 feet wide. Leaves are narrow, 1 inch long, medium green and glossy. Clusters of pink and white flowers bloom for six to eight weeks in spring.

Growing conditions. Plant grevillea in full sun in dry, sandy, infertile soil. It is very heat- and drought-tolerant. Prune the plant after it has flowered.

Landscape uses. The spreading habit of grevillea makes it a good plant for a ground cover, bank cover and mass planting.

Grewia (GROO-ee-a)

Fast-growing, sprawling shrub with serrated leaves and star-shaped, 10-pointed flowers. Zones 7-10.

Selected species and varieties. *G. occidentalis,* lavender starflower, grows 10 feet tall with slender branches and dark green, narrow leaves 3 inches long. One-inch-long lavender flowers bloom in spring. Zones 8-10.

Growing conditions. Plant lavender starflower in full sun in any well-drained soil. Water when the ground becomes dry. Prune growing tips to keep the plant compact.

Landscape uses. Train lavender starflower against a wall or a fence in either an informal or espaliered form. When pegged down, it will make a good ground cover.

Griselinia (gris-e-LIN-ee-a)

Neat, upright shrub with thick, leathery, shiny foliage. Although the plant does form long, thin clusters of flowers, it is primarily grown for its foliage as its blooms are inconspicuous. Zones 9 and 10.

Selected species and varieties. *G. littoralis:* a tree that can be trained to grow as a shrub 10 feet high and wide. Leaves are glossy, leathery, ovate and 4 inches long. 'Variegata' has white markings on the foliage. *G. lucida* is a slender shrub 6 to 8 feet tall with 7-inch leaves.

Growing conditions. Plant griselinia in full sun or partial shade in any well-drained garden soil.

Landscape uses. Show off griselinia's foliage in a screen, a hedge or a container.

Guava see *Psidium*

Hakea (HAH-kee-a)

Dense, rounded shrub with needle-like leaves. Zones 9 and 10.

Selected species and varieties. *H. suaveolens,* sweet hakea, is a broad, upright shrub 6 to 8 feet tall with slender branches. Foliage is stiff, dark green and 4 inches long. Fluffy clusters of small, white, fragrant flowers bloom in fall and winter.

Growing conditions. Plant sweet hakea in full sun in well-drained soil. It tolerates poor soil, drought and wind. Prune the plant after it flowers.

Landscape uses. The upright habit of sweet hakea makes it a good hedge, screen or background plant. It tolerates seashore conditions.

Hardenbergia (har-den-BER-jee-a)

Shrubby vine 10 feet tall with small, pealike flowers in clusters during late winter and spring. Zones 9 and 10.

Selected species and varieties. *H. violacea,* coral pea, has narrow, 2- to 4-inch leaves and lilac, rose or white flowers with yellow markings at the base of the petals. Zone 9.

Growing conditions. Grow coral pea in full sun in cool climates and in partial shade where summers are hot. Soil should be light, rich and well drained. Water sparingly. Prune after flowering.

Landscape uses. Train coral pea on a trellis or against a wall or a fence. It can also be trained as a ground cover. It may be used at the seashore, as it tolerates salt spray and wind.

Heath see *Erica*
Heather see *Calluna*
Heavenly bamboo see *Nandina*

Hebe (HEE-bee)

Rounded, spreading shrub with attractive, leathery, glossy, dark green leaves and 2- to 4-inch spikes of tiny white, pink, red, lavender or purple flowers at the ends of the branches in summer. Zones 8-10.

Selected species and varieties. *H. buxifolia,* boxleaf hebe, grows 3 feet tall with ½-inch leaves densely crowded on the branches. Flower spikes are white. 'Patty's Purple' is similar with purple flowers.

Growing conditions. Grow boxleaf hebe in full sun in cool areas and in partial shade where summers are hot. Soil should be well drained and of low fertility. Prune the plant after it flowers.

Landscape uses. Hebe is a good shrub for a low hedge or edging, and may be used singly as a container plant. Its flowers make it useful in a perennial border. It may be grown at the seashore, since it tolerates salt spray.

Hemlock see *Tsuga*

Heteromeles
(het-er-o-MEE-leez)
Christmas berry

Shrub that may be single- or multi-stemmed and has thick, leathery, glossy, toothed leaves. Large, flat clusters of small, white flowers bloom in summer and are followed by clusters of hollylike red berries in winter. Zones 9 and 10.

Selected species and varieties. *H. arbutifolia* grows 6 to 10 feet tall and has oblong, 4-inch leaves.

Growing conditions. Grow Christmas berry in full sun in any well-drained soil. It will tolerate drought but does better if watered, especially in summer. Prune in early spring to keep the plant compact.

Landscape uses. Use Christmas berry as a specimen plant or a hedge where its winter foliage and berries can be seen. It is also an excellent plant for a bank, as its dense roots help control erosion.

Hiba false arborvitae
see *Thujopsis*

Holly see *Ilex*
Honeysuckle see *Lonicera*
Hong Kong orchid tree
see *Bauhinia*

Hop bush see *Dodonaea*

Hypericum (hy-PER-i-kum)
St.-John's-wort

Low-growing, spreading shrub with oval to oblong leaves. In summer it bears cup-shaped yellow flowers that have five petals and many showy stamens that give the center of the flower a crested look. Zones 8-10; semievergreen Zone 7.

Selected species and varieties. *H. beanii* (sometimes designated *H. patulum henryi*), has graceful, arching branches that spread to 3 feet. Leaves are 3-inch ovals; flowers are 2 inches across. *H. calycinum,* Aaronsbeard, grows 12 to 18 inches tall and spreads by underground stems. Leaves are 4-inch oblongs, green with pale undersides, and turn purple in winter. Flowers are 2 inches across. *H. × 'Hidcote'* has 3-inch fragrant flowers, the largest flowers of all St.-John's-worts. The plant grows 2 to 6 feet tall and spreads to 4 to 6 feet wide. Foliage is 2½ inches long, dark green above and pale green underneath. *H. reptans* forms a prostrate, spreading mat 4 inches tall and 2 feet across. Two-inch flowers stand out from small, ½-inch leaves.

Growing conditions. Grow St.-John's-wort in sun or partial shade in a light, well-drained soil. Most species prefer acid soil, but Aaronsbeard will grow in alkaline soil as well. Prune before growth starts. Heavy pruning can keep the plants more compact.

Landscape uses. Use St.-John's-wort as a ground cover on a flat expanse or on a slope. It also makes a colorful informal hedge.

HARDENBERGIA VIOLACEA

HEBE BUXIFOLIA

HETEROMELES ARBUTIFOLIA

HYPERICUM × 'HIDCOTE'

ILEX AQUIFOLIUM 'ARGENTEA
MARGINATA PENDULA'

ILEX CORNUTA 'DWARF BURFORDII'

Ilex (I-lex)
Holly

Broad genus of shrubs and trees grown for their attractive forms, deep green foliage and bright berries. Some evergreen hollies have smooth foliage; others have spiny leaves. Small clusters of inconspicuous white or greenish flowers appear in spring. Only female hollies produce berries, and with few exceptions, there must be a male holly within 100 feet for cross-pollination. Zones 3-10.

Selected species and varieties.
I. aquifolium, English holly, is a pyramidal plant that can be pruned to a 10- to 15-foot shrub. Leaves are dark green, shiny, 1 to 2 inches long and spiny. Round red berries last all winter. 'Argentea Marginata Pendula' has a weeping habit. Leaves are dark green with gray-green blotches and whitish margins; new growth is briefly flushed with pink. Zones 7-9.
I. × *aquipernyi* grows in a conical shape 8 to 10 feet tall, with 2- to 4-inch glossy and spiny foliage and red berries. 'Brilliant' has abundant, exceptionally bright berries. 'San Jose' is similar but denser. Zones 6-9. *I. cassine myrtifolia* is a very tall shrub, to 30 feet, with 1- to 2-inch narrow, dark green leaves and red fruit. 'Lowei' is similar with yellow fruit. Zones 7-9.

I. cornuta, Chinese holly, has glossy, thick, leathery leaves that are almost rectangular in shape. There is a spine at each leaf corner and one at the tip that often curves under. Flowers are bright yellow and quite showy; berries are red. The species grows upright to 10 to 15 feet. Chinese hollies are among the few that will bear berries without the presence of a male shrub. 'Burfordii' is a 15-foot globe-shaped plant with abundant fruit. Its leaves are spiny only at the tips. 'Dwarf Burfordii' is similar but grows slowly to 5 to 7 feet. 'Berries Jubilee' grows to 6 feet and produces larger red berries than most Chinese hollies. 'Carissa' grows 3 to 4 feet high and slightly wider and fruits abundantly. 'Dazzler' grows upright to 6 feet with many large berries. 'D'or' has spineless leaves and yellow berries. 'O'Spring' is globe-shaped, 8 to 10 feet tall, and has variegated yellow and green foliage. 'Rotunda' is 3 to 4 feet high and wide and does not produce berries until it reaches about 25 years of age. 'Willowleaf' is 10 feet tall and bushy with long, narrow leaves that are slightly twisted. Zones 6-9.
I. crenata, Japanese holly, grows 4 to 10 feet high in a neat, rounded, dense habit. Leaves are shiny, dark green, 1 inch across and may be round or oblong. Berries are black and inconspicuous. 'Convexa' grows 6 feet high and 12 feet wide and has ½-inch cupped leaves. 'Dwarf Pagoda' is a rounded plant 15 to 18 inches tall and has rounded leaves. 'Green Dragon' is a broad, upright, compact shrub reaching 4 to 6 feet in height. 'Helleri' is 2 feet tall and 3 to 4 feet wide and has a flat or mounded top. Leaves are dull green and ½ inch long. 'Hetzii' is similar to 'Convexa' but has larger leaves. 'Mariesii' is low-growing, 15 to 18 inches tall, with dense, round leaves at the ends of the branches. 'Repandens' is a low-growing spreading plant with closely spaced, thin, flat leaves. 'Rotundifolia' is upright to 6 feet and has ¼-inch round leaves. 'Stokes' is 3 feet tall and 4 feet wide, flat-topped and has dense, ½-inch leaves. 'Watanabeana' is 4 to 6 feet high and has yellow berries. Zones 6-9. *I. dimorphophylla* has 1- to 1½-inch spiny leaves similar to those of Chinese holly. It is a 5-foot, rounded plant and has red fruit. Zones 9 and 10. *I. glabra,* inkberry, is a multistemmed, rounded plant growing 4 to 8 feet high and slightly wider. Leaves are shiny, narrow and 1½ to 2 inches long. Berries are black and usually not showy. 'Compacta' grows 4 to 5 feet tall, with dark green, dull foliage and abundant berries. 'Ivory Queen' has sparse white fruit. 'Nordic' is similar to 'Compacta' but is less open at the base of the plant. Zones 3-9.

I. × *meserveae,* blue holly, is 8 to 12 feet in height with oval, leathery, shiny, spined, blue to purple leaves and purplish twigs. 'Blue Boy' is erect, grows to 8 feet and does not produce berries. 'Blue Girl' is similar but bears abundant red berries. 'Blue Prince' is a male shrub that forms a compact, 12-foot pyramid and produces no berries; 'Blue Princess', its female counterpart, produces many red berries. Zones 5-8. *I. opaca,* American holly, is a large tree but can be pruned to a 15-foot pyramid-shaped shrub. Foliage is spined, 2 to 4 inches long, dull green on top and lighter yellow-green underneath. Fruit may be red or yellow and persists throughout the winter. Zones 6-9. *I. vomitoria,* Yaupon holly, is a tall multistemmed shrub 15 to 25 feet high with shiny, 1½-inch leaves and profuse red berries. 'Nana' is 1½ to 3 feet tall and round. It does not set fruit until it is about 20 years old. 'Pendula' grows 15 to 25 feet tall but has weeping outer branches and red berries. 'Stokes' is similar to 'Nana' but more compact and 2 to 3 feet high. Zones 7-10.

Growing conditions. Hollies grow in full sun or partial shade, but they will produce more berries and be more compact if grown in sun. Soil should be rich, moist, acidic and well drained. Most species prefer cool, moist climates, but Chinese holly and yaupon holly, once established, withstand drier soil and climate than other species. All species should be pruned or sheared in spring before growth starts.

Landscape uses. Hollies can stand alone as specimens. They are also useful in foundation plantings, as hedges and as screens. Japanese holly can be clipped to formal shapes and topiaries. Any of the low-growing varieties can be used as ground covers and in rock gardens.

—

Illicium (i-LIS-ee-um)
Anise tree

Genus of large shrubs and small trees with oval to elliptical leaves that have a licorice-like aroma. Zones 8-10.

Selected species and varieties. *I. anisatum,* Chinese anise, Japanese anise tree, grows to 25 feet, with thick, fleshy, oval, pointed 4-inch leaves. Flowers are fragrant, yellow, 1 inch across and bloom in spring. *I. floridanum,* purple anise, Florida anise, is 10 to 15 feet high, with 4- to 6-inch dark green leaves. Flowers are 1½ to 2 inches across, red to maroon and bloom in spring. *I. parviflorum* is a broad, upright shrub 10 to 15 feet tall and has light green foliage and yellow flowers.

Growing conditions. Grow anise tree in full sun to partial shade in rich, moist, acid to neutral soil. Keep it well watered.

Landscape uses. Because of its large size, anise tree is best used as a hedge or screen.

—

Indian hawthorn see *Raphiolepis*
Indigo bush see *Dalea*
Inkberry see *Ilex*

—

Itea (IT-ee-a)
Sweetspire

Graceful, arching shrub with small, greenish white flowers with five narrow petals. Blooms appear in long, showy racemes. Zones 9 and 10.

Selected species and varieties. *I. ilicifolia* grows to 10 feet tall with 4-inch, dark green, shiny, hollylike spiny leaves. Flower racemes are 1 foot long and bloom in late summer and fall.

Growing conditions. Grow sweetspire in sun in cool areas and in partial shade where summers are hot. The soil should be rich, moist and well drained.

Landscape uses. Because sweetspire prefers wet soil, it does well near ponds and streams. Its graceful appearance makes sweetspire a good informal hedge. It can also be trained as an espalier.

—

Japanese aralia see *Fatsia*
Japanese cedar see *Cryptomeria*
Japanese yew see *Podocarpus*
Juniper see *Juniperus*

—

Juniperus (joo-NIP-er-us)
Juniper

Vast group of coniferous trees and both upright and prostrate shrubs. Juvenile foliage is sharp and needlelike; mature foliage is softer and scalelike. Some plants have only one or the other; other plants have both. Foliage ranges from light to dark green, to blue-green, to blue or silver and often turns purplish in winter. Female plants produce small, round, blue berries that are used to flavor gin. Zones 2-10.

Selected species and varieties. *J. chinensis,* Chinese juniper, is an upright, broad pyramidal tree with many smaller-growing cultivars. Foliage may be either scalelike or needlelike. 'Ames' is a 6-foot pyramid with blue-green, mostly needlelike, foliage. 'Armstrong' is 4 feet high and wide with soft, scalelike gray-green leaves. 'Blaauw' grows in a vase shape 3 feet high and has deep gray to blue-green scalelike foliage. 'Densa' is a 10-foot, slender, conical shrub with needlelike foliage. 'Gold Coast' has fine-textured golden yellow foliage. It grows 12 to 18 inches high and 4 to 5 feet wide. 'Hetzii' grows 4 to 6 feet tall and spreads to 10 feet wide, and has long, horizontal branches with needlelike foliage. 'Hetzii Glauca' grows somewhat taller and wider than 'Hetzii' and has blue foliage. 'Keteleerii' has medium green, scalelike foliage on a 15-foot, pyramidal shrub. 'Pfitzeriana', Pfitzer juniper, grows 6 feet tall and 15 feet

ILLICIUM FLORIDANUM

ITEA ILICIFOLIA

JUNIPERUS CHINENSIS 'TORULOSA'

111

JUNIPERUS COMMUNIS DEPRESSA

JUNIPERUS CONFERTA

JUNIPERUS VIRGINIANA 'SKYROCKET'

wide, and has feathery, arching, horizontal branches with mostly scalelike foliage. 'Pfitzeriana Aurea' is slightly more compact and has foliage that is golden yellow when new. 'Pfitzeriana Glauca' is similar to 'Pfitzeriana' but has blue foliage. 'Plumosa' has plumed sprays of scalelike leaves on a plant 3 feet tall and twice as wide.

'Procumbens', Japanese garden juniper, grows 1 to 2 feet tall and 10 to 15 feet wide with ascending branches. It has blue-green, needlelike foliage. 'Procumbens Nana' grows only 6 to 12 inches tall. 'Robusta Green' is a slender pyramid 15 feet tall and has tufted, scalelike foliage. 'San Jose' grows 6 to 12 inches high and 6 to 8 feet wide, and has both scalelike and needlelike blue-green foliage. 'Sargentii' and 'Sargentii Viridis' grow 18 inches tall with stiff branches spreading to 10 feet, and have scalelike leaves. The foliage of 'Sargentii' is more blue-green than that of 'Sargentii Viridis'. 'Torulosa' ('Kaizuka'), Hollywood juniper, has twisting branches and bright green, scalelike foliage on a narrow, upright shrub growing to 15 feet. 'Torulosa Variegata' is narrower and more columnar and has both yellow and green leaves. Zones 4-9.

J. communis, common juniper, has needlelike foliage arranged in threes and grows 5 to 10 feet high and 8 to 12 feet wide. 'Compressa' grows 4 feet tall in a narrow, columnar shape. 'Hibernica' ('Stricta'), Irish juniper, is a very narrow, columnar shrub 8 feet high and 1 to 2 feet wide with dark green leaves. 'Hornibrookii' is a dwarf, creeping cultivar. 'Repanda' forms a dense, matted carpet with dull green leaves that turn bronze in winter. Zones 2-8. *J. communis depressa* is gray-green, 4 feet high and 15 feet wide. Zones 2-8.

J. conferta, shore juniper, has soft, blue-green needlelike foliage and grows 1 foot high and 6 to 8 feet across. 'Blue Pacific' and 'Emerald Sea' both grow 9 inches tall and are quite similar except that 'Emerald Sea' has greener leaves. Zones 6-9. *J. davurica* grows 3 feet high and 6 feet wide and has rigid, spreading, horizontal branches. Needles are scalelike. 'Expansa Aureospicata' is similar but slightly smaller, with both needlelike and scalelike foliage and splashes of yellow throughout the plant. 'Expansa Variegata' is similar but has splashes of white. Zones 5-10.

J. horizontalis, creeping juniper, has blue-green, mostly scalelike foliage that turns purple in winter. 'Bar Harbor' grows 8 to 12 inches high and spreads to 8 feet wide. It has thin,

horizontal, mounded branches and foliage that is blue until it turns red in winter. Similar to 'Bar Harbor' in size and form, but different in color, are 'Blue Chip', with a more silvery tone; 'Emerald Spreader', with emerald green foliage; 'Hughes', with silver-blue foliage; and 'Turquoise Spreader', with turquoise-green foliage. 'Plumosa', Andorra juniper, grows 18 to 36 inches tall and 10 feet wide, with gray-green foliage that turns red-purple in winter. Branches turn upward at a 45° angle. 'Prince of Wales' has low, spreading branches in a starburst pattern and bright green foliage. 'Wiltonii', blue rug juniper, is a creeping plant 6 inches high and 8 feet wide and has steel gray foliage. Zones 3-9.

J. sabina, savin juniper, has stiff branches that arch in a vase shape. The plant grows 4 to 5 feet tall and 10 feet wide and has dark green, scalelike foliage. 'Arcadia' has grass green foliage and grows 1 foot high and 4 feet wide. 'Buffalo' is 12 inches tall and 8 feet wide and has bright green leaves. 'Blue Danube' grows 12 inches tall and 4 feet wide and has blue-green foliage. 'Skandia' has dark green foliage and grows 12 inches high and 4 feet wide. 'Tamariscifolia', tam juniper, is mounded and feathery in appearance, 18 inches high and 10 feet across, and has blue-green leaves. 'Tamariscifolia New Blue' has the same growth habit but a richer blue color. Zones 3-9.

J. scopulorum, Rocky Mountain juniper, is a narrow, erect tree that grows to 30 feet and has scalelike, light green to rich blue leaves. Several of its cultivars are useful shrubs. 'Blue Creeper' is mounded, 2 feet high and 6 feet wide, with bright blue coloring on the foliage. 'Emerald Green' is upright, 5 to 6 feet tall and has bright green foliage. 'Moffetii' has dense, blue-green foliage and a pyramidal form. 'Moonglow' is a broad, upright pyramid that grows to 15 feet and has silver-blue foliage. 'Table Top Blue' is a flat-topped shrub 5 feet high and 8 feet wide with silver-blue leaves. Zones 3-9. *J. squamata,* singleseed juniper; is a 3-foot shrub with blue-green, needlelike foliage. Its branch tips arch and slightly nod. 'Blue Carpet' is low and spreading with silver-blue foliage. 'Blue Star' is more rounded, 2 feet high and 4 feet wide, and has blue-green leaves. 'Parsonii' is low-growing with stiff, spreading branches. 'Meyeri' is upright, 6 feet tall and 4 feet wide, with irregularly shaped branches and a silvery appearance. 'Wilsonii' is conical in form with nodding branch tips; it grows to 9 feet. Zones 4-8. *J. vir-*

giniana, eastern red cedar, is a large tree with deep green, scalelike or needlelike foliage. It has several dwarf cultivars. 'Canaertii' and 'Cupressifolia' are dense, conical shrubs growing to 10 to 15 feet with dark green foliage. 'Manhattan Blue' is similar in form but has blue-green foliage. 'Skyrocket' has blue-green foliage but grows to 15 feet in a very narrow column. Zones 3-9.

Growing conditions. Plant junipers in full sun in acid to neutral, dry, well-drained soil. Do not overwater. Prune in spring as growth starts.

Landscape uses. Junipers are so diverse in habit that there is one to fit any landscape need. Low-growing forms make excellent ground covers on flat surfaces and on slopes. They also do well spilling over rocks and walls. Spreading types make excellent hedges and screens. Any of them can find a place in a foundation planting, and those with unique shape or coloration can be used as specimens and accents. They also do well in seashore gardens.

—

Kalmia (KAL-mee-a)
Laurel, calico bush

Dense, rounded shrub that has shiny, leathery, dark green leaves. Flowers are cup-shaped and appear in clusters at the ends of the branches in late spring; they may be white, pink or purple, and the petals are often spotted in purple or maroon. The stamens curl back and are attached to the petals until they are released by bees or other insects. Zones 3-8.

Selected species and varieties. *K. angustifolia,* sheep laurel, grows 2 to 3 feet tall. It has 1- to 2-inch narrow, oblong leaves and 2- to 3-inch clusters of lavender to rose flowers. *K. latifolia,* mountain laurel, is 7 to 12 feet tall. It has 2- to 4-inch oval leaves and 4- to 6-inch clusters of white or rose flowers. Zones 5-8.

Growing conditions. Grow laurel in full sun or partial shade in moist, rich, acid, well-drained soil. It has shallow roots and will benefit from a mulch to keep them cool and moist. Prune the plant after it flowers.

Landscape uses. Use laurels in a foundation planting, in a massed planting or as specimens. They also fit well in a woodland garden beneath tall trees.

—

Kinnikinick see *Arctostaphylos*

Lantana (lan-TAY-na)
Shrub verbena, red sage

Small shrub or vining plant with hairy stems and coarse, toothed leaves that are rough on the upper surfaces and hairy on the undersides. Tiny, ¼- to ½-inch flowers bloom in flat-topped, 1- to 2-inch clusters all summer long. Zones 9 and 10.

Selected species and varieties. *L. camara* grows to 4 feet tall with 2- to 6-inch, oval to heart-shaped leaves. Flowers are yellow when they open, turn orange and then red, so that all three colors are present on the flower clusters at one time.

Growing conditions. Grow lantana in full sun in any well-drained soil. Water deeply but infrequently; too much water or fertilizer inhibits flowering. Lantana tolerates heat and drought. Prune in early spring.

Landscape uses. Use lantana in an informal hedge, in a flower garden or as a container plant. Lantana tolerates the wind and salt spray of the seashore.

—

Laurel see *Kalmia; Laurus*

—

Laurus (LAW-rus)
Laurel, sweet bay

Broad-based, multistemmed shrub that grows in a conical shape. Leaves are dark green, dull, leathery and aromatic. Inconspicuous white flowers bloom in spring and are followed by ½-inch black berries. Zones 8-10.

Selected species and varieties. *L. nobilis,* bay laurel, grows 8 to 12 feet tall. Its 2- to 4-inch leaves are the bay leaves used in cooking.

Growing conditions. Grow bay laurel in full sun or partial shade in any rich, moist, well-drained soil. Water heavily in spring but keep the soil dry the rest of the year. Prune or shear the plant in summer.

Landscape uses. Several bay laurels together make good hedges and good background plantings. They take well to pruning and can be shaped into topiaries. Singly laurel also grows well in containers.

—

Lavandula (la-VAN-dew-la)
Lavender

Small, mounded shrub or perennial with long, narrow, hairy, aromatic,

KALMIA LATIFOLIA

LANTANA CAMARA

LAURUS NOBILIS

LAVANDULA ANGUSTIFOLIA

113

LEIOPHYLLUM BUXIFOLIA

LEPTOSPERMUM SCOPARIUM

LEUCOPHYLLUM FRUTESCENS

LEUCOTHOE FONTANESIANA

gray-green leaves. Fragrant lavender, purple or blue flowers appear in dense spikes during the summer and off and on all year in frost-free areas. Lavender is hardy in Zones 5-10, but will be an herbaceous perennial in Zones 5-8.

Selected species and varieties. *L. angustifolia,* English lavender, grows 2 to 3 feet tall and has 2½-inch leaves. Lavender or purple flowers bloom in 3- to 3½-inch spikes. *L. dentata,* French lavender, is a 1- to 3-foot shrub. It has 1½-inch gray, toothed leaves and 1½- to 2½-inch spikes of lavender flowers. Zones 9 and 10. *L. latifolia* resembles English lavender, except that the leaves are broader and grayer, and the flower spikes are often branched.

Growing conditions. Plant lavender in full sun in loose, well-drained soil. Water and fertilize sparingly. Prune the plant after it flowers to keep it compact. To dry the flowers, cut them as they open and hang them in a cool, dry area.

Landscape uses. Lavender is used as an edging, a low hedge or in the front of a shrub border. It is also used in flower gardens and herb gardens.

—

Lavender see *Lavandula*

Lavender cotton see *Santolina*

—

Leiophyllum (ly-o-FIL-um)
Sand myrtle

Neat, compact shrub with upright branches and shiny, leathery, oval, ½-inch leaves. Waxy, ¼-inch pink or white flowers bloom in 1-inch clusters in late spring. Zones 6-8.

Selected species and varieties. *L. buxifolia* grows 18 to 36 inches high in a rounded form. Foliage turns bronze in the winter.

Growing conditions. Grow sand myrtle in partial shade in acid, moist, rich, well-drained soil. Prune the plant after it flowers.

Landscape uses. Because of its small size and neat appearance, sand myrtle does well in rock gardens and as a low edging. It tolerates seashore conditions.

—

Leptospermum
(lep-toh-SPER-mum)
Tea tree

Tree or shrub of varying sizes and forms having small, rigid, needlelike foliage. The branching structure is irregular, soft and delicate in appearance. Single white, pink or red ½-inch flowers densely cover the branches in spring. Zones 9 and 10.

Selected species and varieties. *L. scoparium,* New Zealand tea tree, can be either a shrub 8 to 20 feet tall, or a ground cover 1 to 2 feet tall. Its leaves are fragrant, ½ inch long, silky when young and hidden by the numerous flowers when the plant is in bloom.

Growing conditions. Plant New Zealand tea tree in full sun and well-drained, acid to neutral soil. It should be watered heavily when it is young but will be drought-tolerant when mature. Prune the plant lightly after it flowers.

Landscape uses. The low-growing New Zealand tea tree is an excellent ground cover; the shrub form is used as a hedge, specimen or accent plant. New Zealand tea tree can also be used in a seashore garden.

—

Leucophyllum (loo-ko-FIL-um)

Rounded, open, informal shrub that has attractive, silver-gray, hairy foliage and bell-shaped flowers of rose, lavender or purple in summer. Zones 9 and 10.

Selected species and varieties. *L. frutescens,* Texas ranger, is 6 to 8 feet high and 4 to 6 feet wide. Leaves are 1-inch oblongs with white, woolly undersides. Flowers are violet to purple and 1 inch across.

Growing conditions. Plant Texas ranger in full sun in any acid or alkaline well-drained soil. It likes hot, dry and windy locations. Water sparingly. Prune the plant in early spring.

Landscape uses. Use Texas ranger as an accent or an informal hedge.

—

Leucothoe (loo-KOTH-o-ee)

Multistemmed mounded shrub that has graceful, arching branches. Foliage is narrow and pointed, bronze in spring, green in summer and red in winter. White, tiny, bell-shaped flowers bloom in slender, drooping clusters at the ends of the branches in midspring. Zones 5-9.

Selected species and varieties. *L. axillaris,* coast leucothoe, grows to 4 feet tall. It has 2- to 4-inch leathery leaves and 1- to 2-inch flower clusters. Zones 6-9. *L. fontanesiana,* drooping leucothoe, is 3 to 6 feet tall.

It has 2- to 5-inch leaves and 3- to 4-inch flower clusters. Young branches are red. 'Girard's Rainbow' has variegated foliage of pink, yellow, green and copper. *L. populifolia,* Florida leucothoe, is 8 to 15 feet tall and has 1½- to 4-inch leaves that do not change color in winter. Zones 7-9.

Growing conditions. Plant leucothoe in partial to full shade in moist, acid, rich, well-drained soil. Shelter it from drying winds. Prune the plant after it flowers. To rejuvenate an old plant, cut out older stems at the base.

Landscape uses. Leucothoe is attractive in a foundation planting, shrub border, a woodland garden or massed on banks and slopes. It is a good foil for taller plants that have lost their lower branches.

Ligustrum (li-GUS-trum)
Privet

Deciduous or evergreen shrub that has a dense, erect habit. The evergreen species have smooth, shiny, leathery, dark green, round to oval foliage and spiked clusters of small, scented, white flowers in late spring or early summer. Zones 7-10.

Selected species and varieties. *L. japonicum,* Japanese privet, is 6 to 10 feet high and has 4- to 6-inch flower clusters. 'Rotundifolia' is 4 to 5 feet high and has round leaves. 'Texanum Silver Star' is 6 feet tall and has leaves edged in creamy white. 'Variegata' has leaves edged with white and grows to 10 feet.

Growing conditions. Plant privet in full sun or partial shade in any soil except one that is constantly wet. It is very tolerant of air pollution and drought. Pruning in early spring will reduce or eliminate flowering. If flowers are desired, wait until after the plant has flowered to prune.

Landscape uses. Privet is used mainly in hedging because it withstands heavy shearing, but it also makes a good background plant. It is also a good plant for topiary.

Lilly-pilly see *Acmena*

Lonicera (lo-NIS-er-a)
Honeysuckle

Deciduous or evergreen shrub or vine that has small, trumpet-shaped flowers that flare at the ends and show prominent stamens. Blooms appear in whorls at the ends of the branches in late spring and early summer. Berries appear in fall and attract birds. Zones 5-10.

Selected species and varieties. *L. nitida,* boxleaf honeysuckle, grows 3 to 6 feet tall and has thin branches and thick, glossy, ½-inch leaves. Flowers are ½ inch long, creamy white and slightly fragrant. Berries are purple. Zones 7-10.

Growing conditions. Plant honeysuckle in full sun to partial shade in any garden soil. Water generously. Prune the plant after it flowers.

Landscape uses. Plant honeysuckle as a hedge, as a foundation plant or as a screen. It tolerates seashore conditions.

Loquat see *Eriobotrya*

Loropetalum (lor-o-PET-a-lum)

Broad, rounded shrub with tiered, arching branches. Flowers have four long, strap-shaped and curled petals and appear in clusters in early spring. Zones 7 and 8.

Selected species and varieties. *L. chinense* usually grows 3 to 4 feet tall but can attain a height of 6 feet. Leaves are oval, 1 to 2 inches across and light green. White, fragrant flowers are 1 inch across. The shrub may be only semievergreen in areas with cold winters.

Growing conditions. In cool areas, plant loropetalum in full sun; where summers are hot, plant it in partial shade. Soil should be rich, acid and well drained. Water heavily. Prune the plant sparingly to preserve the natural form.

Landscape uses. Loropetalum is effective in massed plantings and in shrub borders.

Magic flower see *Cantua*

Magnolia (mag-NO-lee-a)

Genus of trees and shrubs that have large leaves and cup- or star-shaped flowers that bloom in spring and summer. The shrubs are evergreen in Zones 8-10; deciduous in Zones 4-10.

Selected species and varieties. *M. grandiflora,* southern magnolia,

LIGUSTRUM JAPONICUM

LONICERA NITIDA

LOROPETALUM CHINENSE

MAGNOLIA GRANDIFLORA 'LITTLE GEM'

MAHONIA AQUIFOLIUM

MICHELIA FIGO

MICROBIOTA DECUSSATA

has waxy, dark green foliage that is 2 to 10 inches long. Flowers are fragrant, up to 12 inches across and cup-shaped, and bloom in late spring and on and off throughout the summer. 'Little Gem' grows to 15 feet with 4-inch leaves that are rusty bronze-colored on the undersides. Flowers are 6 inches across and appear in early summer and again in late summer. 'Majestic Beauty' has a pyramidal shape and grows to 20 feet tall. Leaves are 10 inches long; flowers are 12 inches across. 'Saint Mary' is 20 feet high and wide with foliage that is rust-colored on the undersides. Flowers are 10 inches across. *M. virginiana*, sweetbay magnolia, grows 25 feet tall. Flowers are fragrant, pale yellow to white, cup-shaped, 2 to 3 inches across and bloom in summer. Leaves are 2 to 5 inches long, gray-green on the upper surfaces and white on the undersides.

Growing conditions. Plant magnolia in full sun or partial shade in rich, moist, acid to neutral, well-drained soil. Prune the plant after it flowers.

Landscape uses. Magnolias are so magnificent on their own that they make excellent specimen plants. They can also be espaliered.

Mahonia (ma-HO-nee-a)

Upright, rounded shrub with stiff, leathery, spiny, compound, dark green or blue-green leaves that turn bronze or purple in winter. Fragrant yellow flowers bloom in terminal racemes in early spring. Clusters of edible, dark blue berries that resemble grapes appear in summer. Zones 5-10.

Selected species and varieties. *M. aquifolium*, Oregon grape holly, grows 3 to 6 feet tall. Each leaf has five to nine very spiny leaflets and is 4 to 10 inches long. Flower clusters are 3 inches high. 'Compacta' grows 18 to 24 inches tall. Zones 5-9. *M. bealei*, leatherleaf mahonia, grows to 12 feet tall in an upright, stiff form. Leaves are blue-green; each one has nine to 15 slightly spined leaflets and is 18 inches long. Flowers bloom in clusters 4 to 6 inches long. Zones 7-10. *M. pinnata*, California grape holly, is similar in appearance to Oregon grape holly but has duller, more crinkled foliage. Zones 7-10. *M. repens*, creeping mahonia, grows 2 feet tall and spreads to 6 feet across by underground stems. Leaves are dull blue-green; each one has has three to seven spiny leaflets and is 3 to 6 inches long.

Growing conditions. Grow mahonia in partial shade to shade in moist, acid, rich, well-drained soil. It can be grown in full sun if the soil is kept constantly moist. Shelter from winter wind and sun to prevent leaf scorch. Prune the plant before growth starts.

Landscape uses. Use shrubby mahonia in a border, a foundation planting or a woodland garden. Creeping mahonia may be used as a ground cover.

Marmalade bush
see *Streptosolen*

Mescal bean see *Sophora*

Mexican orange see *Choisya*

Michelia (my-KEE-lee-a)

Dense tree or shrub that has narrow leaves and fragrant, saucer-shaped flowers that bloom among the leaves. Zones 9 and 10.

Selected species and varieties. *M. doltsopa* grows to 15 to 20 feet and can be either a wide or a narrow shrub. Leaves are dark green, 6 to 7 inches long, thin and leathery. Fragrant 5- to 7-inch whitish flowers bloom in winter and spring. *M. figo*, banana shrub, grows 6 to 20 feet tall with shiny, 3-inch leaves. Dark yellow flowers with maroon edges bloom in spring; they are 1½ inches across and have a strong banana fragrance.

Growing conditions. Plant michelia in full sun or partial shade in moist, acid, fertile, well-drained soil. It is very heat-tolerant. Prune the plant after it flowers.

Landscape uses. Plant michelia as a specimen where its fragrance can be enjoyed, or train it as an espalier.

Mickey Mouse plant see *Ochna*

Microbiota (my-kro-by-O-ta)

Widely spreading conifer with bright green, feathery, scalelike foliage that turns copper in fall. Zones 2-10.

Selected species and varieties. *M. decussata*, Russian cypress, Siberian cypress, grows 18 to 24 inches tall and spreads to 4 to 6 feet across.

Growing conditions. Plant Russian cypress in sun or shade in a dry, well-drained soil. Prune or shear at any time.

Landscape uses. Use Russian cypress as a ground cover, a low hedge or in a massed planting.

Mintbush see *Prostanthera*
Mirror plant see *Coprosma*
Mountain laurel see *Kalmia*
Mugo pine see *Pinus*

Myoporum (my-OP-or-um)

Dense upright or sprawling shrub that has leaves that are covered with translucent dots. Small, white bell-shaped flowers are followed by small but showy berries. Zones 9 and 10.

Selected species and varieties. *M. laetum* grows to 15 feet with narrow, 4-inch, shiny leaves that are brownish when young. Clusters of ½-inch flowers of white spotted with purple bloom in summer, followed by ¼-inch reddish purple berries.

Growing conditions. Grow myoporum in full sun in moist, well-drained soil. Prune the plant before new growth starts in spring.

Landscape uses. The density and wind tolerance of myoporum make it useful as a screen, hedge or windbreak, or in a seashore garden. If its branches are pegged to the ground, it can be trained as a ground cover.

Myrica (mi-RY-ka)
Bayberry

Deciduous or evergreen upright shrub that has aromatic foliage, twigs and berries. Inconspicuous greenish white flowers bloom in spring. Gray or purple, waxy berries form on the female plants. Zones 1-10.

Selected species and varieties. *M. cerifera,* southern wax myrtle, is a multistemmed shrub growing 10 to 20 feet tall. Leaves are 3 inches long, narrow, light green and toothed. Clusters of ⅛-inch, gray berries form along the stems and last throughout the winter. Zones 7-9.

Growing conditions. Plant bayberry in full sun or partial shade in dry, sandy soil. Prune or shear the plant in early spring. Male and female plants together are needed to produce berries.

Landscape uses. Use bayberry as a hedge or screen, or plant it in a seashore garden.

Myrsine (MER-seen)

Upright, dense, rounded shrub that has flat clusters of single flowers among the foliage. Zones 9 and 10.

Selected species and varieties. *M. africana,* African boxwood, grows 3 to 6 feet tall. It has aromatic, dark green, glossy, round, ½- to 1-inch leaves. Clusters of tiny, reddish brown flowers appear in late summer and are followed by red berries.

Growing conditions. Myrsine may be planted in full sun or partial shade in acid or alkaline, well-drained soil. Pinch growing tips to keep the plant compact. It can be pruned into formal shapes.

Landscape uses. Use African boxwood as a low hedge, a foundation plant or a container plant, or train it as a topiary.

Myrtle see *Myrtus*

Myrtus (MER-tus)
Myrtle

Dense, rounded shrub that has shiny, thick, dark green, aromatic leaves. Flowers are saucer-shaped with five petals and several prominent stamens that give the center of the bloom a delicate, fluffy look. Zones 9 and 10.

Selected species and varieties. *M. communis* grows 5 to 12 feet tall with 1- to 2-inch oval, pointed leaves. Fragrant flowers of white or pink are ¾ inch across and bloom in clusters during the summer, followed by showy, ½-inch blue-black berries.

Growing conditions. Grow myrtle in sun or partial shade in any well-drained acid or alkaline soil. It tolerates heat and drought. Prune or shear the plant in early spring before growth starts.

Landscape uses. The neat, dense habit of myrtle makes it useful as a hedge, edging, screen or massed planting. It tolerates salt spray and wind and is a good seashore plant.

Nandina (nan-DEE-na)

Upright shrub with erect, unbranched, ringed stems resembling bamboo. Leaves are delicate and divided, light green in summer, brilliant red in fall. Small flowers bloom in erect panicles at the ends of the branches and are followed by brilliant red berries. Zones 7-10.

MYOPORUM LAETUM

MYRICA CERIFERA

MYRSINE AFRICANA

MYRTUS COMMUNIS

117

NANDINA DOMESTICA

NERIUM OLEANDER

OCHNA SERRULATA

Selected species and varieties. *N. domestica,* heavenly bamboo, grows 6 to 8 feet high and 2 feet wide. White flowers bloom in late spring or early summer. Large clusters of ½-inch red berries last all winter. There are three dwarf cultivars that grow 2 feet tall: 'Harbour Dwarf' has soft green leaflets that are tinged with pink in spring and turn orange to bronze-red in fall; 'Nana Purpurea' has foliage that turns purplish in winter; 'Wood's Dwarf' turns from green to scarlet in winter.

Growing conditions. Grow nandina in sun or partial shade in any well-drained soil, but acid soil is best. Water young plants regularly; mature plants will withstand drought. Plant in groups to improve cross-pollination and increase berrying. Shelter from winter sun and wind in the lower limits of its hardiness range. Cut out leggy stems at the base; otherwise no pruning is necessary.

Landscape uses. Heavenly bamboo can be used as a specimen, in a massed planting or as a hedge.

—

Natal plum see *Carissa*

—

Nerium (NEER-ee-um)
Oleander

Broad, dense, rounded shrub with thick, leathery, glossy, pointed, narrow leaves that appear in whorls of three. Tubular flowers with five petals bloom in showy clusters at the ends of the branches. Zones 8-10.

Selected species and varieties. *N. oleander* grows 8 to 20 feet tall with 4- to 10-inch leaves that are dark green above and light green below. Yellow, red, white, pink or purple flowers 2 to 3 inches across bloom in clusters of four or five blooms during spring and summer. Some flowers are fragrant. All parts of the oleander plant are poisonous if ingested, and the leaves may cause a skin rash.

Growing conditions. Grow oleander in full sun or light shade in any soil. Regular watering in spring encourages flowering, but water should be decreased in fall so the foliage matures before winter. Oleander tolerates heat, drought, wind, air pollution and poor soil. Prune the plant in early spring.

Landscape uses. Oleander's density and wind tolerance combine to make it a good choice for a screen, windbreak, hedge or seashore garden. It also does well in shrub borders and in containers.

—

Night jessamine see *Cestrum*
Nightshade see *Solanum*
Norway spruce see *Picea*

—

Ochna (OK-na)

Broad, tropical-looking shrub with leathery, oblong, toothed leaves. Single yellow flowers with prominent stamens bloom in large clusters during the summer. Zone 10.

Selected species and varieties. *O. serrulata,* Mickey Mouse plant, bird's eye bush, grows 5 to 10 feet tall and has 3- to 6-inch leaves. Flowers are 1 inch across with slightly twisted petals. When the petals fall, the sepals turn bright red. Small green fruits develop in the center of the red sepals; they turn black and resemble the eyes and ears of Mickey Mouse.

Growing conditions. Grow Mickey Mouse plant in partial shade in well-drained, slightly acid soil. It does best when well watered but will tolerate drought.

Landscape uses. Use Mickey Mouse plant as an accent plant or in a container. It can also be espaliered.

—

Oleander see *Nerium*
Orchid tree see *Bauhinia*
Oregon grape holly see *Mahonia*
Oriental arborvitae
see *Platycladus*

—

Osmanthus (os-MAN-thus)

Upright, rounded shrub with foliage that varies in size and shape and may be smooth-margined or toothed. Fragrant white, yellow or orange flowers are ¼ to ½ inch across, tubular to bell-shaped and bloom in clusters. The flowers are not showy, but they emit a strong, sweet fragrance. Zones 7-10.

Selected species and varieties. *O. americanus,* devilwood, grows to 20 feet, and has 4- to 6-inch narrow, shiny leaves. White flowers bloom in spring and are followed by dark blue berries. *O. delavayi* is 6 feet tall and has graceful, arching branches and 1-inch toothed leaves. White flowers are 1 inch across and the largest of any osmanthus, and bloom in spring. Zones 8-10. *O. × fortunei,* fortune's osmanthus, grows 10 to 20 feet tall and has 3- to 4-inch oval, thick, toothed leaves. White flowers bloom in fall. 'San Jose' is similar but has yellow to orange blooms. *O. fragrans,* fragrant tea olive, grows to 10 feet tall and has 2- to 4-inch slightly toothed leaves. Flowers are white, the most fragrant of any osmanthus, and bloom most abundantly in spring and summer and off and on throughout the year where winters are mild. *O. fragrans aurantiacus* is similar, but has foliage that is narrower, less shiny and toothless, and cream to orange fragrant flowers. Zones 8-10. *O. heterophyllus,* holly osmanthus, grows 10 to 15 feet tall, and has 1½- to 2½-inch oval, spiny leaves. White flowers bloom in summer and fall. 'Myrtifolius' is 5 feet tall and has 1- to 2-inch narrow, spineless leaves. 'Rotundifolia' is 5 feet high with round, spineless foliage. 'Variegata' is 10 feet tall with spined leaves that have white margins.

Growing conditions. Grow osmanthus in full sun or partial shade in moist, acid, well-drained soil. Osmanthus can be pruned or sheared at any time.

Landscape uses. Plant osmanthus in a hedge, a screen or a background planting. It can also be grown in containers or espaliered. Locate it where its fragrance can be enjoyed.

—

Paraguay nightshade
see *Solanum*

—

Paxistima (pak-SIS-ti-ma)

Neat, compact, fine-textured, low-growing shrub with small, shiny, dark green leaves. Flowers bloom in midspring or early summer but are inconspicuous. Zones 4-10.

Selected species and varieties. *P. canbyi,* Canby paxistima, grows 12 inches high and spreads 3 to 5 feet across. Leaves are narrow, ½ to 1 inch long and turn bronze in winter. Flowers are tiny and greenish white or reddish.

Growing conditions. Grow paxistima in full sun to partial shade in moist, rich, well-drained soil. It prefers high humidity. Little pruning is required.

Landscape uses. The small size of paxistima makes it useful in a rock

garden, in front of a shrub border or foundation planting, as a low edging or as a ground cover.

—

Pernettya (per-NET-ee-a)

Dense, low-growing shrub with leathery foliage. Small but profuse bell-shaped flowers are followed by large clusters of marblelike, brightly colored berries that last all winter. Zones 7-10.

Selected species and varieties. *P. mucronata* is a multistemmed shrub that has dense clumps of upright branches. It grows 1½ to 3 feet tall with ¾-inch shiny, narrow, pointed leaves that turn bronze to red in winter. White to pink ¼-inch flowers bloom in late spring. Berries are ½ inch across and white, pink, red, purple or black.

Growing conditions. Pernettya will tolerate partial shade, but should be grown in full sun for best growth and berrying. Soil should be rich, moist, acid and well drained. Plant in groups for cross-pollination and heaviest berrying. Prune roots to control lateral growth.

Landscape uses. Use pernettya as a low border or as a ground cover.

—

Photinia (fo-TIN-ee-a)
Photinia, red tip

Genus of large deciduous and evergreen shrubs. The evergreen species are prized for their shiny, leathery, toothed foliage, which is bright red when young. Single, white flowers have five petals and bloom in panicles in the spring. Berries are ¼ inch across and are often inconspicuous. Zones 5-10.

Selected species and varieties. *P. × fraseri,* Fraser photinia, is 15 feet tall and has 3- to 5-inch oblong leaves and 3- to 5-inch flower clusters. Zones 7-10. *P. glabra,* Japanese photinia, is 12 feet tall. It has 2- to 3-inch oval to oblong leaves and 2- to 4-inch clusters of fragrant flowers. Zones 8-10. *P. serrulata,* Chinese photinia, is 10 to 30 feet high. It has 4- to 8-inch oblong, toothed leaves and 4- to 6-inch flower clusters. Berries are red and showy. Zones 8-10.

Growing conditions. Grow photinia in full sun to light shade in rich, fertile, well-drained soil. Chinese photinia will tolerate alkaline soil; other photinias need acid soil. Water heavily in spring and summer, then taper off in fall to allow the foliage

OSMANTHUS HETEROPHYLLUS

PAXISTIMA CANBYI

PERNETTYA MUCRONATA

PHOTINIA SERRULATA

PICEA PUNGENS 'GLAUCA GLOBOSA'

PIERIS JAPONICA

to mature before winter so it will not be damaged. Repeated pruning throughout the year will encourage new, red growth and keep the plants low-growing.

Landscape uses. Because it is so showy, photinia makes a good specimen. It is also useful as a hedge, a screen or a background plant, and can be espaliered.

Picea (py-SEE-a)
Spruce

Genus of conifers ranging in size from very tall trees to dwarf shrubs, most with stiff branches and sharp, dense, ½- to 1½-inch needles. Foliage may be any of several shades of green or blue-green. Cones hang down from the branches. Zones 2-8.

Selected species and varieties. *P. abies,* Norway spruce, has dark green, shiny, ¾-inch needles. 'Clanbrassiliana' is 7 feet high and 12 feet wide. It has a globe shape and dull leaves. 'Pendula' is 1½ feet tall, spreading to 10 feet with weeping branches. 'Pumila' is 3 feet tall, 9 feet wide and flat-topped. The lower branches are prostrate, the upper branches erect. 'Pygmaea' is 12 inches high and spreads to 20 inches wide; new growth is light green. 'Repens' is mounded, 12 to 18 inches tall and 3 to 5 feet across. Needles are blue-green. 'Sherwoodii' has an asymmetrical growth habit, and is 5 feet high and 10 feet across. 'Tabuliformis' grows 1 foot tall and prostrate, having horizontal branches that spread to 8 feet wide. Zones 2-7.

P. glauca, white spruce, has ¾-inch blue-green needles. *P. glauca albertiana,* Alberta spruce, is compact and has a perfect conical shape and ½-inch, bright green needles. It grows slowly to 6 feet tall. 'Densata', Black Hills spruce, is conical and grows 10 feet tall. Zones 2-7. *P. mariana,* black spruce, has ¾-inch dull green or blue-green needles. 'Ericoides' is cone-shaped and grows to 6 feet. 'Nana' is ball-shaped and 1 to 2 feet high. Zones 2-6. *P. orientalis,* Oriental spruce, has ½-inch, shiny, dark green needles. 'Gracilis' is wider than high when young, but becomes pyramidal as it matures and eventually grows 20 feet tall. Zones 4-8. *P. pungens,* Colorado spruce, has 1¼-inch, blue-green needles. 'Compacta' is a flat-topped pyramid that grows to 6 feet tall and has ½-inch needles. 'Glauca Globosa' is irregularly globe-shaped. It grows up to 3 feet tall and somewhat wider. Needles are dense, short and gray-blue. 'Nana' grows 3 feet tall and is mounded in shape. 'Prostrata' grows 3 feet high and 12 feet across and has silvery needles. Zones 2-7.

Growing conditions. Grow spruces in full sun in moist, rich, well-drained soil. Prune them for shape when growth starts in spring.

Landscape uses. Use spruce as a specimen, an accent or a foundation plant. Low-growing varieties are excellent in rock gardens.

Pieris (py-ER-is)
Andromeda

Upright, rounded shrub with dark green foliage that is red or bronze when young. Urn-shaped, ¼-inch, white or pink flowers bloom in clusters in spring. Red flower buds are evident and decorative all winter. Zones 4-9.

Selected species and varieties. *P. floribunda,* mountain andromeda, is 3 to 6 feet tall and has oval, 1½- to 3½-inch dull foliage. Flower clusters are slightly fragrant, white, 2 to 4 inches high and upright. Zones 4-8. *P. forrestii,* Chinese andromeda, is 5 to 10 feet tall and has 4½-inch narrow, shiny leaves and exceptionally red new growth. Flower clusters are slightly fragrant, white, 4 to 6 inches long and pendulous. Zones 8 and 9. *P. japonica,* Japanese andromeda, is 3 to 10 feet tall and has lance-shaped to oval, shiny, 1½- to 3½-inch foliage. Flowers are slightly fragrant and bloom in drooping clusters. 'Bonsai' is compact and 2 feet tall. 'Mountain Fire' has bright red new foliage and white flowers. 'Pygmaea' looks nothing like other andromedas; it grows only 12 inches tall, has ½- to 1-inch leaves and rarely blooms. 'Valley Rose' is 3 feet tall and has pink flowers. 'Valley Valentine' is 4 feet tall and has deep rose flowers. 'Variegata' is 3 feet tall; its foliage is pink when young, then changes to green with white markings. Zones 5-9. *P. japonica* × *floribunda* 'Brouwer's Beauty' is a cross between mountain andromeda and Japanese andromeda. It grows 3 to 6 feet tall. Zones 4-9. *P. taiwanensis,* Formosa andromeda, is 6 feet tall and has oval, dull, 5-inch leaves and 4- to 6-inch clusters of upright flowers. 'Snow Drift' is 3 feet tall and has pure white flowers. Zones 7-9.

Growing conditions. Most andromedas will grow in full sun or partial shade. Chinese andromeda will tolerate full shade. Soil should be rich, sandy, moist, acid and well drained. Roots are shallow and should be mulched to keep them moist and cool. Shelter from winter wind and sun. Prune in spring immediately after the plant flowers.

Landscape uses. Use andromeda in a foundation planting or border, or as an accent.

—

Pine see *Pinus*

Pineapple guava see *Feijoa*

—

Pinus (PY-nus)
Pine

Coniferous tree or shrub with green or blue-green needles that range in length from 1 inch to 1 foot. Needles on pines are found in bundles of two, three or five; in all forms the base of the needles is encased in a papery sheath. Zones 2-10.

Selected species and varieties. *P. densiflora,* Japanese red pine, has two needles per bundle, each 3 to 5 inches long, and red markings on the bark. 'Pendula' grows 1 foot high and 6 feet across, with weeping branches that lie on the ground. 'Prostrata' follows the contour of the ground and lies flat, growing 6 to 12 inches high and 5 feet across. 'Umbraculifera', Tanyosho pine, grows 3 to 6 feet high and wide. It has numerous stems from the base and a flat top, and resembles an upside-down umbrella. Needles are blue-green. Zones 4-8. *P. mugo,* Swiss mountain pine, has two needles per bundle, each ¾ to 2 inches long. *P. mugo mugo,* mugo pine, is a mounded shrub, 2 to 6 feet high and 12 feet across. It has medium green, 1½-inch needles. 'Compacta' forms a dense globe 4 feet high and 6 feet across and has dark green, 1¼-inch needles. 'Pumilo' is a mounded shrub 2 feet high and 4 feet across with erect branches. Needles are rich green, short and stiff. 'Salvinii' has blue-green, 1-inch needles and erect branches, and grows 2 feet high and 6 feet across. Zones 2-7. *P. parviflora,* Japanese white pine, has five needles per bundle, each 1½ to 2½ inches long. 'Nana' grows 18 to 24 inches tall and has short needles. *P. pumila,* Japanese stone pine, has five needles per bundle, each 1½ to 3 inches long. The plant is 24 inches high and spreads to 8 feet. Zones 5-7. *P. resinosa,* red pine, has two needles per bundle,

each 5 inches long. 'Globosa' is a 4- to 6-foot rounded shrub. *P. strobus,* Eastern white pine, has five blue-green, soft needles per bundle, each 3 to 5 inches long. 'Compacta' and 'Densa' are round plants 4 to 6 feet tall and wide. 'Nana' is round to pyramidal in form, 1 to 2 feet tall and 2 to 4 feet across. 'Pendula' is 1 to 2 feet high, with long weeping branches that sweep the ground to a width of 6 feet. 'Prostrata' grows flat on the ground to a spread of 4 to 6 feet. Zones 3-8. *P. sylvestris,* Scotch pine, has two blue-green, twisted needles per bundle, each 1 to 3 inches long. 'Compressa' is extremely narrow and upright, and grows 3 feet tall and 10 inches wide. 'Nana' is conical in shape and 3 to 4 feet tall. 'Glauca Nana' is similar in shape and has blue-green needles. Zones 2-8.

Growing conditions. Most pines require full sun; Eastern white pine and Swiss mountain pine will do well in partial shade. The only requirement for soil is that it be well drained. Fertilize little if at all. Leave fallen needles in place as a mulch. Keep pine compact by cutting back its candles, the new spring growth, by up to two-thirds of their length.

Landscape uses. Pine has many uses in foundation plantings, in borders and in hedges. The smallest cultivars fit into rock gardens. Prostrate forms make excellent ground covers. Pine may also be trained as a bonsai.

—

Pistache see *Pistacia*

—

Pistacia (pis-TAY-shee-a)
Pistache

Upright shrub or tree, one species of which is the source of the pistachio nut. Foliage is fine-textured and divided into many leaflets. Flowers are small and inconspicuous and have no petals. Zones 8-10.

Selected species and varieties. *P. texanum,* Texas pistache, is a tall, rounded shrub growing to 30 feet tall and 15 to 20 feet wide. Leaves have seven to 21 leaflets; they are red-bronze when young and dark green when mature. Red-brown, ¼-inch fruit forms in spring on female plants. 'Pecos Dwarf' grows 8 to 10 feet tall and 4 to 5 feet wide.

Growing conditions. Plant Texas pistache in full sun in any well-drained, acid or alkaline soil. It tolerates wind and drought. Pinch growing tips to strengthen growth and encourage compactness.

PINUS MUGO MUGO

PISTACIA TEXANUM

PITTOSPORUM TOBIRA

PLATYCLADUS ORIENTALIS

PODOCARPUS MACROPHYLLUS MAKI

Landscape uses. Use Texas pistache as a windbreak, a hedge or an accent plant.

—

Pittosporum (pi-TOS-po-rum)

Genus of small trees and shrubs that may be upright or spreading. Leaves are either oval or oblong. Single, fragrant flowers blossom in spring. Zones 8-10.

Selected species and varieties. *P. tobira,* Japanese pittosporum, is a broad, dense shrub 6 to 15 feet tall. Leaves are dark green, thick, leathery, oval and 3 to 4 inches long; the tips are blunt and the edges curl under. They form in whorls at the ends of the branches. Greenish white to yellow flowers, ½ inch across, bloom in 2- to 3-inch clusters at the ends of the branches in spring and summer. Their fragrance is similar to that of the orange blossom. Hairy ½-inch fruits are green when they form, darken to brown and then split open to reveal orange seeds. 'Variegata' is 4 to 6 feet tall and has white markings on the leaves. 'Wheeler's Dwarf' is 3 feet tall and has 1- to 2-inch flower clusters.

Growing conditions. Plant pittosporum in sun or partial shade. Soil should be fertile, rich and well drained. Pittosporum tolerates heat, wind and drought but grows better if it is regularly watered. Pinch out growing tips to encourage bushiness.

Landscape uses. The form and foliage of pittosporum make it useful as a foundation plant, container plant, informal hedge or windbreak. It does well by the seashore, and on slopes it helps to prevent erosion. 'Wheeler's Dwarf' makes a good ground cover.

—

Platycladus (plat-i-CLAD-us)
Oriental arborvitae

Pyramidal or globe-shaped conifer with scalelike green, blue-green or yellow foliage held vertically in flat sprays. Zones 6-10.

Selected species and varieties. *P. orientalis* (formerly classified as *Thuja orientalis)* is a densely branched, erect shrub with sprays of foliage that curve inward. Leaves are slightly fragrant when rubbed. 'Aurea Nana' (sometimes designated 'Berckmannii') is globe-shaped, 3 to 5 feet tall and has foliage tipped in golden yellow. 'Bakeri' is a light green pyramid 8 to 10 feet tall. 'Blue Cone' grows 8 to 12 feet tall in a py-

ramidal shape and has blue-green foliage. 'Fruitlandii' is a 6- to 8-foot pyramid and has dark green leaves. 'Globosus' is a globe-shaped plant 3 to 4 feet tall. 'Sieboldii' is a globe- to cone-shaped shrub 3 feet tall. 'Westmont' is a 3-foot, dense globe and has yellow leaf tips that turn bronze in winter.

Growing conditions. Plant Oriental arborvitae in full sun or light shade in moist, rich, fertile, neutral, well-drained soil. Remove snow and ice from the branches promptly to avoid breakage or disfiguring. Oriental arborvitae is more heat- and drought-resistant than American arborvitae but less winter-hardy. Prune or shear the plant in spring.

Landscape uses. Use upright forms of Oriental arborvitae as hedges, screens, foundation plants and at entryways. Globe-shaped varieties fit well into rock gardens.

—

Plumbago see *Ceratostigma*
Plum yew see *Cephalotaxus*

—

Podocarpus (pod-o-KAR-pus)

Coniferous tree or shrub that may be columnar or broad. It has narrow to slightly oval, soft needles 1 to 3 inches long. Zones 7-10.

Selected species and varieties. *P. gracilior,* fern podocarpus, is a tree or large shrub 25 feet tall with graceful, slightly drooping branches and 1- to 2-inch blue-green or gray-green leaves. *P. macrophyllus,* Japanese yew, has a stiff, upright, irregular, columnar growth habit. Leaves are dark green, 3 inches long and slightly oval. *P. macrophyllus maki,* Chinese podocarpus, grows 6 to 8 feet tall and has 3-inch, dark green, narrow leaves. *P. nivalis* is 6 feet tall and has ¾-inch olive green leaves. The branches are limber enough to train the plant as a ground cover. Zones 9 and 10.

Growing conditions. Plant podocarpus in full sun in cool areas, or in partial shade where summers are hot. Soil should be rich, fertile, moist and well drained. Prune or shear the plant at any time.

Landscape uses. Use podocarpus as a hedge or a windbreak. It can easily be trained as an espalier or a bonsai. Podocarpus is tolerant of seashore conditions, and is one of the best shrubs available for containers because it does not mind a restricted root area.

Polygala (po-LIG-ga-la)

Annual, perennial or shrub with lance-shaped leaves and showy clusters or spikes of pealike flowers at the ends of the branches. Zones 5-10.

Selected species and varieties. *P. × dalmaisiana,* sweet pea shrub, is an upright, spreading shrub 3 to 6 feet tall. Stems are bare of foliage at the base. Leaves are oval and 1 inch long. Flowers are purple-red, with one white lower petal; they bloom abundantly in spring and off and on throughout the rest of the year. Tufted stamens project from the flower centers. Zone 10.

Growing conditions. Grow sweet pea shrub in full sun or light shade. Soil should be acid and well drained. Prune the plant to keep it compact.

Landscape uses. Sweet pea shrub may be used as a background to low, bushy plants.

—

Powderpuff see *Calliandra*
Pride of Madeira see *Echium*
Privet see *Ligustrum*

—

Prostanthera
(pros-TANTH-er-a)
Mintbush

Dense, rounded shrub with aromatic foliage and abundant, small, tubular, two-lipped flowers. Zone 10.

Selected species and varieties. *P. rotundifolia,* round-leaf mintbush, grows 4 to 10 feet tall and has ½-inch, round leaves that are dark green with pale green undersides. Flowers are purple-blue, ½ inch long and bloom in short clusters in spring.

Growing conditions. Plant mintbush in full sun or light shade in well-drained, acid soil. It tolerates drought, and heavy pruning after the flowers bloom helps to keep the plant compact.

Landscape uses. Use mintbush as a hedge or foundation plant or in a shrub border.

—

Prunus (PROO-nus)

Deciduous or evergreen tree or shrub. The evergreens are dense, upright, rounded shrubs that have lustrous, oblong, dark green leaves. White, ½-inch flowers bloom in erect spikes in spring and are followed by ½-inch fruit in autumn. Zones 3-10.

Selected species and varieties. *P. caroliniana,* Carolina cherry laurel, usually grows 8 to 12 feet tall, but may attain a height of 20 feet. It can be pruned into either an oval or a pyramidal shape. Foliage is 2 to 4 inches long. Fragrant flowers are followed by black fruit. Zones 8-10. *P. laurocerasus,* cherry laurel, English laurel, reaches a height of 6 to 8 feet in the colder limits of its hardiness and may reach 20 feet in warm zones. Foliage is 2 to 7 inches long. Fragrant flowers are followed by fruit that changes in color from red to purple to black. 'Otto Luyken' grows 4 to 6 feet tall and 6 feet wide with smaller flowers and foliage. Zones 7-10.

Growing conditions. Plant cherry laurels in full sun to partial shade in any acid, well-drained soil. Prune them for shape after they flower.

Landscape uses. The dense growth of cherry laurel makes it a good hedge or screen. It is also effective as a foundation planting. It can be pruned into formal shapes and topiaries.

—

Pseudotsuga (soo-do-SOO-ga)

Genus of conifers ranging in size from large trees to compact shrubs. All have aromatic needles that are light green when new and may be soft blue-green or dark green when mature. Four-inch brown cones hang from the branches. Zones 4-8.

Selected species and varieties. *P. menziesii,* Douglas fir, has several dwarf cultivars. 'Compacta' is rounded and 3 to 4 feet tall. 'Densa' is a flat-topped spreading shrub that grows 2 feet tall. Needles are dark green and ½ inch long. 'Fletcheri' is 4½ to 6 feet high, 7 to 9 feet wide and flat-topped. Needles are blue-green. 'Glauca Pendula' is a mounded shrub with drooping branches growing 18 to 24 inches high and spreading to 4 feet wide. Needles are blue-green. 'Pyramidalis' is upright and 8 to 10 feet tall. Zones 6-8.

Growing conditions. Grow dwarf Douglas fir in full sun to partial shade in rich, acid, moist, well-drained soil. Reduce watering in the fall so that the foliage will mature before winter sets in. Dwarf Douglas fir tolerates wind. Prune to shape the plant during the spring growing season.

Landscape uses. The dense branching of the dwarf Douglas firs

POLYGALA × DALMAISIANA

PROSTANTHERA ROTUNDIFOLIA

PRUNUS LAUROCERASUS 'OTTO LUYKEN'

PSEUDOTSUGA MENZIESII 'FLETCHERI'

PSIDIUM LITTORALE LONGIPES

PYRACANTHA COCCINEA

RAPHIOLEPIS INDICA 'SPRINGTIME'

makes them good for low hedges and screens. 'Glauca Pendula' can be used as an accent or in a rock garden. They all tolerate seashore conditions.

Psidium (SID-ee-um)
Guava

Dense shrub that has 1-inch, white spring-blooming flowers with prominent stamens. Clusters of berrylike, round to pear-shaped fruit follow in fall and winter. Zones 9 and 10.

Selected species and varieties. *P. littorale longipes,* purple guava, is a dense 8- to 10-foot shrub that has 2- to 3-inch, oblong, leathery, golden yellow leaves with heavy veining. Young foliage is bronze. Bark is gray-green to golden brown. Fruit is round, 1½ inches across, purple-red and edible; its white flesh has a strawberry flavor.

Growing conditions. Plant purple guava in full sun in rich, moist, well-drained soil. Prune to shape the plant when growth starts in spring.

Landscape uses. Plant purple guava as an informal hedge or screen. It also grows well in a container.

Pyracantha (py-ra-KAN-tha)
Fire thorn

Thorny, upright or spreading shrub that has dark green leaves. Small white flowers bloom in 1- to 1½-inch clusters in spring and are followed by showy clusters of red, orange or yellow berries in fall and winter. Zones 6-10.

Selected species and varieties. *P. angustifolia* may be either a low-growing shrub 3 feet high or an upright grower to 12 feet tall. Leaves are narrow and ½ to 2 inches long. Fruits are orange-red. Zones 7-10. *P. coccinea,* scarlet fire thorn, grows from 6 to 12 feet tall with an irregular branching habit. Leaves are oblong and 1 to 1½ inches long. Fruits are bright red. 'Kasan', 'Lalandei' and 'Wyatti' are 6 to 9 feet tall and have orange-red berries. Zones 5-10. 'Lowboy' and 'Rutgers' grow 3 feet high, spread to 6 feet across and have orange-red berries. Zones 6-10. *P. fortuneana* 'Graberi' grows 10 to 15 feet tall and has 1- to 3-inch leaves that are broad at the tip. Bright red fruit forms in clusters that are larger than those of most fire thorns. Zones 7-10. *P. koidzumii,* Formosa fire

thorn, is 8 to 12 feet high and wide. Leaves are dark, oblong and 1 to 3 inches long. Red berries are produced in large clusters. 'Santa Cruz' is 3 feet tall and spreading. 'Victory' is upright and similar to the species with berries that turn dark red late in the fall. Zones 8-10. The hybrid 'Mohave' is 8 to 10 feet tall and has berries that turn orange-red very early in the fall. Zones 7-10.

Growing conditions. Plant fire thorn in full sun in fertile, well-drained soil. Protect the plant from winter wind. It will tolerate drought and air pollution once it is established. Prune back leggy branches at any time to keep the plant bushy.

Landscape uses. Fire thorn makes a good barrier plant since it is so thorny. It may also be grown as a hedge, in a massed planting or against a north or east wall, as it does not like reflected heat. Fire thorn is very easy to espalier.

Raphiolepis (raf-i-OL-e-pis)

Dense, compact shrub that has thick, glossy, leathery leaves. Showy clusters of single, white or pink flowers bloom at the ends of the branches from midwinter until late spring. There can be a second bloom in the fall. Blue-black or purple round berries follow the flowers. Zones 7-10.

Selected species and varieties. *R. indica,* Indian hawthorn, is 3 to 5 feet high and wide and has 1- to 3-inch toothed, oblong leaves. New foliage is often bronze. 'Springtime' has pink flowers. Zones 8-10.

Growing conditions. Grow Indian hawthorn in full sun; it will tolerate light shade but will flower less. Soil should be fertile and well drained. Once established, Indian hawthorn will tolerate drought but will grow better if it is well watered. Prune the plant after it has flowered to keep it compact.

Landscape uses. Plant Indian hawthorn as an informal hedge, as a tall ground cover or in a shrub border. It will also grow well in a container.

Red cedar see *Juniperus*
Red pine see *Pinus*
Red sage see *Lantana*
Red tip see *Photinia*
Redwood see *Sequoia*

Rhamnus (RAM-nus)
Buckthorn

Thorny, deciduous or evergreen shrub. Small, inconspicuous, greenish flowers bloom in spring among heavily veined leaves. Berries are showy and black. Zones 3-10.

Selected species and varieties. *R. californica,* coffee berry, grows 3 to 6 feet tall in either an upright or a spreading habit. Leaves are oblong to oval, 1 to 4 inches long, finely toothed, and may be either shiny or dull. Berries are red when they first appear in fall, and darken to black.

Growing conditions. Grow coffee berry in sun or partial shade in any well-drained soil. Prune for shape when growth starts in the spring.

Landscape uses. Coffee berry makes a good barrier plant because of its thorniness. It can also be grown as a low hedge or as ground cover on a bank. Coffee berry tolerates seashore conditions.

—

Rhododendron
(ro-do-DEN-dron)
Azalea, rhododendron

Extremely large genus of deciduous and evergreen shrubs known commonly as rhododendrons and azaleas. Plants vary in size, foliage and form, but all have showy flowers that bloom from early spring to midsummer in all colors of the rainbow.

All azaleas are rhododendrons, but not all rhododendrons are azaleas. One way to distinguish between them is that azaleas generally have leaves that are small, narrow, pointed and hairy along the midrib; rhododendron leaves occur in whorls and are generally large, broad, long and leathery. Azalea flowers are borne along the sides and at the tips of the branches; some are single, having one ring of petals, some are double, having numerous overlapping petals, and some have one single flower set inside another single flower, a configuration called hose-in-hose. Rhododendron flowers are generally single; they are borne in dome-shaped clusters known as trusses and appear only at the ends of the branches. Azalea flowers are generally funnel-shaped and have five to 10 stamens; rhododendron flowers are usually bell-shaped and have 10 or more stamens. Azaleas are usually smaller than rhododendrons and grow in a spreading form; rhododendrons generally grow upright.

For the purposes of description, evergreen azaleas and rhododendrons may be divided into four categories: azalea species, which are found in nature; azalea hybrid groups, which have been bred by crossing two or more species; rhododendron species, which occur in nature; and rhododendron hybrids, which have been bred by crossing two or more species. Zones 2-10.

Azalea species. The following azalea species bloom in mid- to late spring. *R. kaempferi,* torch azalea, grows 6 to 8 feet high and has 2½-inch hairy, oblong to oval leaves that often turn bronze during winter. Flowers are 2 inches across and may be white, pink, orange, red or salmon. Zones 6-8. *R. kiusianum,* Kyushu azalea, grows 3 feet high and has dense, 1-inch, oblong, bright green foliage. Flowers are 1 inch across and purple or pink. Zones 7-9. *R. macrosepalum,* big sepal azalea, grows 4 to 6 feet tall, has oval leaves and white to pink flowers with large sepals. The cultivar 'Linearifolium', spider azalea, grows 3 feet tall and has long, narrow leaves. Flowers are 2 inches across, fragrant and pink; petals are long and narrow and resemble a spider's legs. Zone 8; semievergreen or deciduous Zone 7. *R. otakumii yakuinsulare* grows 6 feet tall and has 2½-inch-long leaves. Flowers are 1½ inches across and reddish orange; they bloom in small clusters in late spring. Zones 7 and 8. *R. serpyllifolium,* wild thyme azalea, grows 4 feet tall. Leaves are ¼-inch oblongs; flowers are ½ inch across and light pink. Zones 6-8. *R. yedoense poukhanense,* Korean azalea, is 6 feet tall. Leaves are 3 inches long and lance-shaped. Flowers are 2 inches across, fragrant and pale lilac to purple with darker spotting. Korean azalea is often confused with the early-blooming Korean rhododendron, *R. mucronulatum,* which is deciduous in all zones. Zone 8; semievergreen or deciduous Zones 6 and 7.

Azalea hybrid groups. Back Acre Hybrids have single to double flowers. 'Margaret Douglas' grows 4 to 6 feet tall and has 3-inch flowers of salmon with white throats; they bloom in midspring. Zones 7-9. Belgian Indian Hybrids are 6 to 10 feet tall and bloom in middle to late spring. Flowers are single to double and 2 to 3 inches across; some have frilled petals. 'Chimes' has dark red semidouble flowers in midspring. Zones 8 and 9. Beltsville Hybrids are 12 to 18 inches high and 36 inches across.

RHAMNUS CALIFORNICA

RHODODENDRON YEDOENSE POUKHANENSE

RHODODENDRON × 'ROSEBUD'

RHODODENDRON × 'MARTHA HITCHCOCK'

RHODODENDRON × 'HINODE GIRI'

RHODODENDRON × 'GUMPO WHITE'

RHODODENDRON CATAWBIENSE

RHODODENDRON × 'BLUE DIAMOND'

'Pink Elf' has hose-in-hose flowers of shell pink. 'White Doll' has white flowers. Zones 8 and 9. Carla Hybrids are characterized by small foliage and early blooming. 'Carla' is 3 to 4 feet tall and has orange-red, double flowers. 'Pink Cloud' is 5 to 6 feet tall and has pale pink flowers. 'Sunglow' grows to 5 feet high and has purple-red flowers. Zones 6-8. Eden Hybrids have both hose-in-hose and double flowers. Zones 6-9. Gable Hybrids bloom in midspring with flowers of pink to purple. 'Purple Splendor' is 3 to 4 feet tall and has 2-inch light purple flowers in midspring. 'Rosebud' grows 3 feet tall and has double pink flowers in early to midspring. Zones 6-8. May be semievergreen in Zones 6 and 7. Girard Hybrids are low-growing plants that bloom in midspring. 'Hot Shot' has ruffled, scarlet flowers. 'Variegated Gem' is 2 feet tall and has variegated foliage and red flowers. Zones 7 and 8. Glenn Dale Hybrids have large flowers; bloom times vary from early to late spring. 'Fashion' has hose-in-hose, 2-inch, rose pink to salmon flowers. 'Glacier' has white 2½-inch flowers that have green throats on a medium-sized plant. 'Martha Hitchcock' has 3-inch flowers of white with magenta margins. 'Treasure' has pale pink buds that open to white with pale pink throats. Zones 7 and 8.

Greenwood Hybrids were developed for cool, cloudy areas and bloom in early to middle spring. 'Greenwood Cherry' is 4 to 5 feet tall and has double red flowers. 'Tina' is 12 inches tall and 2 feet across and has purple-red flowers. Zones 7-9. Harris Hybrid 'Pink Cascade' is low-growing and spreading and has 2-inch, blotched red flowers in midspring. 'River Mist' grows 3 to 4 feet tall and has early-blooming, pale lavender, 1½-inch flowers. Zones 7 and 8. Kaempferi Hybrids are upright plants growing 5 to 6 feet high. Pink to red, 2-inch flowers bloom in early spring. Zones 7 and 8; may be semievergreen in Zone 6. Kurume Hybrids are 3 to 6 feet tall. Foliage is small and glossy; a profusion of 1- to 1½-inch flowers cover the plant at bloom time. 'Coral Bells' has hose-in-hose flowers of shell pink that have deep pink centers in early to middle spring on a 5-foot plant. 'Hino' has brilliant red flowers in middle to late spring on a 4- to 6-foot plant. 'Pink Pearl' has salmon-rose hose-in-hose flowers on a 5- to 6-foot plant. 'Sherwood Red' is 5 feet tall with orange-red flowers in midspring. 'Snow' has pure white, hose-in-hose flowers in midspring on a 5-foot plant. Zones 7-9. North Tisbury Hybrids are very low-growing,

about 12 inches high and bloom from late spring to early summer. 'Alexander' has salmon-red, 2-inch flowers in early summer. 'Late Love' has bright pink flowers in early summer to midsummer. 'Pink Pancake' grows almost flat on the ground and has bright pink, wavy-petaled flowers in early summer. 'Wintergreen' has deep pink flowers in early summer. Zones 7-9.

Pericat Hybrids are 2 to 6 feet tall and have 2- to 2½-inch flowers in early to midspring. 'Hampton Beauty' has carmine-rose flowers. 'Hiawatha' has hose-in-hose red flowers. 'Pinocchio' has double pink flowers. 'Sweetheart Supreme' has semidouble deep pink flowers. Zones 7-9.

Robin Hill Hybrid 'Conversation Piece' is 2 to 4 feet tall and has 3-inch flowers of pale pink with lighter margins in middle to late spring. 'Watchet' is 3 to 4 feet tall and has light pink, 2-inch flowers in midspring. Zones 7 and 8. Satsuki Hybrids bloom in late spring. 'Gumpo' is 3 feet high with frilled, 3-inch flowers of white with red spots. 'Wakaebisu' is 4 to 6 feet tall and has hose-in-hose, 2½-inch salmon-pink flowers. Zones 7-9. Schroeder Hybrids grow 3 to 5 feet tall and have single or hose-in-hose flowers. Zones 5-8. Southern Indian Hybrids grow 6 to 10 feet tall. 'Formosa' has 3½-inch flowers of purplish red in midspring. 'Pride of Mobile' has 2½-inch flowers of deep pink in midspring. Zones 8-10.

Rhododendron species. *R. augustinii* is 6 feet tall and has 3-inch leaves. Flowers of blue or purple are 2 to 2½ inches across in 4-inch trusses. Zones 7-9. *R. carolinianum*, Carolina rhododendron, grows 3 to 6 feet high. Leaves are glossy, oval, 2 to 3 inches long, have rust-colored undersides and turn bronze in winter. Flowers of light pink to rose purple bloom in 1½- to 3-inch trusses in midspring. *R. carolinianum album* has white flowers with green blotches and smaller, lighter green leaves. Zones 5-8.

R. catawbiense, Catawba rhododendron, is 6 to 8 feet high and wide. Leaves are oval, 3 to 6 inches long and pointed, and have white undersides. White to purplish pink flowers that have olive green throats appear in late spring and early summer and are 2 inches across in 6-inch trusses. Zones 5-8.

R. chapmanii, Chapman's rhododendron, is 6 to 8 feet tall, erect and rigid. Clear pale pink to rose flowers, each 2 to 3 inches across, bloom in 4- to 6-inch trusses in late spring. Zones 5-9. *R. decorum* is 20 feet tall and has 6-inch oblong leaves that have rust-colored undersides. Flowers are white to pink, fragrant, each 3½ inches across in 6- to 8-inch trusses and bloom in late spring to early summer. Zones 6-8. *R. fortunei* is 12 feet tall and has 4- to 8-inch, oblong leaves that have gray undersides. Flowers are fragrant, pale purple to pink, 3½ inches across in 8-inch trusses and bloom in late spring. Zones 6-9. *R. impeditum* is 18 inches high and has ½-inch gray-green leaves. Flowers are blue or purple, ¾ inch across and bloom in midspring. Zones 5-8. *R. keiskei*, Keisk rhododendron, grows 8 feet tall and has 2½-inch olive green leaves. Flowers are pale yellow, 2 inches across and bloom in midspring. There is also a dwarf form 12 inches high. Zones 6-8. *R. maximum*, rosebay rhododendron, grows 12 feet tall. Leaves are 4- to 10-inch oblongs and have brown undersides. Pale rose or white, 1½-inch flowers that have yellow or green spots bloom in 6-inch trusses in early summer to midsummer. Zones 4-8.

R. metternichi grows to 8 feet. It has light pink to dark pink spotted flowers that are 3 inches across in very large trusses appearing in midspring. Leaves are shiny, 6-inch oblongs and have rust-colored undersides. Zones 6-8. *R. minus,* Piedmont rhododendron, is a loose, spreading plant that grows 6 to 10 feet tall. Leaves are narrow, 2 to 4 inches long and turn reddish in winter. Flowers are 1½ inches across, pink to magenta and bloom in early summer. Zones 5-8.

R. racemosum is 6 to 8 feet tall and has 2-inch, oblong leaves. White, pink or rose-colored flowers are 1 inch across and bloom in small trusses in midspring. Zones 6-8. *R. yakusimanum* is a 3-foot, spreading plant that has narrow, 3-inch leaves. Pink or white, 2½-inch flowers bloom in late spring. Zones 6-8. *R. yunnanense* is 10 to 12 feet tall and has 3-inch, oblong leaves. Flowers are 2 inches across, pink or white spotted with red, and bloom in late spring. Zones 7-9.

Rhododendron hybrids. 'Anna Rose Whitney' is 5 feet tall and has rich, deep pink flowers in late spring. Zones 7-9. 'America' is 6 feet tall and has clear, dark red blooms in late spring. Zones 4-8. 'Blue Diamond' is 3 to 5 feet tall and has deep lavender-blue flowers in midspring. Zones 7-9. 'Blue Peter' is a broad, 4-foot plant and has light lavender-blue blotched flowers in early summer. Zones 6-8. 'Boule de Neige' is 5 to 6 feet high and has white flowers in

midspring. Zones 4-8. 'Bow Bells' is 4 feet high and has bright pink buds that open to light pink; instead of blooming in typical large, round trusses, they bloom in small open clusters. Flowering occurs in late spring. Zones 7-9. 'Chikor' is 3 to 4 feet tall and has primrose yellow flowers. Zones 4-8. 'Cotton Candy' is 6 feet tall and has large, light pink trusses in middle to late spring. Zones 7 and 8. 'Cynthia' is 6 feet tall and has rose to crimson flowers in late spring. Zones 7-9. 'Donna Totten' is 3 to 5 feet tall and has a multitude of small white flowers in very early spring. 'Dora Amateis' is 3 feet tall and has scented white flowers spotted with gold or green in late spring. Zones 6-8. 'English Roseum' is 5 to 6 feet high and has bright lilac to purple flowers with yellow-green throats in early summer. Zones 6-8.

'GiGi' has rose red flowers with deep red spots in midspring. Zones 5-8. 'Gomer Waterer' is 6 feet tall and has white flowers blushed with pink or lilac in early summer. Zones 5-8. 'Janet Blair' is 4 to 6 feet tall and has clear pink flowers in middle to late spring. Zones 5-8. 'Jean Marie Montague' is 5 feet tall and has bright red flowers in middle to late spring. Zones 7 and 8. 'Loderi King George' is 8 feet tall and has large trusses of white flowers in midspring. Zones 7 and 8. 'Loder's White' grows to 5 feet and has flowers that open pink and fade to white in midspring. Zones 7 and 8. 'Mary Fleming' is a low-mounded plant 1½ to 3 feet tall. Flowers are pale yellow with salmon blotches and streaks and bloom in early to midspring. Zones 6-8.

'Molly Fordham' is 1½ to 3 feet tall and has white flowers in midspring. Zones 6-8. 'Mrs. C. S. Sargent' grows to 12 feet and has carmine-rose flowers in late spring. Zones 5-8. 'Mrs. Furnival' is 4 feet tall and has light pink flowers with red to brown blotches in late spring. Zones 6-8. 'Mucronatum', snow azalea, forms a 6-foot mound and has 2¼-inch oblong, dull gray-green foliage. Flowers are white and 2 inches across. Zones 6-9. 'Myrtifolium' is 1½ to 3 feet tall. Pink to purplish pink flowers appear in early summer. Zones 6-8. 'Nova Zembla' is 5 feet tall and has red flowers with dark centers in midspring. Zones 4-8.

'Olga' is 3 to 4 feet high and has clear pink flowers in midspring. Foliage turns bronze in winter. Zones 6-8. 'Pink Diamond' is 3 to 4 feet tall and has semidouble pink flowers in early spring. Zone 6-8. 'Pink Pearl' is 6 to 8 feet tall and has rose pink flowers in middle to late spring.

RHODODENDRON × 'BOULE DE NEIGE'

RHODODENDRON × 'CHIKOR'

RHODODENDRON × 'LODER'S WHITE'

RHODODENDRON × 'MRS. FURNIVAL'

127

RHODODENDRON × 'SCINTILLATION'

RHODODENDRON × 'SHAMROCK'

RHUS INTEGRIFOLIA

ROSMARINUS OFFICINALIS

Zones 6-8. 'P.J.M.' is 3 to 5 feet tall and has purplish pink flowers in early spring. The plant may bloom in fall in warmer areas. Foliage turns bronze in winter. Zones 5-8. 'Pioneer' is 4 feet tall and has clear, light pink flowers in early spring. Zones 6-8. 'Ramapo' is 1½ to 3 feet high and has violet-blue flowers in early spring. Zones 6-8. 'Roseum Elegans' is 6 to 8 feet tall and has rose pink to purplish pink flowers in late spring. Zones 4-8. 'Scintillation' is 8 feet tall and has light pink flowers with gold throats in late spring. Zones 7 and 8. 'Shamrock' is 3 feet tall and has yellow-green flowers. Zones 6-8. 'Tom Everett' is 5 to 8 feet high and spreading. Flowers are frilled, soft pink with pale yellow throats and bloom in early summer. Zones 7 and 8. 'Trude Webster' is a 6- to 8-foot plant that has large trusses of medium pink flowers in middle to late spring. Zones 7 and 8. 'Victor' is 2 to 4 feet tall and has early-spring-blooming, lavender-pink flowers. The small foliage turns bronze in fall. Zones 5-8. 'Vulcan' is 4 to 6 feet tall and has brick red flowers in early summer. Zones 7 and 8. 'Wheatley' is a 6- to 8-foot plant that has flowers of light pink with green throats in middle to late spring. Zones 6-8.

Growing conditions. Plant azaleas and rhododendrons in partial shade. Azaleas will tolerate full sun if the ground is constantly moist, and rhododendrons will tolerate full shade. Soil for both should be rich, moist, high in organic matter, acid and well drained. Roots are shallow and should be mulched to keep them cool. Do not cultivate around the roots or they will be damaged.

Feed lightly and infrequently. If leaves become yellow, check to make sure that the soil is acidic and correct the pH if it is not. Application of chelated iron to the soil will also correct yellowing leaves.

Prune azaleas and rhododendrons immediately after they flower to control size and shape the plants. On rhododendrons, cut to the next lower whorl of leaves; on azaleas cut just above a leaf. Faded flowers of azaleas will fall cleanly from the plant. Faded trusses of rhododendrons should be manually removed; be careful not to damage the new growing tips.

Protect from drying winds and winter sun. Apply an antidesiccant to large rhododendron leaves at the beginning of winter in the colder limits of their hardiness.

Landscape uses. Rhododendrons and azaleas make good foundation plantings. They are also effective lining driveways and walkways, as hedges, in massed plantings and in woodland gardens. The small varieties do well in rock gardens. They will also grow well in containers, a fact that is useful in areas where the soil conditions are not conducive to their growth.

Rhus (RUSS)
Sumac

Broad genus of deciduous and evergreen shrubs having small flowers that bloom in panicles at the ends of the branches during the spring. Upright clusters of red or orange hairy berries follow in the fall. Zones 3-10.

Selected species and varieties. *R. integrifolia,* lemonade sumac, grows 5 to 10 feet high and wide. Leaves are leathery, oval and 2 inches long. Flowers are pink or white in 3-inch clusters. Berries are deep red and often used as flavoring. Zones 9 and 10. *R. terbinthifolia,* temazcal, is 7 feet tall and has compound leaves with three to fifteen 2½-inch leaflets. Berries are red or orange. Zone 10.

Growing conditions. Grow sumac in full sun in any well-drained soil. It tolerates poor, dry soil but performs better if watered during the summer. Prune when growth starts in spring.

Landscape uses. Evergreen sumac is best grown as a bank or ground cover. It may be espaliered and is tolerant of seashore conditions.

Rice paper plant see *Tetrapanax*
Rockrose see *Cistus*
Rosemary see *Rosmarinus*

Rosmarinus (ros-ma-RY-nus)
Rosemary

Upright or trailing shrub that has aromatic stems and foliage. Leaves are needlelike, ½ to 1 inch long, glossy green on the upper surfaces and gray on the undersides. Fragrant, pale blue, tubular, ½-inch flowers appear in upright spikes during winter and spring. Zones 7-10.

Selected species and varieties. *R. officinalis* grows upright, 2 to 6 feet tall. Foliage has white hairs on the undersides. 'Lockwood de Forest' grows 2 feet high and spreads to 4 to 8 feet wide. 'Prostratus' is similar in growth habit, but has lighter blue flowers and darker foliage. Zones 8-10.

Growing conditions. Plant rosemary in full sun in dry, well-drained soil. It tolerates heat, drought and poor soil. Water sparingly and do not fertilize. Pinch out growing tips to control plant size.

Landscape uses. Rosemary is useful as a border plant or a hedge. It may also be grown in a flower garden or an herb garden. The trailing cultivars may be used as ground covers or to spill over walls, and all varieties tolerate seashore conditions.

Rubus (ROO-bus)
Bramble

Broad genus of deciduous and evergreen thorny shrubs that include raspberry, blackberry, loganberry and dewberry. Zones 3-10.

Selected species and varieties. *R. calycinoides,* creeping rubus, spreads at the rate of 1 foot a year, rooting its branches as they creep along the ground. Foliage is 1½ inches across, glossy green on the upper surfaces, gray on the undersides and has three to five lobes. Inconspicuous white flowers bloom singly or in clusters during the summer, and are followed by amber berries. Zones 7-10.

Growing conditions. Grow creeping rubus in sun or shade in any well-drained soil. It tolerates poor soil. To control plant size, prune branches to the roots in early spring.

Landscape uses. The low-growing habit of creeping rubus makes it an excellent ground cover. It can be grown on banks as well as on level ground.

Ruscus (RUS-kus)
Butcher's broom

Low-growing shrub that spreads into a thick clump by underground stems. The actual leaves are tiny and scalelike; what look like leaves are flattened stems. Small, greenish flowers bloom on the middle of the flattened stems in spring, and are followed by ½-inch red or yellow berries on the female plants. Zones 7-10.

Selected species and varieties. *R. aculeatus* grows 1½ to 3 feet tall. The leaflike branches are oval, thick, leathery, ¾ to 1 inch long and dull green, and have spiny tips. *R. hypo-*

glossum grows 1½ feet tall. The leaflike branches are oval, 4 inches long and glossy green. Zones 8-10.

Growing conditions. Butcher's broom may be grown in full sun in cool climates and in partial shade where summers are hot. Soil should be moist and well drained. Both male and female plants are usually necessary to produce berries. Cut out branches at ground level to control plant size.

Landscape uses. The upright spreading habit of butcher's broom makes it useful as a ground cover and as a low hedge; its unusual blooming habit makes it a good accent plant.

Russian cypress see *Microbiota*

St.-John's-wort see *Hypericum*

Sakaki see *Cleyera*

Sand myrtle see *Leiophyllum*

Santa Cruz Island buckwheat see *Eriogonum*

Santolina (san-toh-LEE-na)

Mounded, aromatic shrub with finely divided, ½-inch gray or green leaves. Small, buttonlike flowers bloom in summer at the top of leafless stems. Zones 6-10.

Selected species and varieties. *S. chamaecyparissus,* lavender cotton, grows 1 to 2 feet tall and has woolly, silver-gray foliage. Flowers are golden yellow, ¾ inch across and bloom on 6-inch stems.

Growing conditions. Lavender cotton may be grown in full sun in any dry, well-drained soil. Do not fertilize. Prune the plant in early spring to shape it and cut off flowers as they fade.

Landscape uses. Lavender cotton makes a good edging plant. It may also be grown in an herb garden or a flower garden.

Sarcococca (sar-ko-KOK-a)
Sweet box

Small genus of shrubs that may be erect or spreading. Leaves are thin, leathery and glossy dark green. Small, white, fragrant flowers bloom in racemes among the leaves in late winter and spring. Berries are ¼ inch across and may be black or red. Zones 6-9.

Selected species and varieties. *S. confusa* is a dense, spreading shrub

RUBUS CALYCINOIDES

RUSCUS ACULEATUS

SANTOLINA CHAMAECYPARISSUS

SARCOCOCCA HOOKERANA HUMILIS

SCIADOPITYS VERTICILLATA

SEQUOIA SEMPERVIRENS
'ADPRESSA'

SEQUOIADENDRON GIGANTEUM 'PYGMAEUM'

SKIMMIA JAPONICA

that grows 4 to 6 feet tall and 7 feet wide. Young twigs are hairy. Leaves are 2½ inches long and pointed. Berries are black. Zones 7-9. *S. hookerana* grows erect to 6 feet tall and equally wide and has hairy young twigs. Leaves are lance-shaped and 1 to 4 inches long and ½ to ¾ inch wide. Berries are black. *S. hookerana digyna* is more slender in shape and has narrower leaves. Zones 7-9. The variety *humilis,* dwarf Himalayan sweet box, grows 2 feet high and spreads to 8 feet wide. It has 2- to 3½-inch narrow leaves. Zones 6-9. *S. ruscifolia,* fragrant box, is identical in appearance to *S. confusa* but has dark red berries. Zones 7-9.

Growing conditions. Grow sweet box in partial to full shade in rich, fertile, moist, acid or alkaline, well-drained soil. Prune out old stems to the ground in early spring.

Landscape uses. Sweet box is best used as a hedge or a border, and is easy to train into an espalier. Dwarf Himalayan box makes a good ground cover.

—

Sciadopitys (sy-a-DOP-i-tus)
Umbrella pine

Slow-growing coniferous tree or large shrub that has a dense pyramidal shape. Foliage is shiny, leathery, narrow, flat, dark green, 3 to 5 inches long and whorled in groups of 20 to 30 around the stems. Zones 5-10.

Selected species and varieties. *S. verticillata* will grow to 25 feet tall. Branches droop as the plant matures.

Growing conditions. Umbrella pine needs full sun in cool areas and afternoon shade where the climate is hot. Soil should be rich, slightly acid to neutral, moist and well drained. Prune if necessary after the plant has produced its spring growth.

Landscape uses. Umbrella pine is a magnificent lawn specimen. It can be grown in a container and may be pruned into a sculptural form.

—

Scotch pine see *Pinus*

—

Sequoia (se-KWOY-a)
Redwood

Broad genus of conifers from large trees to small shrubs. Needles are arranged in a flat plane on both sides of the branches. They are pointed, ¼ to 1 inch long, and blue-green or

dark green with two white lines on the undersides. Bark is reddish brown. Cones are round and 1 inch in diameter. Zones 7-9.

Selected species and varieties. *S. sempervirens* 'Adpressa', dwarf redwood, is a 6-foot, broad pyramidal shrub; growing tips are creamy white in spring and summer. 'Nana Pendula' has very tiny, blue-green foliage that clings closely to long, slender branches. The plant grows 3 to 6 inches high and 24 inches across. 'Prostrata' grows flat on the ground with some erect shoots and has ½-inch needles.

Growing conditions. Grow dwarf redwoods in full sun or partial shade in very moist, rich, well-drained soil. They do best where humidity is high. Prune in spring to keep compact.

Landscape uses. Use dwarf redwoods as accent plants or in foundation plantings. The low-growing cultivars may be used as ground covers and in rock gardens.

—

Sequoiadendron
(se-kwoy-a-DEN-dron)
Sequoia

Broad genus of conifers that includes large trees to large shrubs. Foliage is scalelike, pointed, dark blue-green, ½ inch long and has two white bands on the upper surfaces. Cones are 2 to 3 inches long and red-brown. Zones 6-10.

Selected species and varieties. *S. giganteum* 'Pygmaeum' is a spreading, 3- to 4-foot shrub.

Growing conditions. Grow dwarf sequoia in full sun in moist, rich, acid, well-drained soil. Prune in spring to keep the plant compact.

Landscape uses. Dwarf sequoia can be used in a rock garden or as an accent plant.

—

Sheep laurel see *Kalmia*

Shrub verbena see *Lantana*

Siberian cypress see *Microbiota*

Silk-tassel see *Garrya*

Silky-leaved woodwaxen
see *Genista*

Silverbush see *Convolvulus*

—

Skimmia (SKIM-ee-a)

Dense, mounded shrub that has oblong, 3- to 5-inch leaves and small white flowers that bloom in 3-inch panicles in spring. Round, ½-inch red berries form in clusters in fall and winter and may last until spring. Zones 7-9.

Selected species and varieties. *S. japonica,* Japanese skimmia, is a densely branched shrub 2 to 4 feet high and 6 feet wide. Foliage forms at the ends of the branches; it is yellow-green, leathery and has wavy margins. There are separate male and female plants. Flowers on the male plant are larger than those on the female plant, and are also fragrant. Bright red berries form on the female plants. *S. reevesiana,* Reeves skimmia, is 18 to 24 inches tall and wide. Foliage is dull green; berries are dull red. Male and female flowers bloom on the same plant.

Growing conditions. Plant skimmia in partial to full shade in moist, rich, acid, well-drained soil. It tolerates air pollution. Little if any pruning is necessary. Both male and female plants are needed to produce berries on the Japanese skimmia; plant one male for every six to eight females.

Landscape uses. Skimmias are effective in foundation plantings, shrub borders, mass plantings, edgings and hedges. Reeves skimmia is also used in rock gardens. Both skimmias can be used in seashore gardens.

—

Snow azalea see *Rhododendron*

—

Solanum (so-LAY-num)

Evergreen or deciduous shrub, vine, annual, perennial or vegetable. Trumpet-shaped flowers bloom singly or in clusters among the leaves. Zones 3-10.

Selected species and varieties. *S. rantonnetti,* Paraguay nightshade, can be grown either as a vine 12 to 15 feet tall or as a 6- to 8-foot shrub. Leaves are oval, 4 inches long and bright green. Flowers are 1 inch across, fragrant, and dark blue or lavender with yellow centers. Blooms appear in clusters in summer and off and on all year in the warmest areas. Fruits are red, heart-shaped, drooping and 1 inch long. Zones 9 and 10.

Growing conditions. Grow Paraguay nightshade in full sun in any rich, well-drained soil.

Landscape uses. When grown on a trellis, Paraguay nightshade is useful

as a screen. It can be heavily pruned into a shrubby shape and used as an informal hedge.

—

Sophora (so-FOR-a)

Large, upright deciduous or evergreen shrub that has finely divided leaves and hanging clusters of pealike flowers at the ends of the branches. Zones 4-10.

Selected species and varieties. *S. secundiflora,* Mescal bean, grows 15 feet tall. Leaves are glossy, dark green on the upper surfaces and silky on the undersides; each leaf is 4 to 6 inches long and has six to ten 2-inch leaflets. Four- to 8-inch clusters of fragrant, violet-blue flowers bloom in late winter and spring. Eight-inch, dark seedpods follow the flowers and later open to reveal poisonous red seeds. Zones 8-10.

Growing conditions. Plant Mescal bean in full sun in well-drained, alkaline soil. Water deeply but infrequently. Do not fertilize. Prune in early spring to shape the plant and control its growth.

Landscape uses. Mescal beans make good screens and mass plantings. They can be easily espaliered.

—

Spider azalea see *Rhododendron*
Spruce see *Picea*
Starflower see *Grewia*

—

Stranvaesia (stran-VEE-zee-a)

Wide-spreading, upright shrub. Clusters of white flowers bloom at the ends of the branches in late spring and early summer and are followed by round, red, ¼-inch berries in late fall and winter. Zones 7-10.

Selected species and varieties. *S. davidiana* grows 6 to 20 feet tall and equally wide or wider. Leaves are dark green, leathery, oblong and 4 to 5 inches long. They are red when new and bronze in fall and winter. New twigs are hairy. Flowers are ¼ inch across and bloom in 4-inch clusters. *S. davidiana undulata* grows 5 feet high and 10 feet wide and has wavy leaf margins. 'Prostrata' is lower-growing and is twice as wide as it is high.

Growing conditions. Grow stranvaesia in full sun to partial shade in any well-drained soil. It tolerates

SOLANUM RANTONNETTI

SOPHORA SECUNDIFLORA

STRANVAESIA DAVIDIANA UNDULATA

STREPTOSOLEN JAMESONII

SYCOPSIS SINENSIS

SYZYGIUM PANICULATUM

TAXUS BACCATA 'ADPRESSA AUREA'

poor soil but should be heavily watered. Protect it from hot winds. Prune to control size and to shape the plant in early spring.

Landscape uses. The dense habit of stranvaesia makes it a useful background plant, hedge or screen.

Strawberry tree see *Arbutus*

Streptosolen (strep-to-SO-len)

Vining shrub that has 1¼-inch oval leaves and funnel-shaped, four- to five-lobed flowers that bloom in loose clusters at the ends of the branches. Zones 9 and 10.

Selected species and varieties. *S. jamesonii,* marmalade bush, grows 4 to 6 feet high and wide if grown as a shrub and 12 feet tall if trained as a vine. Flowers are orange-red, 1¼ inch across, and bloom abundantly in spring and summer; some bloom on and off during the rest of the year.

Growing conditions. Plant marmalade bush in full sun in any moist, well-drained soil. Thin or prune the plant to shape it in early spring.

Landscape uses. Marmalade bush is best grown against a wall or a trellis or in a mass planting on a slope. It can also be grown in a container or in a hanging basket.

Sumac see *Rhus*
Sweet bay see *Laurus*
Sweetbay magnolia
see *Magnolia*
Sweet box see *Sarcococca*
Sweet pea shrub see *Polygala*
Sweetspire see *Itea*

Sycopsis (sy-KOP-sis)

Large, dense, upright shrub that has prominently veined leaves and clusters of small flowers at the ends of the branches. Zones 7-9.

Selected species and varieties. *S. sinensis* grows 20 feet tall and has 4-inch, leathery leaves. Hairy brown bracts enclose yellow flowers that bloom in late winter. Flowers on male plants have prominent red stamens; those on female plants have none.

Growing conditions. Grow sycopsis in full sun or light shade in rich, moist, well-drained soil. Prune the plant after it flowers in spring.

Landscape uses. Plant sycopsis as a large hedge or screen.

Syzygium (sy-ZIJ-ee-um)

Genus of 400 to 500 trees and shrubs that have deep green foliage that is often tinged with copper, especially when young. Flowers have tufts of stamens that look brushy. Berries are soft and edible. Zone 10.

Selected species and varieties. *S. paniculatum,* brush cherry, is a 40-foot tree that can be pruned into a 20-foot shrub. Leaves are oblong and 2 to 3 inches long. Flowers are white, ½ to 1 inch wide and appear in clusters in spring. Berries are purple and ½ to ¾ inches across. 'Globulus' is compact, globe-shaped, tightly branched and has foliage that retains its coppery color all year.

Growing conditions. Grow brush cherry in full sun or partial shade in any well-drained soil. Prune both the branches and the roots frequently to keep the plant in shrub form.

Landscape uses. Use brush cherry in a background planting or in a hedge. It can be pruned into formal shapes.

Taxus (TAK-sus)
Yew

Coniferous tree or shrub that may be pyramidal, globular or spreading in growth habit. Needles are ½ to 1 inch long and very dark green with lighter undersides. Leaves may spiral around the branches, lie in a flat plane or form a V. Bark is reddish brown, thin and flaky. Female plants produce red berries; the seed inside the berry, not the pulp, is toxic, as are the leaves and the bark. Zones 3-8.

Selected species and varieties. *T. baccata,* English yew, has shiny, slightly curved needles that have two pale green lines on the undersides. Needles are usually arranged in a flat plane. Most English yews are upright plants. 'Adpressa' is rounded, 5 to 6 feet high and 3 to 6 feet wide and has ½-inch needles. 'Adpressa Aurea' is slightly smaller and has golden yellow foliage. 'Brevifolia' is 2 to 3 feet tall and has small leaves that turn bronze in winter. 'Compacta' is dwarf and cone-shaped with ½-inch needles. 'Pendula' is a spreading plant with drooping branches and no berries. 'Prostrata' is a spreading plant that grows 3 to 6 inches high. 'Repandens' grows 2 to 4 feet high and 12 feet wide and has a flat top. Branches are slightly pendulous. Zones 6-8. 'Stricta' (sometimes designated 'Fastigiata'), Irish yew, grows in a narrow, upright column 6 to 12 feet tall. Zones 7 and 8.

T. canadensis, Canada yew, has dark, greenish yellow needles and forms very few berries. 'Stricta' has stiff, upright branches and grows 2 to 4 feet high and as wide or wider. *T. cuspidata,* Japanese yew, has soft, dull green needles with two whitish yellow lines on the undersides. Needles are usually arranged in a V shape. Most Japanese yews are spreading plants. 'Aurescens' is 1 foot high and 3 feet wide and has yellow new growth. 'Capitata' is a broad pyramid growing 15 to 20 feet tall. 'Densiformis' grows 2 feet high and 6 feet wide. 'Depressa' is a low-growing, spreading plant. 'Expansa' grows 10 feet high and wide in a vase shape with an open center. 'Intermedia' is a broad, upright plant that grows 4 to 6 feet tall. 'Nana' is 3 to 6 feet high and 6 to 10 feet wide. 'Nana Pyramidalis' is a broad pyramid 8 to 12 feet tall. 'Prostrata' is a spreading plant 18 to 24 inches high. 'Vermeulen' is a rounded shrub 8 feet high and 10 feet across. Zones 5-8. *T.* × *media* is a cross between the Japanese and English yew. Needles are shiny green and spaced farther apart on the branches than on other yews. 'Andersonii' is spreading with upright branches. 'Brownii' is rounded, 9 feet high and 12 feet wide. 'Densiformis' is compact and vase-shaped and grows 3 to 6 feet high. 'Hatfieldii' has a pyramidal shape and grows 12 feet high. 'Hicksii' grows 10 to 15 feet high in a columnar form. Zones 5-8.

Growing conditions. Most yews will grow in full sun or partial shade. Canada yew will tolerate full shade. Soil should be fertile, moist, acid to neutral, and must be well drained; no yews will tolerate constantly wet soil. Protect from winter wind and sun. Prune or shear at any time to shape the plants and keep them compact.

Landscape uses. The many sizes and forms of yews make them suitable for many different landscape uses. They can be used in foundation plantings, as hedges, as screens and as ground covers. They can be pruned into formal shapes. The cultivar 'Brevifolia' is often used in bonsai.

Tea tree see *Leptospermum*

Tecoma (te-KO-ma)

Large, upright shrub that has finely divided leaves and yellow or orange funnel-shaped, five-lobed flowers that bloom in clusters. Zone 10.

Selected species and varieties. *T. stans,* yellowbells, grows 15 to 20 feet high. Each leaf has five to thirteen 4-inch serrated leaflets. Two-inch, bright yellow flowers bloom during the summer and early fall, and are followed by an 8-inch seedpod.

Growing conditions. Plant yellowbells in full sun in any well-drained soil. They tolerate heat and drought. Prune the plant in early spring.

Landscape uses. Plant yellowbells in a shrub border for summer color or use them in a large screen.

Tecomaria (tek-o-MAIR-ee-a)

Vining shrub that has finely divided leaves and yellow, red or orange flowers that bloom in loose clusters at the ends of the branches. Blooms are trumpet-shaped and five-lobed. Zones 9 and 10.

Selected species and varieties. *T. capensis,* cape honeysuckle, is a sprawling 15-foot semivine that can be pruned to a 6-foot shrub. Flowers are 2 inches long, bright orange, and appear in fall and winter. Leaves are glossy, 6 inches long and have five to nine 2-inch leaflets. Two-inch seedpods follow the flowers.

Growing conditions. Plant cape honeysuckle in full sun in sandy, well-drained soil. It is tolerant of heat and wind, and of drought once it is established.

Landscape uses. If unpruned, cape honeysuckle can be grown on a trellis, against a wall or as a ground cover on a bank. Pruned, it is used as a hedge, screen or espalier. It is tolerant of seashore conditions.

Temazcal see *Rhus*

Ternstroemia
(tern-STRO-mee-a)

Rounded shrub that has leathery leaves arranged in whorls at the ends of the branches. Small flowers bloom among the leaves at the branch tips and are followed by ½-inch berries. Zones 7-10.

Selected species and varieties. *T. gymnanthera* is 4 to 6 feet high and 6 to 8 feet wide. Foliage is thick, glossy, oval, 3 inches long; it is deep green when the plant is grown in shade and bronze or purple when the plant is grown in sun. New growth has a bronze cast; leafstalks are red.

TECOMA STANS

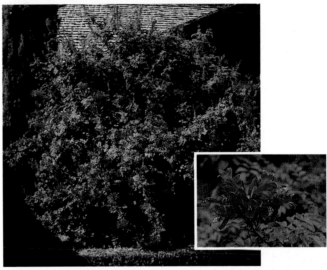
TECOMARIA CAPENSIS

TERNSTROEMIA GYMNANTHERA

TETRAPANAX PAPYRIFERUS

TEUCRIUM CHAMAEDRYS

THUJA OCCIDENTALIS 'HETZ MIDGET'

Flowers are fragrant, narrow, tubular, ½ inch long and appear in summer. Berries are yellow or red.

Growing conditions. Ternstroemia may be grown in full sun or full shade in moist, acid, well-drained soil. It likes to be heavily watered, especially when it is grown in full sun. Prune in early spring to keep the plant compact.

Landscape uses. Ternstroemia makes a good shrub border or an informal hedge. It also grows well in a container.

━

Tetrapanax (te-TRAP-a-naks)

Large, multistemmed shrub that spreads by underground stems. Leaves are dark green, deeply lobed, white and hairy on the undersides, and whorled at the ends of the branches. Flowers bloom in branched clusters at the ends of the stems. Evergreen in Zone 10; deciduous in Zones 8 and 9.

Selected species and varieties. *T. papyriferus,* rice paper plant, grows 15 feet tall. Leaves are 12 to 15 inches across and have five to 14 toothed lobes. Flower clusters are white, 3 feet long and appear in winter.

Growing conditions. Grow rice paper plant in full sun in cool climates, in partial shade where summers are hot, in any well-drained garden soil. Protect from winds, which may tear the foliage. To keep the plant from becoming invasive, plant it in a large container and sink the container into the ground.

Landscape uses. Because of the bold, strong statement made by rice paper plant, it can serve as a focal point or an accent in the garden.

━

Teucrium (TOO-kree-um)
Germander

Small shrub that has white or silver hairs on the stems and leaves. Two-lipped, tubular flowers bloom in showy spikes at the ends of the stems. Zones 5-10.

Selected species and varieties. *T. chamaedrys,* chamaedrys germander, grows 10 to 12 inches tall and spreads to 2 feet from underground stems. Leaves are dark green, toothed and ¾ inch long. White or purplish red flowers bloom in summer. *T. fruticans,* bush germander, grows 4 feet high and

wide and has 1¼-inch, oval, gray-green leaves. Flowers are pale blue or lilac, ¾ inch across and appear off and on throughout most of the year. Zone 10.

Growing conditions. Plant germander in full sun in any well-drained soil. It tolerates heat and poor soil, but does not like to be in drying winds and needs deep but infrequent watering. Prune the plant in early spring.

Landscape uses. Chamaedrys germander tolerates shearing and may therefore be used as a neat edging and as a low, formal hedge. Bush germander is used as an informal hedge or in massed plantings.

━

Texas ranger see *Leucophyllum*

━

Thuja (THOO-ya)
Arborvitae

Coniferous tree or shrub that has soft, scalelike leaves in flat sprays. Plant shapes vary from pyramidal to globular. Foliage can be medium or dark green, or green tipped with gold. Zones 3-9.

Selected species and varieties. *T. occidentalis,* American arborvitae, has shiny medium to dark green foliage that often turns brown in winter. Bark may be reddish brown or gray. 'Emerald' is a narrow pyramid 20 feet tall with emerald green foliage. 'Filiformis' grows 2½ feet high and slightly wider and has leaves that closely hug long, slender, pendulous branches. 'Golden Globe' is a rounded shrub 3 feet high and wide and has golden foliage. 'Hetz Midget' is dense and globular, growing 12 inches high and across. 'Nigra' is a 20-foot, broad pyramid that holds its green color all winter. 'Pyramidalis' is a 20-foot, narrow pyramid. 'Rheingold' is 4½ to 6 feet tall, pyramidal in shape and has golden foliage. 'Spiralis' is a narrow, 10-foot pyramid. 'Woodwardii' is globe-shaped and 3 feet high and wide. *T. plicata,* Western red cedar, has aromatic, shiny dark green leaves. Shredding bark is red or brown. 'Cuprea' is a broad pyramid 3 feet tall that has bronzy foliage that is yellow when new. 'Hillieri' is round and 4 to 5 feet high and across. 'Rogersii Aurea' grows 3 feet tall and has golden tips. The plant may be either round or conical. 'Stoneham Gold' forms a broad cone 6 feet tall and has golden tips. Zones 5-9.

Growing conditions. Grow arborvitae in full sun in moist, well-drained, acid or slightly alkaline soil. It prefers a location that is high in humidity and protected from drying winds. Prune the plant before growth starts in spring.

Landscape uses. Tall, upright species of arborvitae can be used in foundation plantings or screens, or as hedges. Low-growing cultivars can be used in rock gardens and at the front of shrub borders. The golden forms are especially attractive as accent plants.

See also *Platycladus*

—

Thujopsis (thoo-YOP-sis)
Hiba false arborvitae

Coniferous tree with dwarf, shrubby cultivars. All have bright, glossy green, soft, scalelike foliage striped in white on the underside. Cones are round and flat-topped. Zones 7-9.

Selected species and varieties. *T. dolobrata* 'Aurea' grows 10 feet tall and has golden foliage. 'Nana' is 2 feet high and 5 feet wide and has bronze-tipped foliage. 'Variegata' grows in a broad pyramidal form, 10 feet tall, and has creamy white foliage.

Growing conditions. Plant dwarf Hiba false arborvitae in partial to full shade in cool, rich, moist, acid, well-drained soil. Prune or shear the plant in spring.

Landscape uses. Use dwarf Hiba false arborvitae in a foundation planting or a rock garden. It also grows well in a container.

—

Tibouchina (tib-oo-KY-na)
Glory bush

Large, loose, spreading shrub that has oval leaves with prominent veins. Large, showy flowers appear singly or in clusters at the ends of the branches. Zones 9 and 10.

Selected species and varieties. *T. urvilleana* grows 15 feet tall and has velvety green leaves with pale undersides. Vivid purple, five-petaled flowers 3 to 4 inches wide bloom off and on throughout the year.

Growing conditions. Grow glory bush in full sun in well-drained, acid soil. Roots like to be cool and should therefore be mulched. Fertilize in spring and again after each heavy blooming. Prune the plant after it flowers to keep it compact.

Landscape uses. Because of its height, glory bush is best used as a background planting or as a tall hedge. It is attractive enough to be used as a tall accent plant.

—

Tree anemone see *Carpenteria*
Tree ivy see *Fatshedera*

—

Trochodendron
(trok-o-DEN-dron)
Wheel tree

Large shrub that has lance-shaped leaves clustered at the ends of the branches. Flowers are bright green, ½ inch across and bloom in 3- to 6-inch erect clusters above the foliage. The blooms are showy because of the many stamens that radiate from the flower like the spokes on a wheel. Zones 8-10.

Selected species and varieties. *T. aralioides* is a spreading shrub that grows 15 to 20 feet tall. Foliage is shiny, apple green to yellow-green, 6 inches long and scalloped at the margins. Leafstalks are 3½ inches long. Foliage turns bronze in the winter if the plant is grown in the sun. Flowers bloom in early summer.

Growing conditions. Grow wheel tree in full sun to full shade. Soil should be rich, fertile, acid and well drained. Water heavily. The plant may be pruned in early spring.

Landscape uses. Use the unusually flowered wheel tree as an accent plant or as a tall hedge or screen.

—

Tsuga (SOO-ga)
Hemlock

Coniferous tree or shrub that has soft-textured, ¼- to ¾-inch, shiny dark green needles that have two white bands on the undersides. Most hemlocks are pyramidal in shape; some cultivars have different growing habits. Zones 3-8.

Selected species and varieties. *T. canadensis,* Canadian hemlock, is a large tree that can be pruned to a large shrub. Needles are arranged in a flat plane along the drooping branches. New foliage is light green in spring. Brownish gray, ¾-inch cones form at the branch tips. 'Cole's Prostrate' has twisted branches that lie flat on the ground and spread to 4 feet across. 'Geneva' is a narrow pyramid with drooping branches, growing 6 to 8 feet tall. 'Gracilis' is a

THUJOPSIS DOLOBRATA 'AUREA'

TIBOUCHINA URVILLEANA

TROCHODENDRON ARALIOIDES

TSUGA CANADENSIS 'PENDULA'

135

UGNI MOLINAE

VIBURNUM × BURKWOODII

rounded plant 3 to 4 feet high. 'Lewis' is an upright shrub 4 to 6 feet tall. 'Minuta' is globe-shaped and grows to 18 inches high and wide. 'Pendula', Sargent's weeping hemlock, is a broad, weeping shrub with overlapping branches. The plant grows 5 to 6 feet high and 10 to 12 feet wide.

T. caroliniana, Carolina hemlock, is an open pyramid with short branches and grows to a height of 15 feet. Needles radiate around the stem. 'Compacta' reaches 3 to 4 feet in height. 'Nana' is rounded and 3 feet high and wide. Zones 5-8.

T. diversifolia, Northern Japanese hemlock, has the densest foliage of any hemlock. Needles are notched. The plant grows into a broad, 20-foot pyramid. Zones 6-8.

Growing conditions. Grow hemlock in full sun or light shade; the latter is preferred where summers are hot. It likes cool, acid, moist, well-drained soil and high humidity. Protect from winter winds in the colder limits of its hardiness. Carolina hemlock is the only species that tolerates air pollution and salt spray.

Landscape uses. Grow hemlock as a hedge, screen or windbreak. Sargent's weeping hemlock is a magnificent lawn specimen.

—

Ugni (UG-nee)
Chilean guava

Compact, rounded, densely leafed shrub that has ½-inch, oval, leathery foliage. Flowers are showy because of their many brushy stamens. Berries are small and round. Zones 9 and 10.

Selected species and varieties. *U. molinae* is 3 to 6 feet tall and has dark green foliage with bronze shading and white undersides. Flowers of white or light pink bloom in late spring and early summer. Purple to red, ½-inch berries are edible, with an applelike fragrance.

Growing conditions. Plant Chilean guava in full sun where summers are cool and in partial shade where it is hot. Soil should be moist, acid to neutral and well drained. Water heavily. Prune the plant in early spring to keep it compact.

Landscape uses. Its compactness makes Chilean guava a good plant for edging a driveway or a walkway.

—

Umbrella pine see *Sciadopitys*

Viburnum (vy-BER-num)

Deciduous or evergreen, upright, rounded shrub with lush foliage, showy clusters of bell-shaped, white or pink flowers that bloom in spring, and bright clusters of berries in autumn and winter. Zones 4-10.

Selected species and varieties. *V. × burkwoodii,* Burkwood viburnum, grows 6 to 8 feet high and wide. Leaves are pointed, dark green, 4 inches long, glossy on the top surfaces and hairy on the undersides. Flower clusters are white, fragrant and 3 inches long. Fruits are red at first and change to black. Evergreen in Zones 8-10; semievergreen in Zones 5-7.

V. davidii, David viburnum, grows 4 feet high and wide. Leaves have three prominent veins, are dark green, leathery, oblong and 3 to 6 inches in length. Off-white flowers bloom in 2- to 3-inch flat clusters. Berries are blue; more than one plant is needed to ensure berry production. Zones 7-9.

V. japonicum, Japanese viburnum, grows 10 to 15 feet tall. Leaves are shiny, leathery, dark green and 3 to 6 inches long. Fragrant white flowers bloom in 3- to 4½-inch clusters. Berries are red and are not reliably produced. Zones 7-10. *V. macrocephalum,* Chinese snowball, is 6 to 10 feet tall. Leaves are dull green and 2 to 4 inches long. Flower clusters are white and 8 inches across. The plant produces no berries. Evergreen in Zones 8-10; semievergreen in Zones 6 and 7.

V. × pragense, Prague viburnum, is 8 to 10 feet tall and has arching branches. Leaves are dark green, shiny, 2 to 4 inches long and have white undersides. Creamy white flowers bloom in 2- to 3-inch clusters. Fruits are black and sparsely produced. Evergreen in Zones 8-10; semievergreen in Zones 6 and 7. *V. rhytidophyllum,* leatherleaf viburnum, is 6 to 12 feet high and wide. Foliage is shiny, oblong, wrinkled, 5 to 7 inches long, dark green on the upper surfaces and white on the undersides. Yellowish white flowers bloom in 4- to 8-inch clusters. Fruits are red at first and later turn black. More than one plant is needed for cross-pollination and an abundant crop of berries. Zones 6-8.

V. tinus, laurestinus viburnum, is a narrow, 7- to 12-foot shrub. Leaves are shiny, oval to oblong, dark green and 2 to 3 inches in length. Fragrant white or light pink flowers bloom in flat, 3-inch clusters. Berries are blue to black. Zones 7-10. *V. utile* is 6 feet tall and has long, slender stems. Leaves are oblong, 3 inches in length, glossy and dark green with white undersides. Fragrant white flowers bloom in 3-inch, flat clusters and are followed by blue-black fruit. Zones 7-10.

Growing conditions. Plant viburnum in partial to full shade in moist, rich, slightly acid, well-drained soil. Mulch to keep the roots cool. Protect from drying winds. Decrease watering in autumn to let foliage mature before winter cold sets in. Prune to shape the plant and stimulate branching in early spring before growth starts.

Landscape uses. Plant the fragrant viburnums near a window where their sweet scent can be enjoyed. They serve well as foundation plantings, screens, hedges or accent plants. Burkwood viburnum can be trained as an espalier.

—

Wattle see *Acacia*

Wax myrtle see *Myrica*

Wheel tree see *Trochodendron*

White cedar see *Chamaecyparis*

White pine see *Pinus*

Wild lilac see *Ceanothus*

Wintercreeper see *Euonymus*

Wintergreen see *Gaultheria*

Xylosma (zy-LOS-ma)

Large, spreading shrub grown for its oval, pointed, yellow-green foliage, which is bronze in early spring. Branches are spiny. Inconspicuous flowers blossom in racemes. Zones 9 and 10.

Selected species and varieties. *X. congestum* is 6 to 10 feet high and has asymmetrical branching. Leaves are toothed, glossy and 3½ inches long. As new leaves grow each spring, the leaves from the year before drop off.

Growing conditions. Xylosma may be planted in full sun or light shade in any well-drained, fertile soil. It is heat- and drought-tolerant once established but will perform better if it is regularly watered. Prune to control the shape of the plant in early spring.

Landscape uses. Xylosma is one of the best shrubs to espalier against a south or west wall because it tolerates reflected heat. Because of its spines, it is a good barrier plant. It can also be grown as an informal hedge or as a ground cover on a bank.

—

Yaupon see *Ilex*

Yellowbells see *Tecoma*

Yesterday-today-and-tomorrow see *Brunfelsia*

Yew see *Taxus*

XYLOSMA CONGESTUM

PICTURE CREDITS

The sources for the illustrations in this book are listed below. Cover photograph of rhododendron hybrid by Horticultural Photography, Corvallis, OR. Watercolor paintings by Nicholas Fasciano and Yin Yi except pages 82, 83, 84, 85: Lorraine Moseley Epstein. 86, 87: Lorraine Moseley Epstein and Yin Yi. Maps on pages 76, 77, 79, 81: digitized by Richard Furno, inked by John Drummond.

Frontispiece paintings listed by page number: 6: *Landscape with Rider,* 16th century, by Girolamo or Francesco da Santa Croce, courtesy The Phillips Collection, Washington, D.C. 32: *Red Camellia,* Chinese painting: Sung Dynasty, courtesy Philadelphia Museum of Art: Purchased: Museum Funds. 54: *The Terrace at Méric,* c. 1867, by Fréderic Bazille, courtesy Cincinnati Art Museum, gift of Mark P. Herschede.

Photographs in Chapters 1 through 3 from the following sources, listed by page number: 8: Bob Grant. 10, 14, 18: Horticultural Photography, Corvallis, OR. 20: Saxon Holt. 22: Pamela Zilly. 26: Bob Grant. 28: Pamela Zilly. 34, 36, 38: Horticultural Photography, Corvallis, OR. 40: Mark Gibson. 42: Horticultural Photography, Corvallis, OR. 44: Thomas Eltzroth. 46: Pamela Zilly. 50, 52: Horticultural Photography, Corvallis, OR. 56: Bob Grant. 58: Renée Comet. 62: Horticultural Photography, Corvallis, OR. 64: Thomas Eltzroth. 66, 70: Horticultural Photography, Corvallis, OR.

Photographs in the Dictionary of Evergreen Shrubs by Pamela Harper, except where listed by page and numbered from top to bottom. Details in the dictionary designated as A. 90, 3, 3A: Horticultural Photography, Corvallis, OR. 4: William D. Adams. 91, 1: Saxon Holt. 1A: R. G. Turner Jr. 2: Nancy Degenkolb. 3: Horticultural Photography, Corvallis, OR. 4, 4A: Saxon Holt. 92, 1, 1A: Horticultural Photography, Corvallis, OR. 3: Saxon Holt. 3A, 4, 4A: Gordon Courtright. 93, 2: Derek Fell. 2A: Ann Reilly. 3, 3A: Bob Grant. 94, 1, 1A: Horticultural Photography, Corvallis, OR. 2, 2A: Thomas Eltzroth. 4, 4A: Robert Fincham/Mitsch Nursery. 95, 2, 2A: Saxon Holt. 3, 3A: Horticultural Photography, Corvallis, OR. 96, 1, 1A: Michael Dirr. 2, 2A: Horticultural Photography, Corvallis, OR. 3, 3A: Michael Dirr. 4: Horticultural Photography, Corvallis, OR. 97, 1, 1A: Michael Dirr. 2: Steve Rannels/Grant Heilman Photography. 3, 3A: Michael Dirr. 98, 1, 1A: Horticultural Photography, Corvallis, OR. 2, 2A: John N. Trager. 3, 3A: Horticultural Photography, Corvallis, OR. 99, 1, 1A, 2, 2A: Michael Dirr. 3A, 4: Thomas Eltzroth. 100, 1: Horticultural Photography, Corvallis, OR. 1A: Thomas Eltzroth. 2: Horticultural Photography, Corvallis, OR. 2A: Thomas Eltzroth. 3, 3A: Michael Dirr. 101, 1, 1A: Saxon Holt. 2, 3: Horticultural Photography, Corvallis, OR. 102, 1, 1A: Monrovia Nursery. 2: Fred Galle. 2A, 4A: Michael Dirr. 103, 2: Horticultural Photography, Corvallis, OR. 3, 3A: Michael Dirr. 4: Horticultural Photography, Corvallis, OR. 4A: Mark Gibson. 104, 1: Michael Dirr. 1A: Darrel Apps. 3: Horticultural Photography, Corvallis, OR. 3A: Michael Dirr. 105, 1: Horticultural Photography, Corvallis, OR. 3, 3A: Darrel Apps. 106, 1, 1A: Michael Dirr. 3, 3A: Eugene Memmler. 4: Thomas Eltzroth. 107, 1, 1A: Horticultural Photography, Corvallis, OR. 3: Michael Dirr. 108, 1: Horticultural Photography, Corvallis, OR. 2, 4, 4A: Thomas Eltzroth. 109, 1: Thomas Eltzroth. 2: Horticultural Photography, Corvallis, OR. 3: Thomas Eltzroth. 4, 4A: Michael Dirr. 111, 3: Horticultural Photography, Corvallis, OR. 112, 1, 1A: Steven Still. 2, 2A: Horticultural Photography, Corvallis, OR. 3: Dan Clark/Grant Heilman Photography. 113, 3: Horticultural Photography, Corvallis, OR. 3A: Eugene Memmler. 4: Horticultural Photography, Corvallis, OR. 114, 1, 1A: Michael Dirr. 2, 2A: Horticultural Photography, Corvallis, OR. 3: Michael Dirr. 115, 1, 2, 2A: Steven Still. 3, 3A: Michael Dirr. 4: Dr. J. C. Raulston. 4A: Michael Dirr. 116, 1: Horticultural Photography, Corvallis, OR. 1A: Grant Heilman Photography. 2, 2A, 3: Michael Dirr. 117, 1, 1A: Thomas Eltzroth. 2: Michael Dirr. 3: Thomas Eltzroth. 4: Michael Dirr. 118, 2A: Horticultural Photography, Corvallis, OR. 3, 3A: Saxon Holt. 119, 3, 3A: Horticultural Photography, Corvallis, OR. 120, 1: Barry L. Runk/Grant Heilman Photography. 120, 2, 2A: Horticultural Photography, Corvallis, OR. 121, 2, 2A: Paul Cox/San Antonio Botanical Gardens. 122, 1: Michael Dirr. 2, 3: Horticultural Photography, Corvallis, OR. 3A: Robert Lyons/Color Advantage. 123, 1: Horticultural Photography, Corvallis, OR. 2, 2A: Brett Hall, UCSC Arboretum. 3: Horticultural Photography, Corvallis, OR. 4, 4A: Alan Craig/Iseli Nursery. 124, 1: William M. Houghton/Fairchild Tropical Garden. 1A, Thomas Eltzroth. 125, 1, 1A: Thomas Eltzroth. 3, 3A: Horticultural Photography, Corvallis, Or. 126, 1, 1A, 4: Horticultural Photography, Corvallis, OR. 127, 3, 3A, 4, 4A: Horticultural Photography, Corvallis, OR. 128, 2, 2A: Jerry Pavia. 3: Gordon Courtright. 3A: R. F. Thorne. 4: Horticultural Photography, Corvallis, OR. 129, 1: Horticultural Photography, Corvallis, OR. 2, 2A: Saxon Holt. 4: Michael Dirr. 130, 1, 1A: Michael Dirr. 2: Robert Fincham/Mitsch Nursery. 2A: Saxon Holt. 3: Dr. J. C. Raulston. 131, 1: Derek Fell. 1A: Thomas Eltzroth. 2, 2A: Scooter Cheatham. 132, 1, 1A: Horticultural Photography, Corvallis, OR. 2, 2A: Michael Dirr. 3, 3A: Horticultural Photography, Corvallis, OR. 133, 1: Thomas Eltzroth. 2: Horticultural Photography, Corvallis, OR. 134, 1, 1A: Thomas Eltzroth. 2: Michael Dirr. 135, 1: Steven Still. 2, 4: Michael Dirr. 136, 1, 1A: Thomas Eltzroth. 137, 1, 1A: Michael Dirr.

ACKNOWLEDGMENTS

The index for this book was prepared by Lee McKee.
The editors also wish to thank: Dr. Walter Bloom, Bloomland Echota Farms, Chatsworth, Georgia; Sarah Brash, Alexandria, Virginia; Sarah E. Broley, Washington, D.C.; Peggy Dessaint, The Behnke Nurseries Company, Largo, Maryland; Rudi Fuchs, Fox Hill Nursery, Murphy, North Carolina; Leon E. Greene, Fairfax, Virginia; Kenneth E. Hancock, Annandale, Virginia; Elizabeth S. Head, International Oleander Society, Galveston, Texas; George Hockney, Wight's Nursery, Cairo, Georgia; Mary Kay Honeycutt, Crofton, Maryland; Betty Hotchkiss, American Camellia Society, Fort Valley, Georgia; Alice E. Knight, Heather Acres, Elma, Washington; Mr. and Mrs. Larry Moffi, Alexandria, Virginia; Ed Moulin, Brooklyn Botanic Garden, Brooklyn, New York; Wolfgang Oehme, Baltimore, Maryland; Jayne E. Rohrich, Alexandria, Virginia; Vicky and Bill Salin, Washington, D.C.; Candace H. Scott, College Park, Maryland; Lucille Shifrin, Gaithersburg, Maryland; Mr. and Mrs. Kenneth M. Stewart, Fairfax, Virginia; Karen Bentley Upton, The Behnke Nurseries Company, Largo, Maryland; John Wight Jr., Wight's Nursery, Cairo, Georgia.

FURTHER READING

Allen, Oliver E., *Gardening with the New Small Plants*. Boston: Houghton Mifflin, 1987.

Bailey, Liberty Hyde, and Ethel Zoe Bailey, *Hortus Third: A Concise Dictionary of Plants Cultivated in the United States and Canada*. New York: Macmillan, 1976.

Bloom, Adrian, *Conifers for Your Garden*. Antony, France: Éditions Floraisse, 1986.

Brickell, Christopher, *Pruning*. New York: Simon and Schuster, 1988.

Brooklyn Botanic Garden, *Bonsai for Indoors*. Brooklyn, New York: Brooklyn Botanic Garden, 1987.

Brooklyn Botanic Garden, *Dwarf Conifers*. Brooklyn, New York: Brooklyn Botanic Garden, 1977.

Brooklyn Botanic Garden, *Flowering Shrubs*. Brooklyn, New York: Brooklyn Botanic Garden, 1983.

Brooklyn Botanic Garden, *Pruning Handbook*. Brooklyn, New York: Brooklyn Botanic Garden, 1977.

Brooklyn Botanic Garden, *Rhododendrons and Their Relatives*. Brooklyn, New York: Brooklyn Botanic Garden, 1984.

Brooklyn Botanic Garden, *Trained and Sculptured Plants*. Brooklyn, New York: Brooklyn Botanic Garden, 1976.

Browse, Philip McMillan, *Plant Propagation*. New York: Simon and Schuster, 1988.

Davis, Brian, *The Gardener's Illustrated Encyclopedia of Trees and Shrubs*. Emmaus, Pennsylvania: Rodale Press, 1987.

Dirr, Michael A., *All about Evergreens*. San Francisco: Ortho Books/Chevron Chemical Company, 1984.

Dirr, Michael A., *Manual of Woody Landscape Plants*. Champaign, Illinois: Stipes Publishing, 1983.

Dirr, Michael A., and Charles W. Heuser Jr., *The Reference Manual of Woody Plant Propagation: From Seed to Tissue Culture*. Athens, Georgia: Varsity Press, 1987.

Fell, Derek, *Trees and Shrubs*. Tucson, Arizona: HP Books, 1986.

Flint, Harrison L., *Landscape Plants for Eastern North America*. New York: John Wiley and Sons, 1983.

Galle, Fred, *Azaleas*. Portland, Oregon: Timber Press, 1987.

Galle, Fred, and Derek Fell, *All about Azaleas, Camellias, and Rhododendrons*. San Francisco: Ortho Books/Chevron Chemical Company, 1985.

Hamilton, Geoff, *The Organic Garden Book*. New York: Crown Publishers, 1987.

Hastings, Don, *Gardening in the South*. Dallas, Texas: Taylor Publishing, 1987.

Hill, Lewis, *Pruning Simplified*. Pownal, Vermont: Storey Communications, 1986.

Hill, Lewis, *Secrets of Plant Propagation*. Pownal, Vermont: Storey Communications, 1986.

The Hillier Colour Dictionary of Trees and Shrubs. North Pomfret, Vermont: David and Charles, 1984.

Hoobler, Dorothy, and Thomas Hoobler, *Pruning*. New York: Grosset and Dunlap, 1975.

Leighton, Phebe, and Calvin Simonds, *The New American Landscape Gardener*. Emmaus, Pennsylvania: Rodale Press, 1987.

Seabrook, Peter, *Shrubs for Your Garden*. Antony, France: Éditions Floraisse, 1985.

Sinclair, Wayne A., Howard H. Lyon and Warren T. Johnson, *Diseases of Trees and Shrubs*. Ithaca, New York: Cornell University Press, 1987.

Sinnes, A. Cort, *How to Select and Care for Shrubs and Hedges*. San Francisco: Ortho Books/Chevron Chemical Company, 1980.

Smith, Michael D., ed., *The Ortho Problem Solver*. San Francisco: Ortho Books/Chevron Chemical Company, 1984.

Street, John, *Rhododendrons*. Chester, Connecticut: Globe Pequot Press, 1987.

Sunset Editors, *Bonsai: Culture and Care of Miniature Trees*. Menlo Park, California: Lane Publishing, 1976.

Sunset Editors, *Pruning Handbook*. Menlo Park, California: Lane Publishing, 1983.

Taylor, Norman, *Taylor's Guide to Shrubs*. Boston: Houghton Mifflin, 1987.

Wyman, Donald, *Shrubs and Vines for American Gardens*. New York: Macmillan, 1969.

Wyman, Donald, *Wyman's Gardening Encyclopedia*. New York: Macmillan, 1986.

INDEX

REDEFINITION

Senior Editors	Anne Horan, Robert G. Mason
Design Director	Robert Barkin
Designer	Edwina Smith
Illustration	Nicholas Fasciano
Assistant Designers	Sue Pratt, Monique Strawderman
Picture Editor	Deborah Thornton
Production Editor	Anthony K. Pordes
Research	Barbara B. Smith, Gail Prensky, Mary Yee, Elizabeth D. McLean
Text Editor	Sharon Cygan
Writers	Gerald Jonas, Ann Reilly David S. Thomson
Administrative Assistant	Margaret M. Higgins
Business Manager	Catherine M. Chase
PRESIDENT	Edward Brash

Time-Life Books Inc.
is a wholly owned subsidiary of

TIME INCORPORATED

FOUNDER	Henry R. Luce 1898-1967
Editor-in-Chief	Jason McManus
Chairman and Chief Executive Officer	J. Richard Munro
President and Chief Operating Officer	N. J. Nicholas Jr.
Editorial Director	Ray Cave
Executive Vice President, Books	Kelso F. Sutton
Vice President, Books	Paul V. McLaughlin

TIME-LIFE BOOKS INC.

EDITOR	George Constable
Executive Editor	Ellen Phillips
Director of Design	Louis Klein
Director of Editorial Resources	Phyllis K. Wise
Editorial Board	Russell B. Adams Jr., Dale M. Brown, Roberta Conlan, Thomas H. Flaherty, Lee Hassig, Donia Ann Steele, Rosalind Stubenberg
Director of Photography and Research	John Conrad Weiser
Assistant Director of Editorial Resources	Elise Ritter Gibson
PRESIDENT	Christopher T. Linen
Chief Operating Officer	John M. Fahey Jr.
Senior Vice Presidents	Robert M. DeSena, James L. Mercer, Paul R. Stewart
Vice Presidents	Stephen L. Bair, Ralph J. Cuomo, Neal Goff, Stephen L. Goldstein, Juanita T. James, Hallett Johnson III, Carol Kaplan, Susan J. Maruyama, Robert H. Smith, Joseph J. Ward
Director of Production Services	Robert J. Passantino
Supervisor of Quality Control	James King

Editorial Operations

Copy Chief	Diane Ullius
Production	Celia Beattie
Library	Louise D. Forstall
Correspondents	Elisabeth Kraemer-Singh (Bonn), Maria Vincenza Aloisi (Paris), Ann Natanson (Rome)

THE CONSULTANTS

C. Colston Burrell is the series consultant for The Time-Life Gardener's Guide. He is Curator of Plant Collections at the Minnesota Landscape Arboretum, part of the University of Minnesota.

Fred C. Galle, consultant for *Evergreen Shrubs,* is a horticulturalist in Hamilton, Georgia, and an authority on azaleas, rhododendrons and camellias. He served as horticultural director at the 2,500-acre Callaway Gardens in Pine Mountain, Georgia, from 1953 to 1983.

Library of Congress Cataloging-in-Publication Data
Evergreen shrubs.
   (The Time-Life gardener's guide)
   Bibliograpy: p.
   1. Ornamental shrubs—North America.
   2. Ornamental evergreens—North America.
I. Time-Life Books.   II. Series.
SB435.6.N7E94 1989   635.9'76'097   88-24801
ISBN 0-8094-6624-4
ISBN 0-8094-6625-2 (lib. bdg.)